Langtree Parish
History and Memories

Compiled by Margaret Knapman

Part one is a reprint of Allan Edgcombe's book
A Short History Of Langtree

God bless you always
Margaret Knapman

With best wishes
Allan Edgcombe

DEC. 11th 03.
VILLAGE HALL

TARKA·COUNTRY
MILLENNIUM AWARDS

Millennium Awards

This project is funded by the Tarka Country Millennium Awards, which are partially funded with lottery money through the Millennium Commission.

Edward Gaskell *publishers*
Old Gazette Building
6 Grenville Street
Bideford
Devon
EX39 2EA
isbn 1 -898546 -64 -9
First published 2003

Langtree Parish

History and Memories
Margaret Knapman

This book is sold subject to the condition that it shall not be re-sold, lent, hired out
or otherwise circulated in any binding or cover other than that in which it is published
and without a similar condition being imposed upon the subsequent purchaser
without the express consent of the publishers. The overall aim of this book has been to
paint a picture of Langtree throughout the years and across the span of its activities.
Memories will vary. Those included here are a cross-section of the pictures people who grew up,
or lived here for a considerable length of time, have carried in their minds and now choose to share with us.
Much other information has been gathered from Parish and other available records.
Whilst every care has been taken to ensure the accuracy of the information contained in the book,
the compiler disclaims responsibility for any mistakes which may have been inadvertently included.

©Margaret Knapman and those who have contributed articles

Typeset, Printed and Bound by
Lazarus Press
Unit 7 Caddsdown Business Park
Bideford
Devon
EX39 3DX
WWW.LAZARUSPRESS.COM

Acknowledgements & Thanks

Without Allan Edgcombe's 'Short History of Langtree' to use as a foundation the rest of this book would never have happened, so firstly, thank you to Allan for allowing his work to be reprinted here. Thank you to Mike Cole for help with the original application for the Award, to Richard Clark, my mentor, whose practical help and encouragement has been invaluable, to Paula Fuller for letting me draw on her previously researched articles on Mary Richards and Berry Cross. Deirdre Lloyd and Sarah Ward for doing the bulk of the typing with back-up from Julia Ward. Trish Shaw for scanning images, Patricia Soby, Mary Goaman, Tony Glover, Philip Jenkinson, Paul Wheeler our postman, David and Bernard Hill for specific research, Sam Mills and Fritz Takken for computer back-up, and to the proof readers who have sought out mistakes. A very big thank you to all who have shared memories, given information, loaned photographs, family albums and scrapbooks, and to all the parish organisations that have given me full access to their records. Without everyone's willing help the book could not have happened. A special thank you to my husband Les who took on some of my tasks in the home as well as helping to gather information, thus enabling me to put whatever time was needed compiling articles and bringing it all together. This has become his project as well as mine and his photographic exhibition, which will accompany the launch of the book, is the perfect compliment to the written word. Thank you one and all.

I am grateful to Langtree Women's institute for allowing me to use the picture of the parish map, which they created with help from community members, on the front cover. Also thanks to Brian Leverton and Tony Carey respectively for supplying the aerial photographs of Stibb Cross and Langtree used on the back cover.

Thank you to Carin, Kate and Cherie at the Tarka Office for believing in this project from the very first day, for all their enthusiasm and help, and for being there when I needed a listening ear. Thanks also to Lazarus Press for all helpful suggestions and guidance, and for the care they have taken in turning my efforts into the finished book.

In addition to the above I would also like to acknowledge the following sources of reference and information; Barnstaple Records Office, Torridge District Council, The North Devon Journal Herald, Bideford Gazette, The Western Morning News, The Western Times and Clinton Estate Sale catalogue.

Throughout the second part of the book I have not used titles of Mr or Mrs unless the Christian name has been unknown. I trust no-one will find this inappropriate, the aim has been to give a sense of community and family, where most people know each other fairly well. Gerald and Austin Mills have been referred to by their most often used names of Tinky and Jock, with Jock's agreement.

Dedication

*To all the people who have made Langtree Parish their home,
whether in the past or present,
and thus have contributed to making this place what it is today*

About the author

Margaret Knapman (née Dunn) was born in 1941, the third child in a family of eight. The house she was born in, Higher Coombe Park is now the warden's headquarters at Roadford Lake, and part of the ground her parents farmed lies beneath the water. At the age of four she moved with her family to Exbourne and a bigger farm; she attended the village Primary School, and then completed her education at the Secondary Modern School in Okehampton. Marriage to Les in 1962 brought her to a farm in Langtree, which remains the family home. They have two married daughters and five grandchildren. In retirement Les and Margaret still live in the farmhouse but most of the land has been sold to neighbours. Margaret's other interests include gardening, needlework and reading. She is a member of the Women's Institute, a former school Governor, and has been a youth worker, Sunday School teacher and continues to be a preacher within the Methodist Church and elsewhere. Having always had an interest in writing, including poetry, this project has been a challenging and satisfying experience.

Margaret Knapman and Allan Edgecombe (seated).
Back left Leslie Knapman, who did a photographic exhibition to accompany
the launch of the book. On the right is Richard Clark who was Margaret's mentor
during the compilation of this History.

Contents

PART ONE

Chapter 1 *From the Beginning* 9
Some Early Place Names 9
The Domesday Book 9
Other Notes on Early History 10
The Castle 10

Chapter 2 *Lords of the Manor* 11
Early History 11
The Hankfords 11
The St. Legers 12
The Brownes 12
The Rolles 13

Chapter 3 *Medieval Manor of Langtree* 15
The Church 15
Life in the Early Manor 15
How the Manor Spread 18
Witchcraft 18
The Langtree Rolls 19

Chapter 4 *Tudor Langtree* 20
Changes in the Church 21
The Subsidy Roll 1524/1527 21
Village Life in Tudor Times 21
Brute Browne 21
Devon Muster Roll 1569 22
Communications 23
Master William Baylie, Rector 23

Chapter 5 *The Stuart Period* 25
The Civil War 25
The Battle of Torrington 1646 26
Conclusion of Civil Wars 27
Rectors of Langtree during the Civil War 27
Nicholas Monck 27
Theophilus Powell 27
John Elston 27
Doctor John Handford 28
Other 17th Century Characters 28
The Barnfields 28
The Tuckers 29
The Abbotts 29
Devon Hearth Tax Roll 1674 30
The Phipps Charity 30
Employment 31
Glovemaking 31
Craftsmen 31
The Mariners' Way 32
The Plague 32

Chapter 6 *The 18th Century* 33
The Poor 33
The Great Storm 34
Langtree Mills 34
The Green Dragon 34
Roads and Highways 34
Rectors of Langtree during the 18th Century 34
Elston Whitlock, Rector 34
Adam Flaxman 35
Thomas Morrison 35
Charles Hammett 35
Peter Glubb 35
Non-conformity 36

Chapter 7 *The 19th Century* 37
Early 19th Century Church Records 37
The Rolle Canal 38
Development of the Non-conformist Church 39
John Guard, Rector 39
The Devonshire Directories 40
The Churchwarden's Vestry Books 41
Some 19th Century Characters 42
The Railway 44
Rev. Herbert Barnes 44
Rights for All Men 45
The Commons Riots 45

Chapter 8 *The 20th Century* 46
Aspects of Village Life 46
The Green Dragon Fire 46

Appendices 49
1 Devon Subsidy Roll 1524-1527 49
2 Devon Muster Roll 1569 50
3 Devon Protestation Return 1641/42 51
4 Charities 52
5 Devonshire Directories Entries 53
    Farmers 53
    Tradesmen 54
    Landlords 57
    Shopkeepers 57
    Teachers 58
6 Rectors of Langtree 59
7 Glossary of Local Place Names 60
8 Lords of the Manor 61

PART TWO
Chapter 9 — *Public Facilities* — 64
Langtree School — 64
School Acquisitions & Landmark Occasions — 66
The Parish Hall — 72
Langtree Post Office — 74
Parish Church — 75
Zion Chapel — 78
Stibb Cross — 81
Siloam — 82
Union Inn – Stibb Cross — 83
The Green Dragon — 84
Jubilee Playing Area — 84
A Song for Langtree — 86
Parish Newsletter — 86
Stibb Cross Market — 87
Watergate Halt — 89
Meals on Wheels — 90

Chapter 10 — *Clubs & Organisations* — 93
Parish Council — 93
Men's Social Club & Reading Room — 94
Women's Institute — 96
Over 60s Club — 98
Pre-School and Out of School Activities — 99
Langtree Players — 103
British Legion — 104
Young Farmers — 104
The Hunt — 105
Langtree Band — 106
Langtree Choir — 106
Mother's Union — 107
Bellringers — 107
AA Patrol Man — 108
Police — 109
Neighbourhood Watch — 109
Sports Activities — 109
School Sports — 111
Women's Institute Office Holders — 113
Jubilee Play Area Committee — 113
Social Club Office Holders — 114
Parish Council Chairmen & Clerks — 115
Parish Hall Committee — 115

Chapter 11 — *Events* — 116
The War Years — 116
Langtree Home Guard — 117
School War Effort — 118
Evacuees — 118
Plane Crash — 120
Bad Snow Falls — 121
Land Riots or Wars — 124
A Brave and Faithful Missionary — 125
The History and Murder of Mary Richards — 127
Gymkhana — 129
Parish Hall Annual Fun Day — 130
Collective Farm Sale — 131
Miss Langtree — 132
Carnival — 132
Sheep Dog Trials at Collacott — 133
Royal Garden Party May 31st 1965 — 133
Open Gardens Weekend — 134
Foot and Mouth — 135
National Events — 137
School Camp — 139
Summer Daze — 139
Cook of the Realm — 139
Airship 101 — 140
Transformer — 140
Resident's Association — 140
Church Fête — 141
New Year's Eve — 141

Chapter 12 — *Social Changes* — 144
Population of Langtree — 144
Community Buildings Closed or Sold Off — 145
Housing Development — 145
Traffic & Roads — 145
Reasons for Absence from School — 145
School Health — 146
Wells in the Parish — 146
Standpipes — 147
Stibb Cross by David Hill — 147
Langtree by Bernard Hill — 149
Changes at Berry Cross by Paula Fuller — 153
Land Sale — 155
Farming — 156

Chapter 13 — *Business and Employment* — 158
Scott's Bakery — 158
Horn's Flour to PHC — 159
Harris's Hauliers — 161
The recent history of Stapleton — 161
Tarka Springs – water from the rocks — 162
Withacott Dried Flowers — 163
Nicholls Poultry Appliances — 164

Chapter 14 — *Memories* — 165
John and Eleanor Folland — 165
Joe and Joyce Bond — 165
Richard Bray DSM — 166
Jock Mills — 166
Edna and Harold Daniel — 167
Bryan Ley — 167
Mr & Mrs Jack Beer — 168
Ben Copp — 169
Ethel Huxtable — 170
Daisy Watkins — 172
Barbara Babb — 172
Ron & Sandra Juniper — 173
Bernard Hill — 173
Norman Hill — 175
Olive Hill — 175
Peter Johnson — 175
Karen Pollard — 177
Sylvia Martin (Nèe Richards) — 177
Mary Geary (Nèe Harris) — 178
The Holmans by Mary Geary — 179
Alma Carter (Nèe Daniel) — 180
Rose and Ray Isaac — 181
Alice Beckley (Nèe Gerry) — 181
Shirley Clegg (Nèe Knapman) — 181
Sam Braunton — 181
Edgar Pett — 182
Bill Brooks — 182
The Hancock Family — 182
Eric Bond — 182

Introduction

Writing in 1985 in his original introduction Allan Edgcombe quoted the Reverend Richard Polwhele from his book 'History of Devonshire' (1793). When speaking of Langtree, Rev Polwhele said: 'there is little worth observing'. Mr Edgcombe then continued with the observation that, at first glance, Rev Polwele would appear to have been correct, as very little documentation of the parish seems to exist. However he discovered that the more he searched the more he found, and with a little imagination here and there he was able to trace the history of the parish with fair accuracy.

Having come to live in the parish more than forty years ago as a young bride, I myself have listened with growing interest to the tales of people and events, and 'how it used to be'. I've also seen the work and aspirations of today's generation seeking to build a meaningful future for the children and grand-children to come, be it their own or other people's, and felt an increasing need for something more of the last hundred years to be recorded whilst those who have first-hand experience can still share their stories with us. I am much indebted to all those who have talked so freely about memories and events long-past, and also those who have given me access to prized photographs and even whole family albums and scrapbooks to assist in compiling this story of Langtree. Thanks are also expressed to all who helped with the research, they are named elsewhere.

The aim of this book has been to record a general overview of what Langtree has been and is becoming as it grows, develops and changes with the passing years and generations. It was not 'my scene' to do the deep research of long ago times that Allan Edgcombe did so successfully in his original project for the benefit of the primary school children of Langtree with whom he had been associated for twenty five years. He on the other hand, did not have the time nor opportunity to cover what I have researched. Together, we have hopefully recorded a picture of the whole parish, encapsulating its history and its present identity, as well as giving a glimpse of its future hopes and aspirations.

Margaret Knapman

September 2003

Chapter One

FROM THE BEGINNING

There is not a great deal in the way of firm evidence, but I feel that there can be little doubt, that the area around Langtree was populated long before the Norman Conquest in 1066. Certainly, evidence of Stone and Iron Age Peoples have been found, dating back to prehistoric times. Flint tools have been discovered, tumuli, ancient stones and sites and several Saxon place names surround the parish. By the time of the Domesday Survey in 1086 Langtree was established as a prosperous manor. It was held by the Earls of Gloucester during the reign of Edward the Confessor.

Some Early Place Names

During Saxon times the Rivers Taw and Torridge were major landmarks in North Devon. Torridge means 'torri' – rough and violent. This was probably not a reference to the river itself but instead described the surrounding countryside which was clay, rough pasture and moorland. Locally we find the place name 'dun' as in Suddon which meant land enclosed from downs, and 'worthig' or ' worthy', as in Muffworthy or Bulkworthy which was land enclosed from moorland. During the late Saxon period many areas of wasteland and moorland were enclosed, ploughed and cultivated, and many hamlets and farmsteads owe their origin to this period. The land around Langtree, though wooded in the valleys, was probably moorland on the higher ground. The place name 'stowe', as in Stowford, was frequently used to denote a safe place or hiding place. This was often used at the time of the Viking invasions before the Norman Conquest. It is known that Vikings sailed up the Torridge Estuary at least to Appledore and Bideford in those early days, and some evidence suggests that they actually settled on Lundy.

The old Saxon village would have been quite small and centered around the Church (though not the present one), the Castle and a few dwelling houses between Forches Cross and the present village. Quite possibly the areas around Stowford, Suddon and Muffworthy would have been small farmsteads within the parish but since no written evidence exists, we cannot be sure.

The Domesday Book

In 1086, William the Conqueror ordered a survey to be made of his new Kingdom. This was carried out by Monks who compiled huge books listing everything held by the King in every Manor in the land. It listed land held, animals kept, slaves and other workers and the amount paid in tax each year.

It is at this time that the first documented evidence of the village occurs and we can form a true picture of life in the parish at that time. Langtree appears as LANGETREW (it was later to be spelt Langtrewa). The name as expected means tall tree and since Ash trees appear in other local place names – Ashberry, Hillash, Cholash – it seems probable that the original tree was an ash which stood on some prominent spot on higher ground in the parish. In any event, it is certain that the tree has long since disappeared.

The name Langtree can be found with different spellings at different times, e.g. Langatre or Langetre (1228), Langtrewe or Langtriwe (1350) or Langetree (1366).

The Domesday Book was compiled in a form of latin shorthand and the entry for Langtree is shown below – this is a copy of the original which was written several centuries later.

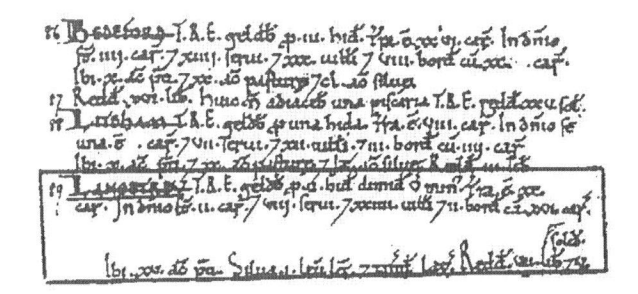

We can see that Langtree can be found with several other North Devon Manors, including Clovelly, Littleham and Bideford, all of whom were held by Brictric (Beorhtric), Earl of Gloucester, and later by Queen Matilda. Langtree was in the Shebbear Hundred and at the time of the Survey was about 4140 acres, much the same as it is today. The entry states that it paid tax for 2 hides, less 1/2 virgate. It had land for 20 ploughs or carucates, i.e. as much land as one team could plough in one year – a common measure of assessment used by the Normans. In Lordship there were two ploughs (the Lords demesne) and 8 slaves. There were 24 villagers and 2 smallholders with 16 ploughs. There were 2 pigmen. There were 15 acres of meadow and there was woodland measuring 1 league long (about 3 miles) and as wide. There were 6 cattle and 60 sheep. The Manor paid £7.5s.0d. *pensam et pansuram* (per year).

The Manor was therefore quite wealthy by Norman standards and almost half the size of Torrington which also included Weare Giffard who paid £20. 0s. 0d. per year. It was well established, of some standing, and quite productive.

Other Notes of Early History

Few, if any, of the early Lords of the Manor ever lived in Langtree or even visited it. In those days lands were held by people who were in favour with the King and they frequently held lands over a very wide area. Langtree was held by the Earls of Gloucester, but other local Barons would, in turn, have held lands for those feudal overlords, paying them annual taxes. Further tithes were paid to the Church which at that time was the Church of Rome.

The name Langtree occurs in other parts of England. One Manor of Langtree was part of the town of Standish, near Wigan in Lancashire, and was the home of Siward de Langtree (mentioned 1190) I am, however, unable to establish any link between this Manor or the family, and our own village. The actress Lily Langtree (1852–1929) was thought to have had some connection with that Manor. Another Langtree is near Oxford, where, I believe, there is another Langtree School. Listed in one of the A.A. Books is a 'Langtree Gardens' near Croyde.

The Ley Subsidy Rolls of the 13th and 14th centuries (these were early Taxation Returns and are still in manuscript form and not generally translated) give some interesting details which relate to present day place names of the parish. A glossary of place names is to be found in Appendix 7. The earliest local place name mentioned is that of Hillash or Hillashmoor, which first appears in 1238 as 'Illeryss'. This would appear to be Langtree's oldest established farm site, although, Suddon, Muffworthy and Stowford all bear Saxon names.

The Castle

An early history of Devon states that . . . .
"within the parish was a long since castle to be seen, but time doth hardly permit the circuit to show what it was."
We know of no date for the castle but its site is known and is near the foot of the lane leading to Langtree Mill. It is likely that it was pre-Norman and probably a wooden structure built on an earth mound. No evidence of stonework can be seen today. However, it is also near the site of the old quarry and it is quite possible that stone from the old castle or its associated buildings had been used for buildings and roads for many years. The castle may well have been an important structure in Saxon and Norman times, probably housing the Lord of the Manor or his representative. Other castles in the district assume greater importance, eg., Launceston or Lydford, but Torrington Castle was not built until some time later. It is known that the Lords of the Manor of Langtree once held the powers of capital punishment (Hundred Roll of Edward I 1272-1307). Could the ancient Manor Courts have once been held in the Castle?

Chapter Two

LORDS OF THE MANOR
(And Noteworthy Landowners)

Early History

Lyson's "Magna Britannia" (1822) states that:
"... the Manor of Langtree which had been Royal Demesne and part of Matilda's Dower belonged at an early period to the Earls of Gloucester".

Who was Matilda? A well documented and presumably true story throws some light on this.

During the reign of Edward the Confessor, Torrington, Bideford and Langtree were under the control of Beorhtric, Earl of Gloucester, a descendent of Alfred the Great, who held lands throughout the southwest of England (at this time all lands were owned by the King and important men held land and controlled it for the King). Beorhtric was sent to France as an ambassador to the Court of the Count of Flanders. There he met Matilda, the Count's daughter, who fell in love with him. However, Beorhtric did not return her affection and instead he returned to England. Spurned by Beorhtric, Matilda eventually married William, Duke of Normandy in 1052. William was later to become conqueror of England.

After the Norman Conquest, Beorhtric's lands were taken from him at the request of Matilda who was now Queen. He was imprisoned in Winchester where he died. His lands were given to the followers of William and many Manors in Devon were given to the Queen. Langtree was one of them, although it would appear that the Manor was restored to the Gloucesters at a later period.

The next account states that:
" . . . . the Manor remained under the Earls of Gloucester until after the death of Gilbert de Clare (Gilbert of Gloucester died 1295) and the Manor then descended to the Spencer family."

Thomas Lord Spencer, the last of these Earls, had a daughter, Isobel, who married Richard Beauchamp (Lord Abergavenny and Earl of Worcester). The Beauchamps were also Earls of Warwick so the Manor passed to the House of Warwick.

The Hankfords

Risdon's "Survey of Devon" (1810) tells of the Hankford family who held lands for the Earls of Warwick around the areas of Torrington, Taddiport, Monkleigh, Buckland Brewer and Langtree in the 1400s.

The Hankfords lived at Annery in Monkleigh and the family was responsible for much of the building of Monkleigh Church. Since Langtree Church is also thought to be late 15th century, it may well be that the family was responsible for its building also. Our Church is a similarly perpendicular style, using similar stone (perhaps Lundy granite), and may even be the work of the same master craftsmen. Other local Churches at Buckland Brewer,. Landcross and Little Torrington were built at about the same period.

A reference to the Hankfords states that:
". . . . in 1419 Richard Hankford died, seised of 1 messuage (buildings), 1 toft and 2 ferlings of land in Langtree, which he held of Thomas Beauchamp. Sir William Hankford died seised of the same in 1423."

Sir William's tomb chest is in Monkleigh Church. It is interesting too that a farm in Putford is still called Hankford. Its original name was Henecheforda (or Henca's Ford). It is an earlier family seat from which the family name derived. Sir William Hankford was Chief Justice of all England under Henry V in the early 1400s. He was doubtless a man of considerable influence and wealth.

The St. Legers

Risdon also mentions that the Manor of Week was sometime the Sackville's inheritance. Riverton and Ilash (Hillash) were the St. Leger lands descended to them from the Hankfords by an heir of Boteler (Butler), Earl of Ormond. The St. Legers, who also lived in Annery, held lands in Torrington and the locality during the late 15th and early 16th centuries. One tenement called Slade which was owned by them (I believe this to be in the Parish of Bucks Mills) was given by Anne, wife of James St. Leger, to the Chantry of Taddiport in Little Torrington.

The Chantry of Taddiport was a hospital for lepers and poor of the town of Torrington and the surrounding district. Leprosy was said to have been brought to England at the time of the Crusades. There were many such colonies in England and it seems unlikely that they housed only true lepers. Indeed, it is more probable 'leper' was used to describe any form of skin disease (often these were brought about by diet, which was mostly salted meat) and that these unfortunate people were removed from towns and villages so that the local people would not have to look at them. The old English word for Taddiport was 'Toad Pitt', a rather cruel way of describing the inmates. The hospital was supported by the charity of wealthy local landowners, and especially Anne St. Leger. With the hospital, which in any event was quite small, was the Chapel of Mary St. Magdalene where a Priest would say Mass one day each week for the poor folk. The Chapel still stands and the site of the leper fields can still be seen.

Much of the St. Leger Lands would have seemed to have passed to the Dennys Family of Orleigh Court. Patrons of Langtree Church between 1550 and 1600 were of this family, who would have held lands within the parish of Langtree as well as Monkleigh and Buckland Brewer. Some of the St. Leger estates in Langtree would have appeared to have been sold to the Browne family.

The Brownes

The Brownes had lived in Langtree for some time. An ancient Charter of about 1290 mentions land sold by Robert de Bulkaworth (note Bulkworthy) to Walter de Stapledon (note Stapleton) and Robert, his brother. The de Stapledons, a well known Devon family, held Annery before the Hankfords. The Charter mentions 'lands of Galhille' (near Forches Cross) and Roveton (Riverton) in the Manor of Langtree with all rents and services of Adam Browne of the lands of Galhille.' Adam Browne was probably a tenant farmer or villein of the estates of Robert de Bulkaworth and the Browne family descended from him.

His family went on to fame and fortune in the wool trade. Histories of Great Torrington mentioned Walter Browne (1394) who was one of Devon's most wealthy wool merchants and was probably from the same family. The fact that the name is found with various spellings, Brown, Browne, Broun, means little as names were frequently mis-spelt in old documents. The name of John Broun is mentioned in the Subsidy Roll of 1330 and several accounts mention that Sir Thomas Browne, Knight, built himself "a gentle (gentlemen's) house, with a park, at an area known as Browns Marsh". This is now known as Browns Lane. It is not known when Sir Thomas built his house, but there is still a farm, in fact two, one at East Browns in Browns Lane and one at West Browns (now called Stibb Hollow). Early ordinance survey maps state that West Browns is built on the site of an ancient Manor House and on the south side of the house is an area known as Deer Park. This I feel, is probably the site of Sir Thomas's 'gentle house'. Another very old building, Puthole, is nearby and is probably connected in some way to the old manor of early times.

The Browne family lived in the parish for many years.

An entry in Rev. J. R. Powell's "Notes on Devonshire and Cornwall Parishes and Families" is interesting:

"1484 Thomas Browne of Langtree. . . . Earl St. Leger (Quizy his landlord), tried at Gt. Tor. (Great Torrington) and executed by Richard III."

It would seem that the landlords of Langtree became a little too involved in the affairs of State and paid the price for it! At that time the manor was held by the Earls of Warwick. We know that in 1460 Sir William Nelme became Rector of Langtree and that his Patron was Richard Neville, Earl of Warwick (in fact Warwick the Kingmaker). The manor was held for the House of Warwick by the St. Legers. Richard Neville was killed at the battle of Barnet in 1471 and it is likely that his army included supporters from his many manors, including Langtree. Support for Royal causes was distinctly dangerous in those days but may well have been 'in the blood' of local lords of the manor such as Earl St. Leger or Thomas Browne. Both possibly fought with Richard Neville.

In 1483 Richard III put down a rebellion in the West Country which was led by the Duke of Buckingham (a former supporter of Neville) who at that time intended to make Henry Tudor (later to become Henry VII) King of England. The rebellion failed and Buckingham and his supporters were executed by orders of the King in 1483/4. Documented evidence shows that one supporter to be executed in Devon was indeed Earl St. Leger although I can find no mention of Thomas Browne. It is likely that lesser supporters were not recorded at the time and that Thomas Browne suffered the same fate as his lord.

In any event the Browne family survived and was mentioned again in the Subsidy Roll of 1524 – 27, when John Browne was listed as a gentleman of considerable means.

A Sir John Browne was a Rector of Langtree. He is listed as a priest who was instituted in 1536. He made the first return to King Henry VIII in 1536 when the Rectory was valued at £29.1s.3d. per annum. This was the tithe payable to the Crown after the separation from Rome and the establishment of the Church of England in 1535. He later became Rector of Bradford and Bradworthy. His Patron was John Browne, gentleman, doubtless of the 1524 Subsidy Roll.

The Devon Muster Roll of 1569 mentions another Thomas Browne. The Brownes probably held their land in leasehold from the Dennys family who were the true Lords of the Manor. Thomas Browne was assessed in 'goods' not 'land' but was clearly the most wealthy man in the parish. Elizabeth I had troubles in Westmoreland and Northumberland and required an army to control this. The Muster Roll was drawn up and men had to provide weapons and armour according to their wealth. The Brownes share was by far the largest from Langtree. We know a good deal about this Thomas Browne. He died in 1596 and is buried in the north aisle of Langtree Church. He and his wife Joan had nine children. There are no records of John, Agnes, Ellen, Margaret or Phillipa – these children possibly died young or married into poorer families. However, Charity married Richard Blackdown of Blackdown, Devon, and Jane married Walter Cottle of Yealmbridge. Brute, his second son was killed at sea off Port Rico (Porto Rico) whilst sailing with Francis Drake in 1595. Thomas, his third son, succeeded him and was knighted at Windsor in 1603. This is the only Sir Thomas Browne I can find – perhaps it is he who built the 'gentle house'. He died in 1613 and desired in his Will to be buried in Langtree Church "near where my father is buried". He left the bulk of his estates to the Harris family of Petersmarland. They remained landowners in Langtree for many years. The daughters of Sir Thomas married into the Stafford family of Stafford and the Brownes became extinct in Langtree.

The daughters of William and Jane Cottle, both married. The elder sister Chary, married Walter Blight of Dipper Mill, Shebbear and they had five children. The younger sister married the wealthy John Arscott of Downsland.

The Brownes certainly purchased some of their lands during the late 1500s and indeed other parts of the parish appear to have been sold off to lesser landowners. The Browne family had become quite large and references to them can be found in Church Registers in Buckland Filleigh, Sheepwash, Bradworthy, Bideford and Holsworthy. The Tavistock poet, William Browne, author of "Britannia's Pastorals" who was born in 1590, was, according to Risdon, 'probably from the Brownes of Langtree'.

The Rolles

At the beginning of the 16th century a new family name emerged as the Lord of the Manor of Langtree. The name of Rolle was to last for over three hundred years.

In 1602 Henry Rolle of Stevenstone (near Torrington) began buying land throughout the area. Bit by bit he brought land in Langtree until the family owned most of it.

The Rolle estates were very extensive and were found throughout Devon and even beyond. The family derived huge revenues from their lands and became very wealthy. Many members of the family became M.Ps. At the beginning of the 20th century the last member of the Rolle family, the

Hon. Mark Rolle, died and the estates passed to the Clintons.

Old documents show how parts of the parish were owned by other landlords. In 1602, an agreement was made between Henry Rolle and Richard Coplestone of Woodland, gentleman, and the Lord of the Manor of Shorneweek in Langtree, regarding a settlement of disputes about land enclosure of part of some wasteland in the Manor of Langtree called Horrage. This I believe to be Orange Hill. It illustrates, however, that Week was in the possession of the Coplestones who also held land in Little Torrington.

Another document relates to Thorne in 1604 which was then owned by John Pincombe of South Molton who died leaving his property to his son John.

Stowford was purchased by the Rolles in 1617 and thereafter remained part of the Rolle estate.

Abraham Barnefilde (Barnefield), Yeoman of Langtree owned Cholash and was given rights to Ashberry Common (Aisheberie) in 1604. The Barnefield's held land in Putford but were closely connected to Langtree. By 1690 they held leases at Riverton, Putshole, Stibb, Cholash, Aisheberry, Withcott, Bearhouse and Caster in Langtree as well as properties in Putford and Millford in Hartland. A memorial to Abraham Barnefield is in Langtree Church.

Other areas in the parish were held as Glebelands by the Church but by the end of the 19th century most of the Parish was owned by the Rolles.

After the Second World War, in the 1950s, most of the estates within the parish were sold off by the Clinton estates and many local farms and properties were purchased by their tenants at that time.

One other family name, that of the Tucker family, is especially worthy of note at this point. The Tuckers can be traced to perhaps as early as the Devon Muster Roll of 1569 and are certainly mentioned in the 1600s. By the end of the 19th century they had become much respected members of Langtree society. Descendents are still alive today and some still live in the village. They are probably Langtree's oldest surviving family.

Chapter Three

THE MEDIEVAL MANOR OF LANGTREE

The Church

A parish was an area served by a single church or ministered over by a single priest. Early churches were built of wood – none survive – and, in the main, it was not until after the Norman Conquest that Churches were built of stone. The Parish Church at Langtree is said to be late 15th century (and for some reason it is built in the style of many South Devon Churches) so it is more than probable that a wooden Church once stood on the present site. Even the present Church has been altered over the centuries and would once have looked somewhat different from today.

There are frequently chapels – often a single room attached to the larger houses – which were used by the local priest for some form of worship. These were usually built by local landowners to ensure that the priest prayed for them after their death. The system of purchasing such religious favours was discontinued after the separation from Rome in the 16th century. One such chapel was at Stowford, (the Chapel of St. Nicholas), which existed in 1412 when a licence was granted to Walter Cook, Chaplain at Langtree, to celebrate in the Chapel at 'Stauford'. Another was at Buda (the Chapel of St. Mary's) built in 1528. A third Chapel was in Brownes Lane near Putshole (not to be confused with the 19th century Methodist Chapel near Frost) and an ancient burial ground is nearby. It was possibly connected to the old Manor House. There is also a tale of a one-time monastery in the area but, since there was a priory at nearby Frithelstock it was possibly no more than a monk's cell, where a man lived a hermit's existence, some distance from his monastery.

The first recorded Rector of Langtree was Elias de Forde, a sub deacon who was instituted in 1285. His patron was Gilbert, Earl of Gloucester, the Lord of the Manor. Taxations of £10.0s.0d. per annum were paid to the Pope Nicholas IV during his time.

The leading social class in England was the landed gentry or squires. Yeomen and merchants later married into this class and the younger sons of manorial lords frequently passed out of it into trade, military service or into the Church. Sons of local barons became priests, often wielding great influence and not infrequently accumulating considerable wealth. Some did not even live in their parish. In Langtree one priest, Sir Simon (1317), obtained a licence of non residence, paying a fine of 40 shillings, and there were undoubtedly others. At that time all priests were given the title 'Sir' unless they were university scholars in which case they were titled 'Master'. In 1295 Edward I Model Parliament compelled all priests to pay taxes. In the century that followed many clergy were unpopular with the people as they became wealthy at the expense of their parishioners, collecting revenues and payments in kind from the people even when they did not live in the parish.

Life in the Early Manor

Early manorial life in Langtree was probably centered around the area of the Church and the present village. The castle too, would have played its part. It is in fact likely that the parish contained at least two manors, one at Stowford and at Langtree itself.

In keeping with many West Country Manors, Langtree probably had a two-field system of crop rotation and the village would have been surrounded by woodland, moorland and wastelands. Doubtless a road ran from Torrington to Holsworthy and Shebbear. Probably another ran from Berry to Newton St. Petrock. A route from Marland to Frithelstock would also have been important since Marland brick and tiles were used in Frithelstock Priory.

Overleaf is an artistic impression of what the Norman Manor of Langtree may have looked like.

At the head would have been the Overlord whose only allegiance was to the King. His estates would have been held for him by a local Lord of the Manor. He may possibly have lived in the Castle, or enjoyed some other more splendid house on the Lord's Demesne (i.e. the land was actually farmed for the Lord's own use.)

Artisitic Impression of the Norman Manor of Langtree (c1100-1200)

Officers were appointed to carry out the affairs of the manor and the chief of these would have been the Bailiff or Reeve. He too would have had a good sized house. In Langtree we have Rivaton (which means Reeve's Farm), the dwelling of the man who ran the manor. He was not the most popular figure since he had to collect revenues for his lord and since he was in charge of agricultural work, he planned the men's weekly tasks. However, when things went wrong he was also blamed by his Lord and master.

The Church owned some land and this was farmed by tenant farmers who paid taxes to the church. This payment was usually 'in kind' and not as money. The priest was not under the direct control of the Lord of the Manor. He was a freeman and would have had his own priest's house.

A small number of villeins or yeoman farmers lived in the parish. These men had some wealth and held the tenancy of their farms and had land which they could work for themselves. However, they were tied to the Lord of the Manor and in return for their farms they undertook to work for him for a number of days each week (week work) and on other occasions throughout the year (boon work) such as harvest time. This work was done on the Lord's demesne. Wheat and barley were the main crops grown and the villagers would have owned a small number of animals: sheep, cattle, pigs, horses and poultry.

All corn was taken to the Lord's Mill. Here the miller worked and since most mills were water mills, Langtree's was probably near the site of the present Langtree Mill. The miller was paid by each farmer with a share of the corn. A further share was given to the Lord of the Manor and the remainder was kept by the farmer. Payments to the Lord of the Manor were usually in kind i.e. in corn or livestock, and very little money changed hands.

Cottars were another social class. These were frequently craftsmen, carpenters, blacksmiths, bowmen etc. Also many were labourers who worked for the villeins or the manorial lord for a small wage. This too was usually paid in kind. There were also a number of slaves or surfs who were paid nothing for their labours but were 'kept' by the manor.

Crop rotation was simple. One system required two large fields which were divided into strips or furlongs. This system probably applied in Langtree. A three-field system was more common in the Midlands. Each farmer had a number of strips spread over the whole parish. One 'great' field was planted with corn whilst the other was left 'fallow' or used for grazing or hay. The following year the system was reversed so that each field was rested every other year. The great fields were often called 'parks'. One area in Langtree, north of the main road, is still called North Park and was probably one of the original great fields. The other may have been called Broad Park (still a local name on some farms) and would have been on the south side of the village.

Ploughing with oxen

The common land was used by the villagers for grazing and for recreation. Langtree Common was once quite extensive but, over the centuries, it has been enclosed into smaller fields and brought into various farms.

Threshing with a flail

The area surrounding the Lord's house was known as the Lord's Demesne and here may have been parkland or agricultural land according to the wishes of the Lord of the Manor. At the time of Domesday it was about one tenth of land under cultivation. The Lord's Demesne was possibly near the Castle, or possibly nearer to Rivaton. The area around Brown's Marsh or Brown's Lane was also favoured.

Surrounding the whole area of cultivated land was woodland (very important for hunting and as a source of timber and fire wood), moorland and and wasteland. This was to become much more important in later centuries as farmers gradually spread from the nucleus of the village. There are signs that this was beginning to happen even before the year 1200.

Life on the manor was hard and with few comforts. Winters were frequently colder than those of today. The River Thames regularly froze over so that annual fairs were held upon the ice. Many animals were killed in the autumn and salted for the winter. Houses were made of wattle and were thatched. Most were not more than one room in which people lived, ate and slept. Not infrequently room was also found for the remaining animals during the coldest part of the winter.

There were few rest days or feast days. Taxes were collected twice a year (Michaelmas and Lady Day) and other feast days included Christmas and the annual fairs days. There were two of these in Torrington: the feast of St. Michael the Archangel and the feast of St. George. Torrington also held a weekly market day and this would have been of importance to the inhabitants of Langtree.

Fairs were usually a time of great rejoicing and merriment and people travelled considerable distances to attend them. Amusements and sports included hunting, wrestling, and the now illegal pursuits of cock fighting and bull and bear baiting. Ale was brewed locally in most households and a sweet wine, called mead, was made from honey.

Market Day

Each manor held a Manor Court which was presided over by the Lord of the Manor or his Reeve. In Langtree the court once had the right of capital punishment. Trial was often by ordeal, for example being ducked in the river. If a man survived he was often proclaimed 'not guilty', if he did not he was thought to have been guilty anyway. There is no evidence of stocks or of a pillory in Langtree but probably some similar device was used. Men accused of very serious offences were usually sent to Torrington for trial.

How the manor spread

Gradually the picture changes. The villein class was probably responsible since they at least had the chance of bettering themselves. Often they had time to clear an area of woodland or moorland, usually with their Lord's permission, and cultivate it. These small areas developed into larger ones and the villeins built their farms on them. This kind of development was quite common in the West Country and it would appear that it happened in Langtree from about 1230 onwards. A succession of smallholdings and farmsteads sprang up around the outskirts of the parish. Records of these places first appear in Subsidy Rolls made for the purposes of taxation.

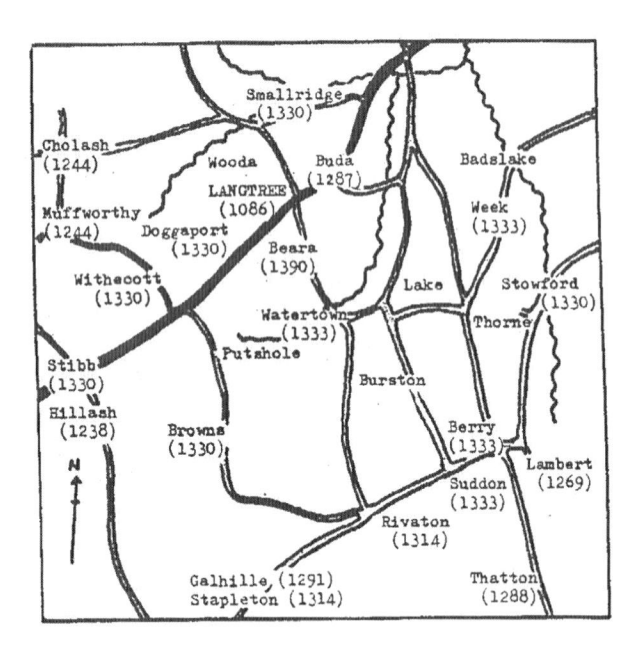

Map showing distribution of early farms and hamlets around Langtree (not to scale)

If we look at a map of the parish we see ancient farms in the centre such as Withecott (1330), Doggaport (1330), Brownes (1330), Buda (1287), Beara (1390), Watertown (1333) and Berry (1333). However, a closer look will show a ring of farms around the edge of the parish, many of even older origin like Cholash (1244), Muffworthy (1244), Hillash (1238), Galhille (later Stapleton) (1291), Rivaton (1314), Lambert (1269), Thatton (1288), Suddon (1333), Stowford (1330), Week (1333) and Smallridge (1330)

It is likely therefore that, even before the Norman Conquest, there was a fairly prosperous manor in Langtree itself and that during the following 300 years, this spread into a manor surrounded by a number of farmsteads and hamlets, some of which developed into manors in their own right e.g. Stowford, Week, Stibb and Stapleton. This development probably accelerated after the time of the Black Death (1349) when almost half of the population of England died. We cannot say for sure that Langtree was affected by this dreadful plague but it is unlikely that it could have escaped entirely. It is said that 17 out of 23 priests died from the Black Death in the Torrington Deanery alone. The list of Rectors (appendix 6) for Langtree shows two priests for the year 1348 and a third in 1351. Perhaps at least one of these died of the plague.

The effect of the Black Death was, initially, to cause manors to withdraw into small clusters since there was insufficient labour to allow them to spread too far. However, it quickly led to the lessening of the power of the feudal barons and that, coupled with the effect of general rural unrest (note the Peasants Revolt in Kent and East Anglia), ultimately led to the breakdown of manorial life in England.

During the 15th Century England was constantly at war. These wars were paid for by the people who worked and lived in the manors of England and, under feudal law, men had to fight for their overlord. Men were continually taken from the land in order to do this. Could men from Langtree have fought in the Wars of the Roses? At first glance this may seem unlikely since these battles were fought between the Houses of Lancaster and York. Yet, the Lord of the Manor of Langtree at that time was Richard Neville, Earl of Warwick, "Warwick the Kingmaker". He was the Patron of Sir William Nelme, Rector of Langtree 1460-61. Warwick was a nephew of the Duke of York and played a prominent part in the wars. He would have raised his army from men from his own estates, possibly including Langtree (remember Thomas Browne). The first battle was at St Albans (not in the North of England) and at which Warwick triumphed. He was eventually killed at the Battle of Barnet. The fate of Thomas Browne and Earl St Leger in 1484 serves to illustrate that national affairs were not far removed from the village in those days. If walls could only talk, those of the church could possibly tell us the answer.

Witchcraft

We cannot pass by this period of our history without mentioning the effect of witchcraft on the people. There were few doctors or physicians in those days and indeed the village barber performed most minor operations. Certainly, the best many of the poorer classes could hope for when they became ill was a visit to the local herbalist or witch. Most of these ladies have been persecuted throughout history but few had anything to do with the occult. The vast majority never engaged in forms of 'black magic' but were frequently old and eccentric and often widowed. Many were skilled at making a living by using the herbs and plants which grew in the hedgerows. It was often their only way of survival since most lived alone. No doubt many remedies failed, and when they did the witch got the blame. It was generally a fear of death and illness that led to their hatred. Many, of course, were poorly dressed and gave the impression of evil so that the ignorant masses felt that they had been cursed by them when things went wrong. Many were greatly trusted and were relied upon to act as midwives, as men knew little of the affairs of childbearing. Witches suffered cruel fates, most in the name of the Lord and always because it was felt to be in their own best interests, though it is hard to see, even in those days, how being burned alive was of benefit to anyone! (Note the fate of Joan of Arc 1428.)

The Langtree Rolls

Before we leave this period of our history, mention should be made of two ancient rolls or scrolls which were discovered in the Langtree parish chest towards the end of the last century. The earliest scroll was a 16th century copy of an aid granted to King Henry III (1216-1272) on his son John (strange since Henry had no legitimate son called John, his eldest son was Edward I) being made Knight - the charter was granted by Baldwin de Redvers, Earl of Devon. Why does Langtree have the honour of this document? It is perhaps significant that one of the leading barons during the reign of Henry III was Gilbert of Gloucester, Lord of the Manor of Langtree.

The second scroll is also a copy, and of an Involvement of Inquisitors of fees made in 1314 at the time of Edward II's invasion of Scotland and his wars with Robert Bruce (Bannockburn). Edward raised a large army for this encounter and would have needed a great deal of money in order to form it. The date coincides with the first mention of Stapleton and is possibly connected with fees paid by the de Stapeldon family at that time. Certainly it would seem that someone in the manor paid something and once again shows how closely the manor was concerned with affairs of state. It is further interesting to note that one of the leading characters during the reign of Edward II was Sir Hugh de Spencer who was also the Lord of the Manor of Langtree.

These scrolls had lain in the parish chest for many years and were discovered by the Rev. Herbert Barnes (Rector of Langtree 1873-1890). He gave them to Mr John Maclean for transcription and Mr Maclean was able to say that they were copies, not originals. They were therefore difficult to value but he offered to buy them, with the permission of the church wardens, for £20, in order to publish them. Although this must have been a tempting sum in those days, the Rev. Barnes and his church wardens were reluctant to part with them and correspondence went on for several years, by which time Mr Maclean withdrew his offer and the scrolls were returned to the rector. Further advice suggested that, since the rolls belonged to the parish and not to the rector, he had no authority to sell them anyway.

No one could say how the rolls came to be in the parish chest or shed any further light as to their origin but they are now kept and can be viewed at the North Devon Records Office in Barnstaple or at the County Records Office in Exeter along with the correspondence relating to them. One of Langtree's unsolved mysteries!

The use of gunpowder signalled the end of the Medieval period in England during the early 1500s but life in Langtree would have changed very little during the century that was to follow.

Chapter Four

TUDOR LANGTREE

Introduction

At the beginning of the 16th Century, England underwent many changes. At that time much of Langtree was owned by, or under the control of, the St. Legers of Annery and the Brownes of Brownes Marsh. The wool trade was still of great importance and the Brownes were wool merchants of considerable wealth. By this time we see the breakdown of early manorial life which was further eroded by the enclosure of land. Great fields were divided up into smaller ones and farms now had their own identity and fields. These fields may still have been widely scattered throughout the parish. By the end of the 16th Century very few open fields were left in Devon. This was not the case in much of the rest of England. Many of our present field boundaries will date from this time and we can also find evidence of the enclosure of common land which was to become such an important issue in the parish in the 19th Century.

Changes in the Church

The Church would have been built around the turn of the century and in 1528 St. Mary's Chapel was built at Crosshill. This was on or near the site of Chapels at Buda and the rector, Master Halnothene Arscott, was licenced to celebrate there. At that time England was still under the control of the Catholic Church in Rome and the village church would have been Roman Catholic.

However, the accession of Henry VIII in 1509 began a major upheaval in the affairs of the Church and the State. Henry objected to paying large revenues to the Pope in Rome and since his kingdom was dominated by the Roman Catholic Church, he had great difficulty in raising the money he needed to defend it. Coupled with this was the Pope's reluctance to allow the King to divorce his first wife, Katherine of Aragon, and marry Anne Boleyn. The culmination of this dispute was the separation from the Church in Rome and the establishment of the Church of England in 1535. This was quickly followed by the Dissolution of the Monasteries between 1536 and 1539, when lands of the Catholic Church were seized by the Crown and many monasteries fell into decay.

The role of the monasteries cannot be overrated before this time since, besides being the only places of learning in some areas (most books were still written by hand), they provided places of sanctuary and the monks played their part in caring for the nation's poor. Following their dissolution, the poor (owing to the breakdown of the manorial system there were an increasing number of these) had nowhere to turn and this necessitated the introduction of the Poor Law, making the responsibility for the poor a 'parish' responsibility. This did little to alleviate the plight of those in need.

At Frithelstock there was a Priory founded by Sir Robert Beauchamp and dedicated to St. Gregory. It was given to Sir Arthur Plantagenet at the time of the dissolution and, whilst it did not immediately disappear, its influence declined after the mid 1500s.

The King became head of the Church of England and thereafter taxes were paid to the Crown. The first of these was paid in 1536 by the then Rector of Langtree, Sir John Browne, when the Rectory was valued at £29.1s.3d. per annum, and the Church in Langtree became Church of England.

The Subsidy Roll 1524-27

General taxation had remained very much the same throughout the medieval period and Subsidy Rolls (taxation returns) were produced from time to time throughout that period. However, in 1524-27 a New Subsidy Roll was produced and is clearly translated. This provides us with names of people and places in Langtree at that time and makes interesting reading. Men were assessed according to their means in terms of land (L), goods (G) and Wages (W). It shows clearly who were the men of wealth and influence.

John Stapeldon (L 5) was the only man rated in 'land' and I can only assume from this that most of the parish was still owned by the St. Legers.

John Browne however was clearly the most influential and wealthy man in the parish and was rated at G 20. Other men were beginning to accumulate some wealth and are sometimes mentioned with the names of their farms. Appendix 1 lists the complete roll but some names worth noting are as follows:

Henry Babecombe	(G10)
William Yoldon	(G10)
John Boberygge	(G10)
*John Holamore	(G10)
*John Whitelock	(G8)
*John Mason of Withecote	(G8)
*John Prodham of Watertown	(G8)
Walter Smythe	(G6)
Richard Dyer	(G6)
Walter Bachelor	(G6)
*Jane Eyer	(G6)
*John Parsons of Birchall	(G2)
*Stephen Toker	(W1)
*John Waterman of Estlake	(W1)

In all 64 names were listed giving an indication of a total population of at least three times that number. No present day family names are found, although Whitlock was a local name until quite recently. Since spelling was rather irregular the names of Eyre (Ayre perhaps!) and Toker (Tucker?) are also interesting. Place names such as Withecote and Watertown had been mentioned in earlier rolls but now we find 'Holamore', Birchall (Birchill) and Estlake (possibly now Badslake).

The total taxation of the parish (spelt LANGTRE) amounted to £7. 5. 4d. – interesting that it had altered little from the time of the Domesday Survey almost 500 years before.

Village Life in Tudor Times

Life in the village would probably have changed very little and when changes came, they came slowly. The main source of wealth was still from agriculture and the wool trade and weekly markets and annual fairs continued to be held at Torrington. During this century also, the plague visited both Torrington and Frithelstock (1538), and it seems unlikely that Langtree could have escaped its effect. These epidemics were common during the 16th and 17th Centuries and frequently had disastrous results. The 'Great Plague' was not until a century later but nevertheless the countryside would have been greatly affected by these unfortunate epidemics.

Life in England in general altered considerably. Dress styles became more elaborate, for the wealthy at any rate, and houses took on a new look, especially in towns where, in some areas, much Tudor architecture remains today. Little remains in North Devon, though locally the Black Horse Inn in Torrington dates from this period. In Langtree itself, parts of a number of farms would have been built in the 16th Century but many new parts have been added since.

Because of the state of the nations poor, rogues and vagabonds began to roam the countryside and pirates sailed the high seas. Henry VIII was also responsible for the development of the navy and, with the exploration of the 'New World', Devon played a leading role in this period of maritime history. Sailors like Sir Francis Drake and Sir Richard Grenville sailed to discover new lands during the reign of Elizabeth I and there is evidence that men from Langtree joined in this. Bideford at that time was emerging as an important shipbuilding port and Drake and Grenville frequently sailed from North Devon ports.

Brute Browne

16th century sailing ship

One of the Browne family, Brute Browne, actually sailed with Drake and was killed at sea by the Spaniards off Puerto Rico, an island off the West Indies, in 1595. This was only 7 years after the defeat of the Spanish Armada though we cannot say that Brute Browne took part in that victory. Sailors in those days were politely called 'gentlemen of fortune' for, in truth, many were little more than pirates since to rob from the arch enemy of the day, the King of Spain, seemed fair game and Queen Eizabeth herself gained huge fortunes from these exploits. Drake plundered many a Spanish ship to take riches home to his Queen. Gentlemen such as Brute Browne may have helped to finance such voyages and frequently sailed on the ship as an officer or a gentleman patron. In any event, most stood to make a great deal of money if the voyage was a success. The venture in 1595 was however less successful and Drake, the General of the voyage, encountered much well organised opposition. Upon the death of Brute Browne who was killed during a Spanish attack, Drake, who was clearly close to him, said:

"I could grieve for thee dear Brute, but now 'tis no time to let down my spirits."

We do not know whether Brute Browne travelled for reasons of valour or fortune but in any event it proved to be his undoing. Drake himself was taken ill and died at sea shortly afterwards.

Devon Muster Roll 1569

Further evidence of family names in Langtree during Tudor times can be found in the Devon Muster Rolls. These were produced early in the reign of Elizabeth I in 1569. They were lists of the able bodied men in the parish who were required to take up arms, or at least to provide them, to serve Queen and Country.

An attempt to restore the power of the Catholic Church by the Earls of Northumberland and Westmoorland brought about a northern rebellion and the Queen required an army to defend her realm. In fact, no major battles took place and it is doubtful that the men of Langtree were called upon to do anything. However, those who were wealthiest once again had to provide most. Men who possessed land which realised a yearly income of between £20 and £40 were rated L8. Only Thomas Browne (son of John Browne) fell into this class and he was required to provide:

1 *harquebus* (an early firearm about 3 feet long which was fired by igniting: gun powder in a pen by means of a lighted wick;
1 *corslet* (a light body armour with metal breast plate and back plate – held together by straps – worn by pikemen
1 *pike*
2 *murrions* (helmets)
1 *bow*
1 *sheaf of arrows*
1 *steel cap*

Four men of the parish were rated L10 and had a yearly income of between £5 and £10 from their lands. These men actually owned their own lands, a departure from earlier records, suggesting that the estates of the St Legers (or maybe the Dennys family) were beginning to be sold off to their tenants. These men were Richard Prodham (now spelt Prudham), John Skynner, Nicholas Stapledon and Alexander Frayne (Frayne or Fraine was to become a longstanding Langtree name). Each of these had to provide:

1 *almein rivet* (similar to a *corslet* but with only a breast plate and apron)
1 *bow*
1 *sheaf of arrows*
1 *steel cap*
1 *bill*

Of the men rated in goods, John Waterman was the most wealthy. Rated as G6 (income between £20 and £40) he had to provide:

1 *almein rivet*
2 *bows*
2 *sheafs of arrows*
2 *steel caps*
1 *bill*

Nine men held goods valued at between £10 end £20 (G7) and each had to provide:

1 *bow*
1 *sheaf of arrows*
1 *steel cap*
1 *bill*

These men were Richard Collacott, John Prodham, Thomas Crocker, John Hunte, Richard Stapledon, John Smytham, Robert Fugars, John Meryfielde and Richard Martyn.

In addition 'the inhabitants not particularly charged by statute' (i.e., those not listed by name but everyone else in the parish) were instructed to find 2 *corslets*, 2 *pikes*, 2 *calivers* (another type of early firearm) and 2 *murrions*.

Tudor Firearm

It is perhaps significant that 14 men of Langtree were harquebusiers ie. they carried firearms (I am unable to say where the remainder of the weaponry came from) whilst only 2 were archers (the age of gunpowder had arrived!) 3 were pikemen and 10 were billmen

Billman

Other names worth noting from the roll were Robert Froste (Frost Cottages!) William and Thomas Dyer, Peter Clyverdon and Amys Whitlock – another longstanding local name (see Appendix 2 for further details)

The returns of a century later continue to mention some of these families whilst others are no longer present. It serves to illustrate how things change in the course of 100 years.

Communications

Most roads during the 16th Century would have been only mud or stone tracks. However, Langtree was on the main route from Barnstaple to Plymouth, a much used highway, especially by sailors. Many of the parish roads which exist today would have been there in Tudor times. Roads in general remained in much the same state until the end of the 19th Century when great steps forward in engineering enabled them to be improved. Hedgebanks marked the boundaries between properties and parishes and these became increasingly important during the periods of land enclosure. Many of Devon's hedgebanks were formed by the continual clearing of mud from the roads and lanes. The road became lower and lower whilst the hedges became higher. There is clear evidence of this in places such as Southcott Lane (field studies suggest that this lane dates from at least the 16th Century – possibly even earlier). The main road from Torrington would have followed much the same path as it does today since Taddiport Bridge dates from the 13th Century. However, hedges did not run the whole length of the road. Even in the 18th Century there were no hedges beyond Stibb Cross for some distance towards Holsworthy, since this was an area of moorland. Brown's Lane dates from Brownes Marsh in the 15th Century and the road to Berry Cross via Watertown is also an ancient lane. Similarly, the roads to the mill and the commons would have been important even in medieval times. Frithelstock and Monkleigh would have been reached via Southcott and also via Watergate (now Clements Hill). No road led from Stibb Cross to Monkleigh according to land maps of 1765, although roads did run through Withecott. Shebbear and Newton St Petrock would have been reached through Stibb Cross but lanes around Berry Cross, Rivaton and Stapleton are also very old. The road from Watergate to Berry and on to Peters Marland is very ancient and could have been the main access to Week and Stowford, both of which are ancient manors.

Master William Baylie – Rector 1594-1624

This was also the time of Shakespeare and of the beginnings of education for the less well off. Most of the wealthy classes had enjoyed an education of some sort for many years, usually under the direction of a private tutor or a priest, but now new schools were opening up for the poor as well. Some schools were beginning at Torrington and it is possible that some form of school existed in Langtree, possibly begun by the local rector. Early churches had been more than a place of worship, they were meeting places for the parish and in medieval times, dances were held in them. Often the early schools were financed by church charities and whilst local church charity records do not date as early as the l6th Century, they undoubtedly existed at that time. In 1601 Master William Baylie (Bailey or Bayley), the Rector, wrote:

"The Rectory enjoyeth about 53 acres of land one and another. . ."

He mentions a 'close' beneath the highway called North Park. North Park is now north of the road and the area mentioned by Baylie is known as Lovelands. This was mentioned as early as 1408 as La Lovelonde. The area is part of what is known as The Loveland Charity and still exists today.

It would be wrong to assume that William Baylie actually ran a school but he did seem to be a very determined gentleman. His writings are perhaps the earliest hand written documents that we can find from a rector in the parish. He was instituted as rector in 1594 and remained so until 1624.

During the early part of his rectorship he brought a complaint in a lawsuit against the widow of Eustace Marshall, the previous rector. He claimed that, although Eustace Marshall collected the tithes and oblations due to him, he let the chancel fall into disrepair. There were no shingles (oak slates) on the roof or tiling on the floor, and one glass window had been blocked up with stones. The estimated cost of repairs was £15

Part of the writings of William Baylie in his complaint against Eustace Marshall

His note of the Glebelands of the parish, written in 1601, also provides interesting reading:

"The Rectory enjoyeth about 53 acres of land one and another..."

"One close lying beneath the highway leading from Holsworthye to Great Torrington called North Park...

"One close lying by the west side of Spurwill Moor, alias Langtree Moor, called Psonage [sic] Meddowe...

"One pcell of ground with one coppes, called Pitt Meddowe, about one acre, the way thither through pcell of lands of John Martyns tenament of Langtree Town... (both William Pytte and John Martyn were mentioned in the Subsidy Roll of 1524 and the Muster Roll of 1569)

"One little pcell called Water Towne meadowe, liing at the foot of the way leading to Watertown.

"One pcell called the Fyrse Park.
"The Towne place close
"The Kyching Park
"The east park
"The wood park
"Woodland or coppes about 3 or 4 acres, with gardens bacsydes and Towne place."

William Bayly, Rector.

There is no mention of the actual Rectory buildings. William Baylie was clearly a rector who tried to record what was his responsibility and put right what had been allowed to deteriorate by those who had preceded him.

Of the other Tudor rectors, most came from the wealthy classes, though it is interesting that one, Thomas Wasshington, was recorded as a 'Public Preacher' when instituted as rector in 1565-6.

Chapter Five

THE STUART PERIOD
The 17th Century

The 17th Century began with the death of Elizabeth I and the accession of James I (the King of Scotland) in 1603. This was quickly followed by further religious unrest and the 'Gunpowder Plot' in 1605.

In Langtree, the Brownes were soon to leave the parish and their estates were inherited by the Harris Family. However, Sir Henry Rolle of Stevenstone began to buy land in the parish at the turn of the century and the Rolles were to remain the principal landowners until the beginning of the 20th century.

The Harris family were not without influence however. In 1629, Frances Toms of Suddon brought a court case in Exeter against Christian Palmer, also of Suddon, for deformation of character. She called upon Christopher and Ephraim Harris to state that:

"In the town place of Suddon where John Toms and Humphrey Palmer live, Christian Palmer called her a whore, mare and bitch."

I cannot say how the case ended but Christopher and Ephraim Harris were called upon to speak up for her.

In 1679, a rate was fixed in order that repairs should be made to the church. Philip Harris was the leading landowner at that time and had to pay 10 shillings. Possibly some of his land was held in 'leasehold' from the Rolle estates.

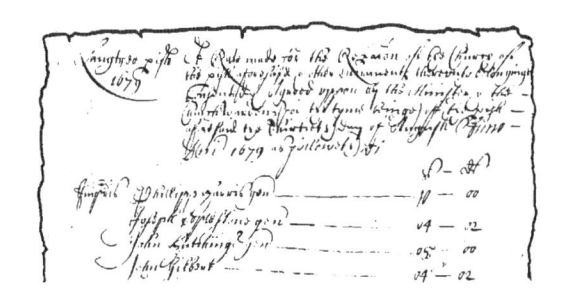

Part of the 'Rate' fixed in August 1679 showing that Philip Harris paid 10 shillings

The Civil War

The century did not start well and things deteriorated further with the accession of Charles I in 1625. Charles taxed the people heavily. Parliament tried to restrict him and the result was a split between King and Parliament which was largely made up of the principal landowners.

In Devon, the King's troops were billeted in Exeter and Plymouth and the townspeople had to maintain them. Their riotous behaviour did not endear them to the local people. The King ignored the many protests and, to add to the discontent, many men from westcountry ports were 'press-ganged' into the navy and army.

Acting without Parliamentary consent, the King levied a tax called 'Ship Money'. This was originally intended to help rid the seas of pirates but Charles used it to strengthen his own navy. The tax was first levied upon the coastal counties and then upon the whole country. Devon's share was £9,000. People objected and many refused to pay.

In addition, a shortage of grain in the 1630s led to further difficulties for the poor until "the roads were crowded with beggars, vagabonds and the wandering Irish". The Irish rebellion of 1641 led to many Irishmen coming to England, many to Devon, providing a new threat from the Catholic Church.

People petitioned their local Justices and, in turn, they themselves petitioned Parliament and urged the King to cooperate. The petition of 1641/2 – the same year, incidentally, as the sundial was placed on the church porch, although I can find no connection – was signed by the Baronets, Justices and Gentlemen of Devon and was known as *The Devon Protestation Return*. It gave overwhelming support for Parliament 'against all popery'. All males over the age of 16 were asked to sign it and in Langtree the return contained the names of 130 men. Only one man, Thomas Bayliese, is recorded as having 'not taken the protestation' though the reason for him not having done so is not given. It is interesting to note that Thomas Baylis followed William Baylie as rector of Langtree in 1624. I cannot say whether or not he was the same man, but we do know that he was not rector of Langtree in 1641, since Nicholas Monck was instituted as rector in 1640. A full list of men who signed the protestation is listed in Appendix 3.

Civil War was becoming inevitable and the country took sides. Most of Devon supported Parliament though many were not anxious to take up arms against the King. During the early battles men from the locality joined forces, either Royalist (Cavaliers) or Parliamentarian (Roundheads) – some changed sides as battles went first one way and then the other. Torrington seemed to have been a Royalist stronghold for most of the war whilst Bideford and Barnstaple were for Parliament, though both changed hands more then once during the war. The final battle of Torrington was to be a decisive turning point in the defeat of the Royalists when their resistance in the westcountry was finally broken.

Local skirmishes undoubtedly took place and, in the main, local people were the losers. Crops were often ruined, food was taken by both armies as foraging parties raided local villages and farms, and men were taken from the land in order to fight.

Local men certainly did fight. One Langtree man, John Fraine, became a major in Cromwell's New Model Army. He probably fought battles all over the country – the army was trained at Windsor – only to be killed at the Battle of Torrington fighting under Sir Thomas Fairfax at the moment of Parliamentary victory. A memorial to him is in Langtree Church. Little remains of it now since it is badly worn. It has been used as a flag stone for many years and is between the font and the main door. The centre of the stone has been used by a family called Gilbert but around the edge runs an inscription:

"Major John Fraine who was slain in battle at Great Torrington fighting under Sir Thomas Fairfax A.D. 1646."

Only part of the inscription can still be seen.

Fraine Family Arms

The Battle of Torrington – 1646

There were many battles fought in and around Torrington but the major, and final, one was fought on 16th February 1646. It began as a result of Sir Ralph Hopton strengthening the Royalist defences there with 4,000 horse and 5,000 foot soldiers. (They were in fact on their way to Exeter to relieve the besieged city and had come up from Cornwall, probably through Langtree.)

Sir Thomas Fairfax, Lord General of the Parliamentary forces, and Oliver Cromwell, his Lieutenant General, were at the time in Exeter and, on hearing the news, set out for Torrington with an army of about 10,000 men. Reaching Stevenstone late in the evening, Fairfax decided to delay further advance until dawn the next day. At about midnight, mistakenly thinking that the Royalists were about to retreat, he sent a small party into the town to investigate. The Royalist guards opened fire and in the confusion both sides brought up further support and the battle began. It was, I believe, the first example of a night battle fought by English troops. The superior training of Fairfax's army finally drove the Royalists back along Calf Street and into the town. Royalist prisoners were herded into the Church. Fairfax was unaware that it had been used to store some 80 barrels of gunpowder and, at the height of the battle, the church blew up killing 200 prisoners and their guards, destroying the church and with it many of Torrington's ancient records.

Cavalier

Roundhead

The explosion shook the town and the Royalists fled with the Roundheads in hot pursuit. Attempting to reach the safety of Cornwall, Hopton's troops crossed Taddiport Bridge and made their way to Launceston, reaching it in amazingly quick time. Many would have passed through Langtree chased by Cromwell and his men who eventually gave up the chase at Woodford Bridge. Doubtless many skuffles took place along the way. It would have certainly been a night to remember in the village.

Conclusion of civil wars

Charles I was eventually executed for treason and Cromwell's 'Commonwealth' ruled England for about 12 years. Further religious persecution followed the Civil Wars and many religious festivals, including Christmas, were abolished as Puritanism established a hold on life in England. The people seemed little better off under Cromwell than they had been under the former King and widespread discontent resulted in a move to restore the monarchy once again. The restoration of the monarchy and the crowning of Charles II was to be the first thing recorded in Langtree's oldest remaining Church Register.

Rectors of Langtree during the Civil War Period

Nicholas Monck

At the outbreak of the Civil Wars the Rector of Langtree was Nicholas Monck (1640), the third son of Sir Thomas Monck of Potheridge in Merton. It would seem that Nicholas Monck probably did not live in Langtree since he had also been given the Rectory of Kilkhampton. He probably allowed curates to officiate on his behalf in the village. The Protestation Return mentions John Badcock (minister) who is not listed as a Rector of Langtree in other publications and Theophilus Powell, who was eventually instituted as Rector in 1662 (he was formerly curate at Great Torrington), certainly was in charge of the church by 1650 and began the oldest surviving Church Register in 1659. Nicholas Monck however, together with his brother General George Monck, played a prominent part in the restoration of King Charles II in 1660. George Monck was to become Duke of Albermarle and Earl of Torrington, whilst Nicholas was rewarded by becoming Provost of Eton and Bishop of Hereford in 1660. He unfortunately died in the same year and was buried in Westminster Abbey.

Theophilus Powell

The Reverend Theophilus Powell became Rector of Langtree in 1662 but he had acted as rector for some years before that time. In 1659 he began the oldest Church Register of the parish that is still in existence. Much evidence and many records of Langtree exist from ancient times and these documents are available for viewing at the North Devon Record Office in Barnstaple or the County Records Office in Exeter. He wrote:

"The Register of Langtree 1659-
Theophilus Powell.

Memorandum

King Charles ye first was beheaded by his subjects Jan. 30, 1648.
King Charles ye second came to England in ye month of May 28, 1660. And was crowned King, April 23, 1661, being St. George's day.

Vivat Rex."

Powell's patron was Sir John Rolle of Stevenstone who was also actively involved in the restoration of Charles II and was knighted by the King in 1660. It would seem from this that the clergy and their patrons were very much on the side of the King during the Civil Wars, even if their parishioners were not always so.

John Elston

John Elston replaced Powell in 1667 and remained rector for nearly 40 years. He is buried at Little Torrington.

In 1679 John Elston wrote a lengthy account of the 'Parsonage'. It is, I believe, the earliest account of the Rectory buildings. It too, is now housed at the North Devon Record Office in Barnstaple.

He describes the house as . . . "A parlour hall and buttery of stone. Over this is a parlour chamber with a chimney. Nearby, at the head of the stairs, is one little chamber and a buttery chamber . . . ."

A Ground Floor plan would have looked like this:

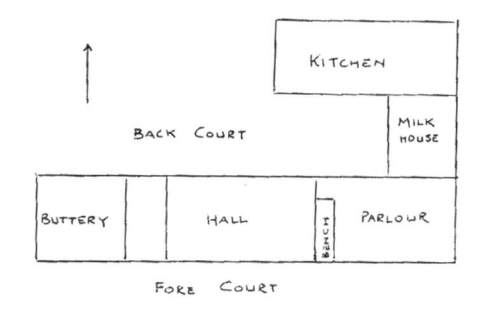

A First Floor plan would have looked like this:

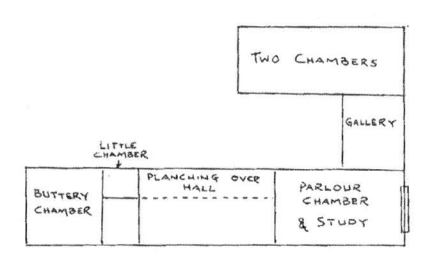

He also writes of an orchard, a barn, a shippen. a stable and over it a tallet with a slee house called Reed House, and a linney. The forecourt was walled all round ". . . a little herb garden and a newe garden."

It was clearly an extensive house and much of it remains today. Alterations were made to the Rectory during the 19th century but the original parts to which John Elston refers are still at the east end of the present building.

He also writes of the 'Glebe Land'. Much of this was mentioned in the earlier account of William Baylie in 1601. There seems to be very little change. The account was signed Jo. Elston, Rector, John Bragg and John Judd, Churchwardens (both of these men were listed in the Protestation Return).

Doctor John Handford
John Elston was an influential figure and a number of documents signed by him are still in existence. One such document was written on behalf of John Handford of Langtree, requesting that he be given a license to practice the art of 'Chirurgy' (surgery). The request was made to the Bishop of Exeter and was signed by John Elston.

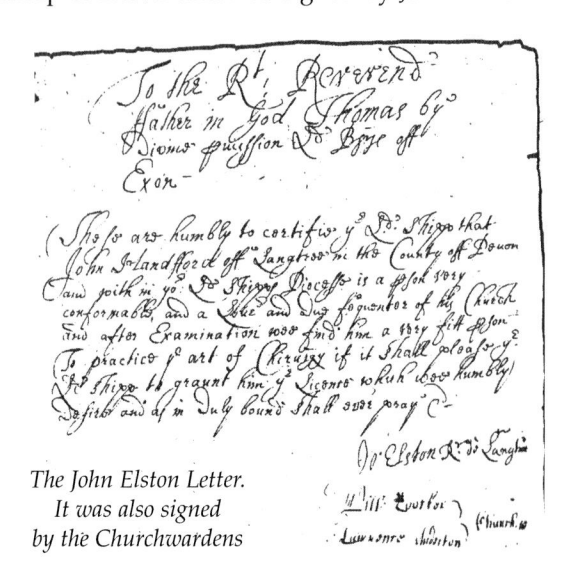

The John Elston Letter. It was also signed by the Churchwardens

Anyone setting up as a doctor, midwife or school teacher in those days had to obtain a license from the Bishop who required to be assured that he or she was a member of the Church of England and a fit person to practice so that they would not influence those in their care towards Catholicism or Non-conformity. I can find no other reference to Doctor Handford however and can only assume that he moved to the village towards the end of the 1600s in order to practice there.

Some other 17th Century Characters
The Barnfields
It is during the first years of the 17th Century that we find the first mention of the name of Barnfield. The Barnfields owned a farm in East Putford called 'Mambury', but in 1604 an agreement gave Abraham Barnefilde, Yeoman of Langtree, rights to 40 acres of land on Aisheberrie Common.

A further agreement in 1616 stated that John Barnefield and Jacott Barnefield should jointly hold lands at Cholash, New Common and Ayshbery. In 1642 John Barnefield made over his lands at Cholash to his son Abraham, his heir (probably the grandson of the Abraham of 1604). It would seem that Abraham was to be the Christian name of several members of the family. This Abraham Barnfield was to become a prominent gentleman in the parish though his name rarely appears on Langtree returns since his 'home' parish was Putford.

He was however 'overseer' to the poor of Langtree and in 1688, together with Daniel and John Tucker, his position was shown when "Joan Vigures, a poor child, was bound to Abraham Barnfield until the age of 21". Such was the lot of the poor that churchwardens and overseers were responsible for their upbringing and frequently children were bound to them in service.

Abraham Barnfield died the same year (1688), his wife Joan having died previously. On the north wall of the Church is a memorial to them both, erected by his son in 1724. The inscription contains a clever 'play' on the family name:

> "Out of God's field into his barn are gone They who whilst here were Barn and Field in one."

The old man left his lands to his son, Abraham junior, and doubtless responsibility for Joan Vigures, and money for the poor of the parish.

By 1690 the Barnfields owned or rented many farms in the parish. A land lease between John Fortescue (probably of Buckland Filleigh) and Abraham Barnfield of Langtree, gent, mentions lands at Rivaton, Putshole, Stibb, Cholash, Caster, Aishberry, Withecott and Bearhouse in Langtree, and also lands at Milford in Hartland. The family were frequently connected with the church and the poor rate in the parish and when Abraham junior died in 1726 he left 20 shillings to the poor of Langtree in his will.

A Gentleman of the Stuart Period

The Tuckers

The Tucker family certainly were mentioned in a number of local Returns. Possibly the earliest mention of the name was that of Stephen Toker in 1524. Arthur, Walter and William Tucker were named in the Protestation Return of 1641, and the "lands of Walter Tucker" were mentioned in the Church Record of 1679 when John Elston states that they were "on the left of the road towards Withecott". By 1726 Matthew Tucker was given a 99 year lease on a building erected at Kings Frost – probably Frost Cottages.

In 1688 Daniel and John Tucker shared responsibility with Abraham Barnfield for the welfare of Joan Vigures, As members of the Church Council they were overseers for the poor.

During the next century, in 1728, William Tucker was to become the first licenced landlord of the Green Dragon.

The Tucker family were to remain leading characters in Langtree for many years, perhaps the most prominent of whom were John Elias Tucker and Miss Peternel Tucker during the 19th Century. Both are buried in the churchyard with other members of the family. Whilst originally at Frost, they were later associated with Rivaton and Lake. Although the original family name does not survive (though off-shoots probably do) descendants of the family still live in the village and indeed at Lake.

The Abbotts

On the north wall of the Church is a large plaster Royal Arms. It is dated at the time of George I (1714-1727) but it is thought to have been originally the Stuart Arms of Charles II (1660-1685) and had been altered during the reign of George I. In Langtree, at about that time, lived a plasterer, John Abbott of Southcott. He was born in 1639 and died in 1727 at the age of 87.

*John Abbott of Frithelstock 1639-1727
Sketched from an original oil painting*

The Abbott family were granted Hartland Abbey at the time of the dissolution of the monasteries under Henry VIII and, later, a branch of the family moved to Frithelstock, the Priory being part of the Abbey estates. The family became plasterers and began what is known as the 'Frithelstock Book' – a collection of drawings and designs used in the trade. The book was continued by John Abbott who is perhaps the best known of the family. Most records for the family are from Frithelstock Church since the family also owned Culleigh in Frithelstock.

It was in Frithelstock Church that John Abbot designed and built the Kings Arms as illustrated overleaf. The illustration is from his original pattern book. The work was begun in 1662 and was completed in 1677 and for which John Abbott received the sum of £13. 6s 8d.

The Arms in Langtree Church is similar and was also the work of John Abbott though I can find no drawings, dates or costings. It would probably have been erected during the time of Rector John Elston.

John Abbott was famous throughout Devon for his work on ceilings – though I can find none surviving in Langtree – and for plaster ornamentals. Some work has been attributed to other members of the family, including his father and his son who succeeded him.

This page from John Abbott's Pattern Book shows his original drawings for the Royal Arms in Frithelstock Church. It is similar to the Langtree Design.

In 1932, during the rebuilding at Putshole, a plaster ornamental of the *Judgement of Solomon* was discovered behind plaster in one of the bedrooms. It was unfortunately damaged beyond repair when attempts were made to remove it. It was dated 1640 and may have been made when the Barnfields owned the house. The date is too early for the work to have been John Abbott's though the design is to be found in the 'Frithelstock Pattern Book' (another example of this work can be found in Stafford Barton, Dolton) so it was either wrongly dated or was the work of his father, Richard, who also lived in Langtree until the time of his death in 1663.

The last surviving member of the Abbotts lived at Westward Ho! for many years and died in the late 20th century. Indeed, it was she who owned the pattern book, several of the plasterer's tools and the oil painting of John Abbott.

Devon Hearth Tax Roll 1674

The Devon Hearth Tax Roll of 1674 provides us with a further list of local names of the Stuart Period. A tax of 2 shillings per hearth was levied and collected twice a year, at Michaelmas and Lady Day. Walter Tucker and Philip Harris were both mentioned, as was the Rector, John Elston. It would seem sad to note the demise of the Fraine family, Anne Fraine now being listed amongst the poor and exempt from the tax. No other Fraines are mentioned so I can only conclude that, following the death of John Fraine at the Battle of Torrington in 1646, the family fell upon hard times. It is certain, however, that the family survived for some time afterwards, indeed, the name Frain appears on the First World War memorial plate in the church. Some other names which survived from an earlier period were, Palmer (now quite a large family), Merrifield, Bowman, Thorne, Collacott and Rowe. The name of Prodham (or Prudham), so prominent in the 16th Century, is no longer present

Illustrations of 'The Judgement of Solomon' and the plaster ornamental similar to that found at Putshole

The Phipps Charity

In 1676, a gentleman by the name of Robert Phipps died. (He was, I believe, not of this parish though a John Phipps was Rector of Little Torrington in 1635. In his will he:

". . . gave to the parish of Langtree £60 to be bestowed in lands of inheritance, the rents and profits whereof were to be employed to buy linen cloth at Easter, for old men and women, such of the said parish as had none or little relief from the said parish, the said linen cloth to be dowlas of 10d a yard and each poor man and woman to have three yards a-piece".

This generous endowment became known as the Phipps Charity and still exists today. Robert Phipps directed his executors (William Edye, William Sumpter and Thomas Cole – again not of this parish) to nominate so many trustees from the parish as they should think fit. In 1681, the executors purchased land called Little Close, Middle Close and North Close, which is part of a tenement called East Hole in Black Torrington, from John Webber. The rents from this land were used by the charity and by 1818 these brought in £13 annually. Cloth continued to be given to the poor of the parish until 1863 when, because of the shortage of cotton brought about by the American Civil War, money was given instead. The practice of giving money on Good Friday from this charity continues to the pensioners of Langtree to this day. For further details see Appendix 4.

Employment

During this period of English History, most forms of employment in rural areas were connected with agriculture. Farms, particularly in North Devon, were quite isolated. They frequently employed a number of farm hands, either on a regular or an occasional basis, but the village centres were not very large. The great fields had by this time been completely divided up in this area, and common land continued to be enclosed. One result of enclosure was that a number of smallholdings were sold to more wealthy Landowners since the tenants were unable to afford to provide hedges or fencing. Many men had no regular work and, because of the enclosure of the commons, nowhere to graze their few animals. The number of families who went 'on the parish' – the poor rate – increased considerably. Methods of agriculture however, had improved very little from manorial times. The horse was now the means of pulling plough, cart and carriage.

A peasant farmer and his horse

Glovemaking

At this time, the practice of glovemaking was fast becoming an important activity in Torrington and women from Langtree may well have been employed in the industry. Merchants from the town would take the locally produced leather and chamois to villages around the district where the women would spend tedious hours sewing together the ready cut shapes into gloves. Torrington gloves were of rough quality in the 17th Century, It was not until the 19th Century that the area became renowned for its fine gloves and by that time most were made in factories in the town. However, this earlier work, probably by candlelight or at the door of their cottages, must have been a hard way for the women to make a little extra money since they were paid according to the quality and the quantity of the gloves they produced when the merchant called to collect them the following week with a fresh supply of 'cut-outs'. A little extra money was nevertheless very necessary to many families since a labourer who worked on a farm received a very low wage. Often he worked for only part of the week, or at harvest time, and even then he was frequently paid in kind and given food instead of money. Labourers often lived in houses belonging to the farmer and although they paid very little rent, families were very badly off. Wages earned from glovemaking often kept the family 'off the parish'.

Craftsmen

Cobblers, tailors, barbers, builders, carpenters and wheelwrights, potters and blacksmiths lived in almost all villages and there were many other skills as well, since the village was in many ways self sufficient even in the 1600s. Thatchers, plasterers, pewterers, gold and silversmiths would also have lived locally and, although these men would have served a number of villages and even small towns, they rarely travelled far.

Local craftsmanship was on the increase in the 17th Century and much fine work was produced. The pulpit in the church is an excellent example of the work of this period, its woodcarving probably done by a local man. There was once a rood screen in the Church, also probably made about this time. It would have been a large oak screen, finely carved, and which divided the chancel from the rest of the church. It was removed in the early 19th Century when repairs were made in the church.

At Arlington Court there is further work of a craftsman of Langtree. His name was Simon Sanders and he was a pewterer in the village in the late 1600s and early 1700s. He probably moved to the village late in the century since his name does not appear on any returns. The name

Sanders (Saunders) does however frequently appear on documents of the 18th and 19th century. Pewter was used for a number of kitchen and dining utensils such as plates, mugs, jugs, tankards and cutlery. On display at Arlington is a set of spoons made by Simon Sanders. There are six in all, three from one mould and three from another, although they are quite similar. They were made to commemorate the reign of Queen Anne 1702-1714, probably at the time of her Coronation. It is said that at least nine different castings of these spoons are known.

The Mariners Way

Langtree was once on a route called the Mariner's Way, which ran from Bideford (or perhaps Appledore) to Dartmouth. Sailors would cross the county by the most direct route – usually on foot and therefore often on footpaths – in order to get from one ship or one port to another. The route probably avoided the meanderings of the Torridge. It is recorded in the Church Records that the Rector or his Churchwardens had to pay any sailor who passed through the village and requested help one shilling for bread.

The Plague

Mention must also be made of the Great Plague of 1665. Plagues were common throughout this period of history and, sadly, they visited different areas at different times. It is not easy to find evidence that Langtree was affected but we do know that at the end of the Civil War period (1646) many people in Bideford died of plague. John Strange, the Mayor of the town, worked with those who were ill – against the advice of many who were afraid to do so – and eventually died from the epidemic himself. It is probably true to say that the whole area of Torridgeside was affected to some extent and Langtree could hardly have escaped completely.

The 17th century was a strange mixture of poverty, misery and unhappy events, and developments in craftsmanship, furniture making, art and architecture, and elaborate costume and custom for those fortunate enough to have been born into the landowning and wealthy classes. It would appear that Langtree was not amongst the more wealthy areas since so little remains of the period today.

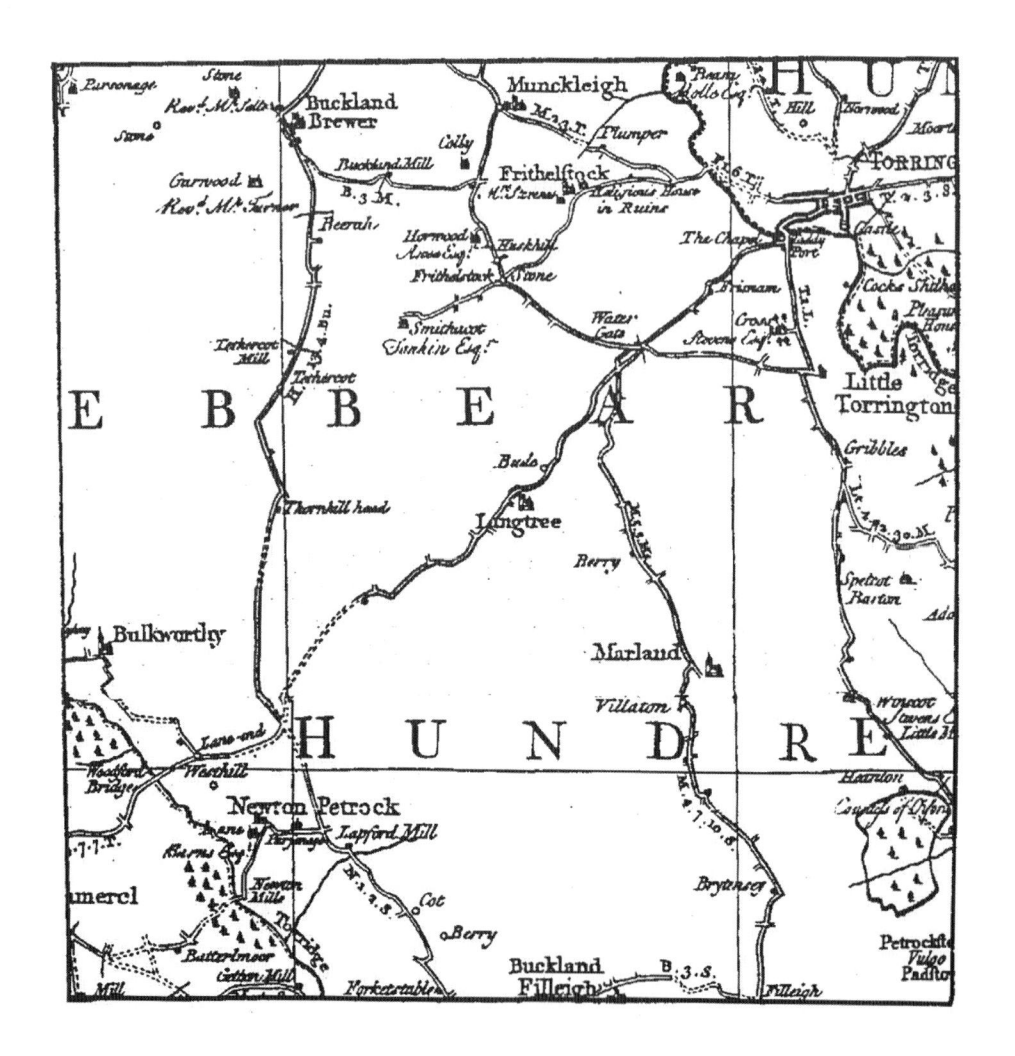

Land Map of 1765

Chapter Six   THE EIGHTEENTH CENTURY

The Agricultural and Industrial Revolutions during the next 100 years brought about many changes in England. In general there was a shift away from the land, into industry. Rural populations declined, some villages disappeared altogether, and towns grew in size. However, the centres of industry were mainly in the North and Midlands and, locally, the population of Langtree tended, if anything, to increase.

Methods of farming were changing everywhere as new crop rotations were introduced and further common land was enclosed. In 1726, for example, John Rolle of Stevenstone, the Lord of the Manor, granted a lease to Thomas Nanskivill for the tenament of Smalridge with common pasture upon the waste called Horridge. Constant erosion of common land in this way was becoming a serious problem for the villagers who were losing their grazing land and areas where they were in the habit of going to trap rabbits and small game. Sheep farming was becoming less important as the wool trade declined in the south west. Yorkshire became the centre of the woollen industry in England as factories and mills were built in the new towns. Mills in Torrington began to close as they ceased to compete with goods produced in the north of England

The Poor
One outcome of this was an increase in the number of people supported by the parish poor rate. If no work was available in their town or village it was a great risk for a man to go to another place. Since the Act of Settlement, any man found in a Town other than his own, without work, could be whipped or placed in the stocks. To help overcome this problem, workhouses were etablished where work was given to the 'ablebodied' poor in return for a very small wage. The first workhouse in Torrington was built in 1736 and the inmates were given weaving to do. It is unlikely that Langtree families ever worked there since each parish was responsible for its own poor. Many people preferred to starve rather than be labelled 'poor' since poor relief was very small and not always given in money. Poor houses were overcrowded and filthy and conditions in the workhouse were even worse.

Some examples of the affairs of local Poor Rates are as follows:

1711. In return for an agreement for part of the 'two Challashes', John Blight had to pay 4d. per month and Abraham Barnfield 3d. per month to the Langtree poor rate. They had to pay other rates and taxes in the same proportion.

1718. John Smythe, a blind fiddler, was given 10s. 0d. from the Torrington Poor Rate for a new fiddle.

1726. Abraham Barnfield left 20 shillings to the 'poor of Langtree' in his will.

1766. Jenson Gilbert gave £10 to the poor of the parish.

1784. Humphrey Futts gave, by his will, £20 to the poor of the parish.

The plight of the poor in the 18th century

The Great Storm

In 1703 there was a 'Great Storm'. Gale force winds throughout Devon and Cornwall caused immense damage to trees – thousands were destroyed. Cattle were drowned and hay and corn ricks were blown down. People were killed by falling masonry and chimneys. Torrington records mention the damage done to the Church and the Schoolhouse there. Since its effect was so widespread, the storm must have caused havoc in Langtree also.

Langtree Mills

During the 18th Century there were two mills in Langtree, one at Higher Mill, on the site of the present dwelling at Langtree Mill, and a second, further down the valley at Watergate, known as Lower Mill. These were grist mills and ceased working at about the middle of the 19th Century when a new mill was built on the Rolle Canal at Town Mills in Torrington. Little is recorded about these mills but it is likely that at least one of them existed in some form during medieval times (probably Higher Mill).

Green Dragon

In 1728 Walter Tucker, Victualler, paid ". . . unto our Sovereign Lord King George II . . ." the sum of £10 as a licence fee for the Green Dragon Inn. This is the earliest surviving licence for the inn although it is thought to have been licenced before that date (1714 or perhaps even earlier). Its original name was probably 'St George and the Dragon' but the King felt that the name was an insult directed at his wife and himself and all inns with that name were renamed 'The George', 'The Old George' or 'The Green Dragon' – the dragon was always displayed in green.

The inn was at that time thatched but a chimney fire in 1924 caused the building to be burnt out, leaving only the original walls. The inn would have been a focal point for the village. Church Vestry Meetings were held there until the Schoolroom (Church Hall) was built in 1840.

After rebuilding in 1924, the cottage next door and other outbuildings were joined to the inn There was once a piggery and a stable, and nearby was a blacksmith's forge. It is worth remembering that there were other inns and ale houses in the village at that time. The consumption of ale and cider was quite considerable.

Roads and Highways

Roads had altered little during the 18th Century and were still the responsibility of the parish. Each year 'Waywardens' were appointed at Vestry Meetings. These were local farmers who were appointed for one year and had the responsibility to see that the highways were kept in good repair throughout the year. They were given few tools and usually had to use their own. They could call on the parish poor to help in the work. The system did not work well since the farmers did not want to do the job and the poor were even less happy about it since they had to work for nothing; consequently, roads were often in a very poor state of repair. A number of small local quarries were used to provide stone for the roads.

Also appointed at the Vestry Meetings were 'Village Constables'. They were also appointed for one year from the ranks of the farmers and tradespeople and this too was not a popular job. They were responsible for law and order and, once again, the task was often poorly done.

The Land Map of 1765 (see page 32) is one of the earliest surveyed maps of the area and shows the route from Great Torrington to Holsworthy. It ran from Taddiport along the valley, north of Frizenham, to Watergate and on through the village to Stibb Cross and Woodford Bridge. There were no fencemarkings beyond Stibb – which is not clearly marked as a junction – and no clearly defined roads to Monkleigh. By 1794, however, things had clearly changed as can be seen by the later Land Map (see page 36).

Rectors of Langtree during the 18th century

Elston Whitlocke

In 1705, Elston Whitlocke became Rector of Langtree. He followed John Elston. It is perhaps only coincidence that the surname of one was the Christian name of the other. Elston Whitlocke remained Rector for 26 years.

The name Whitlocke (Whitelock or Whitlock) was not new to the parish – they were mentioned as early as 1524 and the family name survived until the early part of the 20th century. I cannot say that the Rector was from this family but it does seem probable.

Whitlock Family Arms – two locks on a gold and black background

Adam Flaxman

In 1731 Elston Whitlock was succeeded by Adam Flaxman who was instituted Rector in June of that year.

During his time, in 1752, the Rural Dean sent his annual report on parishes in the Great Torrington district to the Bishop in Exeter. He found fault in most places and his extract on Langtree is shown below.

It reads: "Langtree – indecent communion cloth and surplice. Chancel somewhat ruinous but engaged to be repaired."

I cannot say what repairs were made to the church but in December of the same year Adam Flaxman wrote to the Bishop to report:

"I do certify that a new Surplice is provided with a linnen table cloth; for lack of which our Church was presented."

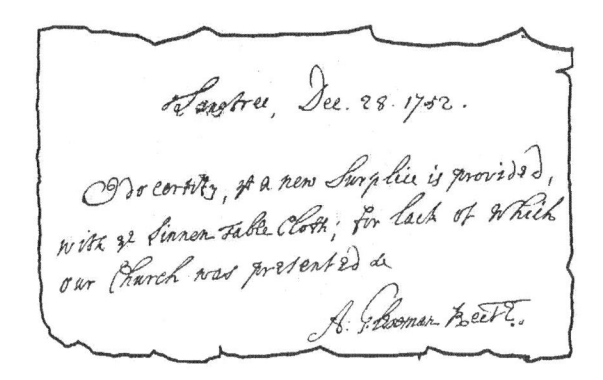

Thomas Morrison

18th century Rectors enjoyed long periods of rectorship. The 27 years of Adam Flaxman were followed by Thomas Morrison who became Rector in 1758. He remained Rector for 19 years and a monument to him is in Great Torrington Church where a mural also records his three marriages.

Charles Hammett

Charles Hammett became Rector in December 1778. It would appear that he came from Woolfardisworthy since monuments to his father and mother are to be found there.

Peter Glubb

In 1795 Peter Glubb succeeded Charles Hammett as Rector. He remained in charge of the church for about 15 years. He was from a well-known Torrington family and left Langtree to become Rector of Little Torrington, where he remained until his death in 1852. A memorial to him is in Little Torrington Church.

Glubb Arms

An entry in one of Langtree's church registers notes:

"Trees planted in Langtree Church in the year 1798 by P. Glubb, Rector."

I believe that some of these trees still survive in and around the churchyard, and that the beech tree beside the Green Dragon, not to be confused with the original Lang 'tree', was one of an avenue of beeches planted at that time. Others which survive include the beech beside the inn car park and some in the churchyard. It is interesting that a further beech tree, perhaps one from the same group, has recently been felled on the way to Watertown.

Peter Glubb was a well known public figure after leaving Langtree and at one time became Mayor of Great Torrington.

A country Gentleman of the 1700s

Nonconformity

During the 18th Century, we see the beginnings of the Methodist Non-Conformist Church in the area. John Wesley, born in 1703, visited North Devon in the 1740s, though he did not come to Langtree. Between 1782 and 1784 preachers of Methodism were appointed to the Bideford Circuit which included areas around Torrington. In 1792, Richard Drew and John Sandoe were appointed to preach in the neighbourhood. The area was somewhat inaccessible to Methodist preachers. The landowning classes were generally much against them and many leases forbade the holding of religious meetings on penalty of the loss of the holding. The treatment of Richard Drew at Taddiport – even though he had been recently welcomed at Merton – was quite unwelcoming. He was first pulled down from the chair on which he was preaching by the local Squire. In the scuffle which followed, both men fell into a nearby quarry pit. Finally, the mob threatened to throw him into the river.

However, over the next 25 years the movement gained much support. The 'Baptist' movement also began and preachers travelled the local villages to preach at 'Meeting Houses'. These were ordinary houses where people met often in secret, to listen to the preachers. Chapels were built in the early 19th Century. One of the first in Langtree was at Siloam which was built in 1830 and which, for many years, was known as the Siloam Meeting House.

Land Map 1794

Chapter Seven — THE NINETEENTH CENTURY

It is during the 19th Century that we find the greatest documentation of life in the parish. It increases as the century progresses and much material can be found in the County Record Office. For some people, this period is almost within living memory and many of the characters of the village are still remembered today. Langtree then, as now, was largely a parish dependent on agriculture and its commercial links with Torrington and Bideford.

Nationally, it was the time of Wellington, Queen Victoria, Gladstone and Disraeli; a century which saw vast changes in communications, steamships, canals, railways, the motor car, telegraph and telephone. England became a great world power and our own modern age was given its springboard at that time.

Early 19th Century Church Records

The Church, incidentally one of the very few churches in England which are undedicated, continued to be the main focal point in the village. Much early 19th Century history is found in the Church Records. The building had already stood for more than 300 years when the 19th century began (today it is about 500 years). Much had been added during its lifetime and much was to be altered during the century.

Perhaps the oldest historic item in the church, maybe even older than the church itself, is the font. It is octagonal and one record says it is Norman, others however date it in the perpendicular period of the 15th Century.

Added during the 17th Century was the sundial (1641) and the pulpit which has fine carved garlands and cherubs heads. Also placed within the church during the late 17th Century was the Royal Arms. Other family monuments have been added throughout the 1800s, some even earlier.

In the chancel are two finely carved wooden chairs with "re-used 16th Century Flemish reliefs" of Christ carrying the cross and Christ being crucified.

At the beginning of the l9th Century the church contained a rood screen which divided the chancel from the rest of the church and stretched from the pulpit to the North Aisle. There may also have been some form of rood loft or gallery where, before the days of the organ, musicians played instruments to accompany the singing. Records of the purchase of instruments can be found:

1807	for Bass Viol	£5. 0s.0d.
1809	for a Clarinet	£1.10s.0d
1818	for a Flute	16s.0d.
1821	lock for gallery door	1s.0d.

Church records also give some idea of the changing fortunes of local agriculture. In Peter Glubb's day he wrote:

"Barley sold in the year 1800 for l6s.0d a bushel, Wheat for 22s.0d. and Oats for 5s.0d."

Yet in the year 1801 barley was sold for 2s.0d per bushel, wheat for 6s.0d and oats for 2s.0d. Prices continued to fluctuate throughout the Napoleonic Wars, but on the whole farmers did well since there was no competition from foreign grain. At the end of the wars, however, the Corn Laws were passed. These were intended to maintain the price of grain at a high level. However, the laws proved a failure and were eventually repealed in 1846, leaving much rural hardship in its wake.

In 1810, John Moore was instituted Rector on the resignation of Peter Glubb. It was during his time that further repairs and alterations were made to the church. In 1816, some of the church bells were re-cast and the sum of £150 was borrowed from a Friendly Society in the parish. Friendly Societies were linked with the early trades union movement and, whilst unions themselves were illegal, Friendly Societies were given legal status by an Act of 1793. Members contributed to a sort of insurance fund from which payments were made to them during times of sickness or unemployment. Those who ran the societies were empowered to use the funds as they thought fit, so a loan to the Church would have included an element of 'interest' in the repayments.

Five bells were hung at this time and Rector Moore wrote:

Weight of new bells 22nd November 1816:
632   638   740   892   1310

Langtree Parish Church

About £40 was raised in Church Rates in 1817 and in each of the following three years, and in 1821 a further £19 was raised. Following repairs to the church, especially the seating – it was at that time too that the rood screen was removed and given to another church – it was agreed by the Church Council that:

". . . in 1823, the expected expenditure of the Church would fully equal the income arising from church lands." Money was difficult to raise in those days too!

In 1821 Bishop William Carey surveyed all parishes in his diocese. John Moore's return throws light on village life at that time.

There were 142 families in the parish – the actual population would have been nearer 1000. Questions related to the affairs of the parish, the Church, Non-conformist activities, education, the poor law and the Church Charities.

One of the first questions concerned the Non-conformists. Meeting houses and preachers were required to be registered and licenced by the Bishop. John Moore wrote:

"There are three farmers who preach to congregations in three farmhouses. The houses are licenced. The preachers are not licenced. They are disciples of a man named Bryant (in fact William O'Bryan, founder of the Bible Christian Movement), violent enthusiasts, but what their intents are it is impossible to say."

He was asked about service times, preparation for confirmation, and whether or not he had a proper rectory. He was also asked for details of education in the parish. He wrote saying:

"There is a private school in which there are about 60 boys and girls. They are taught reading and writing and some are taught arithmetic."

This is, I believe, the earliest record of a school in Langtree but I am unable to say where it was.

He told of provision for the poor:

"There are some lands of the value of about £40 a year left for the use of the Church, they are managed by trustees." (This was the Phipps Charity land.)

"There is a poor house which contains about seven families. There is also the sum of £21 in the hands of the trustees for distribution annually to the labourers not receiving poor relief."

John Moore resigned the living shortly afterwards and moved to Otterton. He was replaced as Rector by Joseph Prust in 1822. It was during his time that the fourth bell was recast (1835). He is buried in Woolsery churchyard.

The Rolle Canal

The Rolle Canal was built in 1823 and linked Torrington to the main River Torridge at Beacon Down Marsh, Landcross. It follows the course of the river and evidence of it can still be seen. It crossed the river at Beam where the old canal aqueduct is now a road bridge leading to Beam House. It ran to Taddiport, where there was a lime kiln, below Castle Hill and on towards Beaford. It was 8 miles in length.

There followed the building of a new corn mill at New Bridge (Town Mills), and this eventually led to the lessening in importance of local mills including those at Lower and Higher Mill in Langtree. The main item transported, however, was limestone which was converted into lime for use on the fields in the numerous lime kilns along the way. The lime, which was 'hot' from the kiln was then taken to local farms and villages by horse and cart. Flat bottomed barges were used on the canal and the building of it led to increased prosperity for Torrington.

Development of the Non-conformist Church

Mention has already been made of some early developments in the Non-conformist movement and John Moore mentioned the work of William O'Bryan who founded the Bible Christian Movement.

In 1830 the Siloam Chapel was built. It was known as the Siloam Meeting House. However, it would appear that it was not licenced until a little later for, in 1838, John Whitlock requested a licence from the Bishop.

He wrote:

"I, John Whitlock, of the Parish of Langtree in the County of Devon, Yeoman, do hereby certify that a building known by the name of Siloam

Siloam Chapel

Chapel, at Suddon . . . is intended forthwith to be used as a place of religious worship by an assembly or congregation of protestants."

The licence was granted and by 1857 it also contained a school for about 20 children, run by Mrs Catherine Kievill. Rebuilding was done in 1865. A small graveyard contains gravestones to a number of the Whitlock family who farmed at Collacott, including that of John Whitlock who died in 1848, aged 71 years.

One interesting gravestone there, is dedicated to Mary Richards. She was a worker at a Torrington glove factory and was attacked and killed by a vagrant on her way to work, illustrating the dangers of walking the highways alone in those days. Her inscription reads:

" A murderous assault was committed on Cross Hill, Little Torrington, May 16th 1854."

She was 21 years old.

Early chapels were often built outside of the main villages. The next to be registered locally would appear to have been Withecott Chapel in 1851.

The Bible Christian Chapel in Langtree village was erected in 1871 at a cost of £200. It provided seating for 150 persons. Another, at Week, provided seating for 100 persons. Stibb Cross Chapel was built in 1896 and the Sunday School was added in 1903. The Non-conformist movement, under the Bible Christians, became very strong in the area and the present Methodist Chapel in the village was also built in 1904. It later became the United Methodist Church. Another point of historical interest is that the doors and some of the windows of this building are faced, I believe, with yellow Marland brick, which was very commonly used in the area.

John Guard

Shortly after the accession of Queen Victoria in 1837, Langtree was to have a new Rector. John Guard was instituted in July 1839 and was to remain Rector for the next 35 years. He was one of Langtree's longest serving rectors and was responsible for a great many changes.

The Rectory as it is today, showing the new portion centre and left. The older part of the building is on the right.

One of his first acts was to engage upon a major rebuilding project at the Rectory. Possibly, very little had changed since John Elston's day but a considerable new portion was added in 1839/40, mainly to the western wing of the house, and modifications and alterations were also carried out to the old eastern wing.

He did not stop there, however, for in 1840 he was responsible for the building of the Church Schoolroom, (later the Church Hall and now a private residence) and the Schoolmaster's residence, the cottage at Beara.

In 1850 the schoolmaster was John Bassett and by 1856 there was a schoolmistress as well, Mrs Elizabeth Short. It was then known as the National School and is also referred to as the Parochial School. Later, in 1874, the school was extended by the Lord of the Manor, the Hon. Mark Rolle and by 1878 it catered for 130 children, although it is doubtful that they all attended at any one time. The building was last used as a school in the early 1960s when the infants' class from the village school was housed there.

John Guard's work was not finished however, for by 1862 the Church itself was badly in need of repair. Vestry Book records tell us that a meeting was held of the parishioners in the Schoolroom to:

". . . consider what steps should be taken to restore the Parish Church, parts of which are. . . not only dilapidated but dangerous."

An estimate for repairs had been obtained by John Guard from a Torrington builder, Walter Cock, for £400. A very substantial sum to raise.

The repairs needed were extensive and included rebuilding the south wall, opening the tower arch and providing a new western window in the tower, 2 new south and one new north-east windows, and other south windows to be restored. There was also repairs to the seating, removing and cleaning the font, removing and varnishing the pulpit, replastering walls, cleaning and colouring the ceiling, the taking down of four arches and re-setting the pillars – stone coping to

The National School – built in 1840

gables – and new doors to be provided for the porch, chancel and vestry. The roof slates and guttering needed attention and the work included re-flooring the aisles and chancel with tiles.

It was a formidable task but the meeting agreed that the work should go ahead. In fact it began in 1865.

The Rector announced to the meeting that the Hon. Mark Rolle had subscribed £200 towards the repairs and that he himself would offer a further £50. Subscriptions from others in the parish amounted to a further £80 but still more money was needed.

The repairs, of course, eventually totalled more than the estimate, £450 in all in fact, so it was necessary to borrow money once again. This was done by means of a loan from the Langtree Female Friendly Society of £120. Repayments for this were to be the annual interest of 5% plus a yearly repayment of the principal sum of not less than £10 per year.

I cannot say whether or not John Guard lived to see the debt repaid for he died in 1873. Upon his death the people of the village erected a further window to his memory and also provided an iron fence around the area of the churchyard where he and his family had been laid to rest.

The Devonshire Directories

In 1850 the first of the Devonshire Directories was published by Whites. It gives useful information about life in the village at that time.

The population of the village in 1850 was 941, almost twice that of today. The parish was 4028 acres and included Stowford and Week.

The Rev. John Guard had 66 acres of Glebe and a good residence (you will remember that it had only recently been rebuilt). The Church had a tower with five bells and several neat monuments.

The village had three inns (although only two were listed). John Clements ran the Green Dragon and William Cleverdon the New Inn – I am unable to say where that was. The Union Inn clearly existed but the landlord was not included until the next directory in 1856. There were also two Beer Houses owned by John Parnicott and William Kivell.

There were two clothes dealers, William Dark and Mr Gabell, and three tailors, William Lang, John Ford and John Thorne (the last two also ran shops).

Two cornmillers were in the village, James Osborne (Lower Mill) and John Perdon (Higher Mill).

Captain Adolphus Slade R.N. lived at Langtree Week. He was followed by a succession of 'gentlemen' who lived at the Manor for short periods until it became the property of the Cole family who have lived there since the early 1880s.

Other tradesmen in the village were also listed. There were three blacksmiths, William and Humphrey Blight (the ancestors of the Blights of Blights Motors, Bideford, I believe) and William Thorne; two boot and shoe makers, John Palmer and James Call (actually Cole). James Cole also ran a shop and there were three carpenter/wheelwrights, Thomas Hadger, Thomas Saunders and John Vanstone.

Farmers were also listed:

George (H) Ackwill, John Andrews, Isaac Barkwell, Jas. and Samuel Bullivant, John Bumberry, William Beer, Samuel Clements, John Copp, William Copp, Henry Copp, Henry Hearn, Thomas Johns, James Ley, John Madge, Humphrey Mallett, Henry Netherway, Robert Saunders, Thomas Symons, John Tucker, John Vanstone, Thomas Ward, George and Richard Whitlock. There were undoubtedly names missed off the list. Their farms are not listed but many come to light in subsequent directories. Most names occur again and again and many can be found on gravestones in Langtree and Siloam churchyards. Several of these names will stir the memories of some readers, since although the characters have long since gone their names remain in the village today.

Directories were published at about 5 year intervals, though not in a regular pattern, until 1939, when it would appear that the last of them was published. An analysis of the main characters listed appears in Appendix 5.

The population of Langtree declined sharply during the next 50 years so that by about 1900 it was in the region of about 650. Various outbreaks of illness accounted for part of this decline, whilst the general trend of rural de-population continued into the 20th century when, by 1919, the population was 504.

The Rolle Family continued to own most of the land although from time to time, the wealthier farmers were able to purchase their own holdings. Billings Directory of 1857 says:

> "Langtree. . . is now the property of the Hon. Mark Rolle, for whom Courts Leet and Courts Baron are held there."

These were Manor Courts, though where or when they were held I cannot say. They probably dealt with contracts for the sale of land.

The Churchwarden's Vestry Books

The Churchwarden's accounts and Vestry Books are full of interesting detail. They were minutes of Vestry Meetings (The Parish Council Meetings of the day, although Parish Councils were introduced later in the century) which were held in the Green Dragon until the Schoolroom was built in 1840. The Vestry Book of 1834 records the many responsibilities of the committee, not just Church affairs but many other matters such as road repairs, the poor rate, and education.

a) *Waywardens*:

From amongst the farmers of the parish, Waywardens were appointed. They were known as 'Surveyors of the Highways'. Extracts read:

> "1852 Waywardens appointed for roads. Mr James Ley (Withecott) and Mr Walter Madge (Stowford) were appointed Surveyors of Highways for the year."

The work done by the Waywardens was frequently under criticism from other members of the Church Council and many requests for road repairs appear in the minutes:

> "1855. It was resolved that the Chapple Quarry should be filled in (or sloped so as to admit the plough) on or before Lady Day 1855."

Evidence of these old quarries which were used to provide stone for the roads can still be seen today. Bridges were also built and maintained.

> "1855 Mr George Whitlock (Collacott) represented the great inconvenience and occasional danger experienced by himself and others, from the want of a bridge over the brook at Gortledge."

General opinion was that a bridge was desired, to be financed by the ratepayers. A committee was formed to report thereon and after a short while the bridge was built.

In 1862, another bridge was built this time at Southcott, and at joint expense between Langtree and Frithelstock parishes.

In 1856 the Waywardens were John Copp (Lambert) and William Beer (East & West Wood). It was determined by the Church Council that they should contract for repairs to the roads "to a responsible party resident in the Parish." A committee was formed and a tender from William Blight (the blacksmith from Stibb Cross) was accepted: "to keep the whole of the parish roads in repair according to contract for a term of 5 years from Lady Day 1856 to 1861 for the yearly sum of £66. 0s. 0d."

This seemed to be a very satisfactory solution to the problem and thereafter fewer references are found in the Vestry Book.

b) *Overseers*

Frequent references occur about the administration of poor relief. The parish was still responsible for its own poor (even bringing families originating from Langtree back from other parishes who refused to look after them). However, relief (which was paid for by the rate payers) was not easily obtained and requests were put to the Overseers who, like the Waywardens, were appointed annually. One account reads:

> "1850. William Martin applied to the Overseers for assistance towards putting his son William to a trade. He is a crippled boy (Rickets was very common) and unable to engage in farm labour."

It was agreed to give one shilling per week for 2 years out of the poor rate. John Palmer (village shoemaker) offered to take the boy for 5 years on the following terms:

> "1st & 2nd Year, the boy was to receive nothing.
> 3rd Year, the boy was to receive 3d. per week.
> 4th Year, the boy was to receive 6d. per week.
> 5th Year, the boy was to receive 1s. per week".

What became of the lad I cannot say, since there are no further references to him and his name does not appear in any of the directories. However, only those who owned or held land, those who were considered tradesmen, professionals or with commercial interests were allowed to be listed in Directories – labourers were not, nor did they have the right to vote. Those who obtained poor relief were unlikely to ever achieve this status.

The case of Albert N'Kievill's family also highlights the plight of the less fortunate. I quote:

> "The man himself did not apply. . . he being somewhat weak in intellect though strong in body."

He had lost many days' work through ill health:

> ". . . partly from unwillingness on the part of the farmers to employ him, in consequence of his wayward temper and his inability to execute his farm work properly."

His wife and family duly suffered. He was 'able bodied' and so was not entitled to poor relief but some relief was granted for the maintenance of his children, one of whom was crippled. This was called 'out relief'.

In 1857 Betsy Wonnacott was granted £3. 10s from the poor rate to:

> ". . . enable her to join her husband in America – who had already sent £11 to her "

A number of people at that time emigrated to America where a 'new life' awaited them. It would be interesting to know what became of this family and of their descendants.

c) *Education:*

Mention was made about education and a list of schoolteachers taken from Directories and school records appear in Appendix 5.

Early schools were either privately owned or were run by the parish. From 1840 the National School at Langtree was run under the direction of the Rector and his Church Committee. In 1870 an Education Act provided education for all, it soon became free, and the school at Langtree was run by the School Board. The 'Board' had certain statutory powers and it was shortly after this date that the Schoolroom was extended by the Hon. Mark Rolle. In those days the difficulties experienced by the schoolteachers and members of the Board were considerable and many are recorded. One problem was that of compulsory attendance since boys especially were frequently in the habit of taking days off in order to help on the farm. Criticism about the behaviour of pupils occurs in the Vestry book, as well as comments about inspections and general standards. The schoolroom was used for other functions and meetings and one complaint relates to the 'leaving of stout bottles and matches in the school-room following a meeting which were discovered by the pupils in the morning.'

Some 19th Century Characters
(listed alphabetically)

John Blight: he was a blacksmith at Stibb Cross. He was mentioned in 1870 and until 1915 when he died aged 75.

William Blight: another blacksmith (there were several others in the family) also from Sibb Cross. He was mentioned from 1850 until 1873 and was the man first contracted to repair the roads.

William Burrows: a carpenter from Watertown between 1878 and 1933, a period of 55 years.

James Cole: a shoemaker in the village, first mentioned in 1850 and finally in 1866. He also ran a shop. He died in 1883 aged 80 years. His tombstone is in Langtree churchyard.

John Tanton Copp: a miller at Higher Mill in 1866 and later a farmer at Clements Week. He died in 1915 aged 81, and is also buried in Langtree churchyard.

William Davey: he was a mason and a boot and shoemaker in the village. He was first mentioned in 1873 and last listed in 1923.

John Ford: he was a tailor and shop keeper in Stibb Cross and was mentioned in directories between 1850 and 1873.

John Goss: farmer from Stowford and Buda. He is listed between 1866 and 1893, he died in 1896 aged 73 years. He was one of the farmers involved in the 'Commons Riots' in the 1890s and is also buried in Langtree churchyard.

George How Hackwill: listed 1850 to 1880, he died in 1881 aged 83.

William Henry Hackwill: listed 1878 to 1933. Both Hackwills were farmers at Collacott. The latter was also at Stapleton and Suddon. Both were key Church figures, Churchwardens and Overseers. The Hackwill family had farmed in Langtree from about 1700.

Elias Holman: born 1851 died 1927 and buried in Langtree Churchyard. His father was a carpenter. His mother died when he was 14 and his brother Thomas went to America. Elias was going too, but decided against it. His father John was mentioned in 1870 as a machinist at Langtree Week, he died the following year. Elias learned his trade as machinist and carpenter. He was listed as a machine maker from 1870 until 1919. It is possible that some people in the village may remember him. His farm machines, or what remains of them, can still be found in the district.

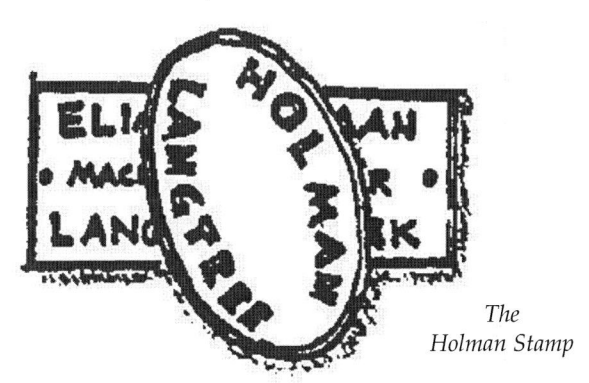

The Holman Stamp

James Ley: a farmer from Withecott who was listed from 1850 until 1866. He died in 1869 aged 82 years. He was the Waywarden mentioned in 1850. The family still farm at Withecott.

James Martin: a boot and shoemaker in the village between 1870 and 1919.

John Mills: One of Langtree's most colourful characters. He and his wife Mary, were schoolmaster and mistress around the period 1870 to 1873. By 1873 John Mills, in addition, was also the Post Office Receiver. Letters were received daily from Torrington, the nearest money order office, at 10.35 a.m. and were despatched at 3.15 p.m. By the 1880s he was no longer in charge of the school but was sub-postmaster and Parish Clerk – a position he held until the beginning of the 20th century. This was when the Parish Council was formed and Samuel Sanders became Clerk for the next 20 years. The Post Office run by John Mills does not appear to have been a shop until it was taken over in 1893 by William Trigger who was also a draper and grocer. John Mills died in 1902 having held key positions in the Parish for over 30 years. He is buried in the churchyard near the graves of his two wives, Mary who died in 1878 and Sarah who died in 1890.

Henry Netherway: farmer, Doggaport. His name first appears in 1850 and lastly in 1893. He died in 1898 aged 83. He too is buried in the churchyard. In view of the great age of some of the village characters, rural life could not have been too disagreeable in those days. Occasionally, the name Ezekiel Netherway also appears and was possibly his brother. In 1910 we find the family name again as Henry Ezekiel Netherway (his son perhaps) who last appears in 1926. Netherways were mentioned in Langtree Returns as early as 1641.

John Palmer: boot and shoemaker listed between 1850 and 1866. He was the man who offered work to the young crippled boy William Martin. Palmers were mentioned in Langtree Returns of the 1600s and were clearly a longstanding village family.

Samuel Richards: listed in 1878 as a coal dealer and carrier. His carrier's cart travelled to Bideford on Tuesdays, Thursdays and Saturdays, and doubtless he also travelled to Torrington, Holsworthy and beyond. He died in 1888 aged 44 years. The 'carriers cart' was the only means of transport out of the village for most people in the 19th century and many a tale has been told and a song sung as the horse plodded its weary way home. It was slow and uncomfortable sitting amongst the sacks and baskets, but when the pace of life was likewise no one minded.

Ned Vanstone once told me a tale about George Bond who was a carrier and colt breaker at the Union Inn in Stibb Cross. George would often go to Delabole in North Cornwall to collect slate for the local builders – a fair distance in those days. He would leave in the early hours of the morning and travel via Launceston. Once loaded he would return home, stopping for an occasional 'ale' at the wayside inns. He would arrive home in the early hours of the next day, exhausted, where his wife would be waiting for him – doubtless forewarned by the sound of the horses hooves on the road well before he actually arrived at Stibb Cross. Ned reckoned that the horse knew the way home better than the carrier – fortunately perhaps!

William Short: a mason in Langtree from 1870 until 1906, He died in 1916 aged 88 years.

John Thorne: a tailor in the village mentioned between 1850 and 1866 when he died aged 82. He is buried in the churchyard.

William Thorne: possibly his son and also a tailor and shopkeeper who was mentioned between 1856 and 1893.

John Elias Tucker: Yeoman farmer at Riverton. He is mentioned from 1866 until 1919. He was a prominent churchwarden and Overseer. His writings in the church vestry book (he was Parish Clerk before John Mills) are in beautiful copperplate style. The Tuckers have been mentioned in village returns as early as the 1500s.

Miss Peternell Tucker: listed as a farmer (and occasionally as 'gentry'). She lived at Riverton and later at Week. She died in 1872 aged 72 years, and her gravestone is near the front path in the churchyard beside other members of the Tucker family. She would have been a most influential lady.

Stephen Saunders: he was a building contractor, paper hanger, carpenter and wheelwright who lived at Sandy Lane. First listed in 1883, he was still working in 1926. He died in 1930 and will be remembered by some present-day villagers. He is buried at Siloam and his gravestone tells that he was a Methodist preacher on the circuit for 43 years.

William Vanstone: he was a carpenter and wheelwright in the village. Listed between 1856 and 1883, he died in 1909 aged 87 and is buried in the churchyard. His son William succeeded him in the same trade and was also an undertaker and glazier between 1889 and 1923. He was the father of Ned Vanstone who is well remembered in Langtree.

Thomas Ward: farmer at Little Comfort between 1850 and 1878. He also ran a shop for a short while. He died in 1897 aged 86 and his gravestone is in the churchyard at Langtree.

William Walters: in the village is a house on which the initials W.W. 1885 appear. The house was built by William Walters. His name can first be found in the directory of 1890 as a grocer, draper, butcher and threshing machine proprietor, clearly a shopkeeper of some ambition. Later from 1902 to 1914, he is listed as a farmer. His descendents, of course, still live in the village.

George Whitlock: farmer from Collacott. He is listed from 1850 until 1893 when he retired to Rose Cottage. He died in 1894 aged 76 and is buried at Siloam. Whitlocks are buried at Langtree and at Siloam. George was a Methodist but nevertheless served on the Church Council. It is he who complained about the lack of a bridge at Gortledge.

[I have doubtless offended someone by omitting their family name. If so, please accept my apologies, but there are so many characters during this period that it is impossible to mention them all].

The Railway

In 1870, the Southern Railway Company brought the Rolle Canal and promptly filled most of it in. The railway line was then built upon it from Bideford to Torrington and the railway took the trade which had previously used the canal. The line ended at Torrington at that time and the Hon. Mark Rolle filled in a further portion of the canal below Castle Hill in order to make a toll road to Town Mills. The Toll House can still be seen beside Taddiport Bridge. The road proved a failure however, since people continued to use Mill Street to avoid paying the toll. The road is now only a footpath. The railway line was later extended, through Watergate and on to Halwill Junction.

At about the same time as the railway came to Torrington, in 1874, the Torridge Vale Buttery was founded by Robert Sandford. This, combined with the railway, was to prove a great boost to local farming.

Rev. Herbert Barnes

In 1872, John Guard, long time Rector of Langtree, died. He was replaced in April 1873 by the Reverend Herbert Barnes. He, too, was a very popular Rector. He had been domestic chaplain to the Bishop of Madras from 1857 to 1861 and had travelled a great deal. He quickly made his mark in the district, becoming Rural Dean of Torrington and later, Archdeacon of Barnstaple in 1885.

It was during his time that the ancient 'Langtree Rolls' were discovered in the Church Chest (mentioned at the end of the section on the Medieval Period). In 1879 another bell was recast and a new treble was added to the peal, making the present six bells. They were, incidentally, rehung in 1905 by a Mr Stokes of Woodbury at a cost of £160.

Herbert Bames was held in high regard by the Bishop of Exeter and became treasurer to the Cathedral in 1890, where he was affectionately known as 'Treasurer Barnes'.

He died in 1893. The Bishop of Exeter said, upon his death:

> "Archdeacon Barnes was one whom all will remember as an eminently good man and the Diocese is poorer now that his generous heart has ceased to beat."

His funeral, in Exeter, was attended by eight bearers from Langtree. They were John Elias Tucker and William Hackwill (Churchwardens), John Mills (Parish Clerk), Jonathan Snow (Schoolmaster), John Darch (farmer, Withecott) William Thorne (tailor), J. Heard and P. Whitlock.

Herbert Barnes was succeeded by the Reverend John Hall as Rector of Langtree, who was instituted in October 1890 following a short period when a curate, the Rev. Houston Pattison, was in charge.

In 1891 the present church organ was purchased. It was made by Brevington and Sons at a cost of £195. It was formally opened at a service on 12th November 1891 when the sermon was preached by Herbert Barnes, the former Rector.

Rights for all men

In 1884, the farm of Alscott (latterly a farm museum but now a working farm again) became part of the civil parish of Peters Marland. This followed a Parliamentary Reform Bill of that year which gave the vote to the labouring classes. Previously only about 40 to 50 people in the village had been entitled to vote. This quickly led to the establishment of elected local councils in the country districts. County Councils were established in 1888 and Parish Councils in 1894. For administrative purposes at any rate, Alscott was lost to Langtree but Muffery (formerly in Frithelstock) was added to the parish.

The Commons Riots

The newfound 'rights' of the labouring classes resurrected an old thorn in the side in the shape of the enclosure of common land. For many years the farmers had been fencing off more and more of the common, believing that it was their right to do so and in any event, there was little the villagers could do about it. However, the villagers now had rights and they objected most strongly about losing the land on which they rabbited. Things came to a head in 1894. An account in the Exeter Gazette appeared on 16th February and reads:

"VILLAGERS' RIGHTS ON LANGTREE COMMON"

"A burning question in the village for some time past has been the right of the villagers to shoot or trap ground game on the tract of land known as Langtree Commons."

The villagers determined to draw attention to the situation so they planned a day's rabbiting, giving notice of their intentions to the farmers.

"On Wednesday afternoon, therefore, over 100 individuals assembled on the Commons, and, after partaking of refreshments, commenced operations."

Confrontations of this nature were common. Fences and gates were erected by the farmers and were promptly torn down by the villagers who sawed off the new gateposts. The events of this day were nothing new until one of the farmers appeared on the scene and threatened prosecution to those whom he found upon the plot of land farmed by himself.

"The villagers, by their actions, have therefore brought about the result they desired."

At not inconsiderable cost the case was taken to court, first through local courts and finally through the High Court where it was eventually settled and the rights of the villagers were upheld. It cost many a farmer dearly, both physically and financially, and some present day deeds still contain clauses which protect the commoners' rights.

So ended the 19th century and a century of massive change was about to begin.

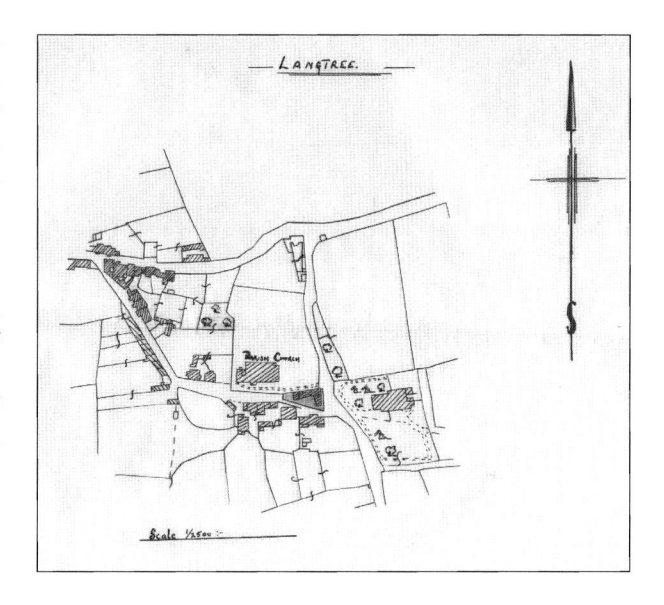

Map of Langtree Village c1850

Chapter Eight THE TWENTIETH CENTURY

What is history? Where does it begin or end? For many of us the mid 20th Century seems like only yesterday, and so it is, but for others it is history. However, for the purpose of these notes, 20th Century History will be essentially brief.

Life everywhere speeded up. Transport and communications were already developing rapidly and, with the coming of the motor car, the aeroplane, radio and television, the world suddenly seemed a much smaller place and the old country ways had little chance of survival. Some changes were clearly needed for the good of everyone, but we will all have some regrets at the passing of other parts of traditional rural life.

Aspects of village life

Early in the century (and probably before), there was a village pound. It was situated on the opposite side of the road to the present Post Office. Animals which strayed upon the highway were impounded by the local constable or police sergeant (there was always one in Langtree and some are listed in Directories) and the owners had to pay a fine in order to recover them.

Early in the century the circus came to Langtree. It was said that the land on which it was held (near the present Council Houses and Crescent) was never the same again after the elephants had trampled it.

In 1903, the new Methodist Chapel, still Bible Christian, was built in the village and a new Sunday School was added to the Chapel at Stibb Cross.

By 1910 the Lord of the Manor was Lord Clinton, following the death of the Hon. Mark Rolle, and the Clinton Estates continued to own most of the parish until the 1950s.

In 1911 the Rev. Charles Burkitt became Rector and in 1912 the Mens' Club was built with reading and billiard rooms and a miniature rifle range.

In 1914, the Rev. Bernard Hallowes became Rector and remained so for 30 years. He is buried at Langtree and is well remembered in the village.

Then followed the 'Great War' of 1914-1918 when 12 men of Langtree perished. A memorial tablet to them is in the Church and in 1918 the present church clock was presented by the Parish in their memory.

Sometime during the early part of the century a new road was built from Stibb Cross to Wonders Corner. This then became the main road to Monkleigh and Bideford. Some may still remember the gangs of navvies working on it.

The Green Dragon Fire

In 1924, a chimney fire completely gutted the Green Dragon Inn and the beech tree beside it was badly scorched. Miraculously, the tree still stands nearly 80 years after the fire which has nevertheless left its scars upon it. Sadly, I have to dispel the 'legend' that it is the tree from which Langtree gets its name. It is not as old as the village itself (the village name is probably nearer 1000 years old) and was probably planted in about 1795, at the time of other churchyard trees. It is, in any event, unknown for beech trees to live as long as 1000 years.

The Green Dragon Inn and the Beech Tree in 1985

The inn was rebuilt, virtually only the original walls remain. Carrier George Bond brought most of the stone from a quarry at Wooda – he was the grandfather of Joe Bond who still lives in the village. The inn was never re-thatched. The cottage next door was added to the inn at the time of the rebuilding. Langtree was well known for many years for its teams of bellringers. Competition judging was sometimes held at the Green Dragon.

By 1923, the directories show the first mention of Samuel Hill, motor engineer, Stibb Cross. Ten years later 'Hills Omnibus Service' ran to Bideford on Tuesdays and Saturdays, Exeter on Mondays, Wednesdays and Fridays and Torrington on Saturdays. Hills Services were owned by the family until the 1970s.

In 1926 we find Horn Bros., flour dealers. Samuel Horn, a tailor, moved to Stibb Cross in 1893 where he ran a shop. After he died, his wife and then his sons took over the business. The family business still survives at Stibb Cross, though no longer as flour dealers.

In 1926, the Church was re-slated and re-decorated four years later.

In 1929, the railway line at Torrington was extended through Watergate and on to Halwill Junction. It was then possible to travel by rail from Bideford to Bude. The line is no longer in use and was closed to passengers in the 1960s. Until about 1975 clay trucks from Peters Marland still used the line, and from Torrington, dairy produce was taken from Torridge Vale Creamery through Bideford and on to Exeter.

Also in 1929 the present school was built. It was known as the Langtree Council School. It was opened on 20th January, 1930. Headmaster Walter Westcott wrote in the school log book:

"A free tea was given the scholars and parents after the opening"

No doubt this was appreciated by all concerned. There were 61 children on roll with two teachers and a monitress.

Langtree Primary School in 1985

Walter Westcott will be well remembered. He remained in charge of the school until 1944 when he retired. He was replaced by Mrs Lucy Fishleigh as headteacher. He died in 1967, at Bideford, aged 88. He is buried in Langtree churchyard.

In 1933, the Cattle Market opened at Stibb Cross. It will be remembered by many and markets were held there on the second Monday of each month. There was also a branch of the National Provincial Bank which opened there on market days.

Besides Hills Services, another garage appears in the Directory of 1933, that of Richard Bray, motor engineer at Wayside Garage.

By 1939, Jas. Scott was the baker at Stibb Cross. Scott's Model Bakery operated there for many years and moved to Bideford in the 1960s.

During the Second World War, 1939-45, a number of evacuees came to Langtree from London. There were also women in the Land Army. Some stayed on after the war and made Langtree their home.

A wartime account by Walter Westcott in April 1944 (the time at which he retired), shows the School's contribution to the War Effort:

Langtree School War Effort to March 31st 1944
Monies raised and given to:

	£	s	d
Red Cross Fund	30	0	0
Aid for China	10	0	
Aid for Russia 5.	5	0	
British Seaman's Society	7	9	2$\frac{1}{2}$
Blind Institute, Exeter	13	8	6
Overseas League			
(Empire Day)	2	5	7
	58	18	3$\frac{1}{2}$
Langtree Knitting Assoc.	6	7	9
Total	65	6	0$\frac{1}{2}$

Money was raised by the collection of salvage, waste paper, rags, bones, iron, sacking and rubber. Over 13 tons was raised.

The amount of National Savings was given as £808. 2s. 0d

There was some additional excitement during the war when a British bomber crashed at Langtree. It was a Halifax bomber of the 1663 Heavy Conversion Unit, based at Rufforth in Yorkshire. It broke up, having been hit by anti-aircraft guns in operations over enemy territory. It crashed near Buda Farm, Langtree, on the evening of 27th August 1943, killing all seven crew. Pieces of the wreckage can still be found from time to time.

After the war, Thomas Gibby succeeded Bernard Hallowes as Rector. Electric lighting was installed in the Church in 1946 and other repairs were carried out. The population of the village in 1961 was 526.

In 1957, Mr R. A. Yeo Jenn became headmaster of the school and two years later Mr Gibby resigned and was replaced as rector by Rev. Harry Neville. At about that time the village school at Newton St. Petrock closed and the children were transported to Langtree where there were three classes, two in the school and the third in the Church Hall which by that time had been given to the Parochial Church Council by the Clinton Estate. The infant class used the hall until a new 'Temporary classroom' was built at the school in 1962 and was still in use at the time of writing (1985).

In 1964, the Rev. Richard Wallington came to Langtree, having formerly been Headmaster of Buckland House School in Buckland Filleigh. We will all remember with pleasure the many Christmas plays performed in the Church, produced by his wife St Claire, during his years as Rector. He retired in January 1985.

In 1974, Allan Edgcombe became Headmaster at the School, having taught in Langtree 1959 and 1969 as an assistant teacher. He retired in December 1990.

I should mention the 700th Anniversary Celebrations of church ministry in the village in June 1985. A Flower Festival, Archive Exhibition and Pageant marked the occasion.

Let me return to the words of the Rev. Richard Polwhele in 1793 he wrote of Langtree "... there is little worth observing. " It depends of course upon which viewpoint you take but I would hope that this collection of notes on the village history has been both interesting and enjoyable to the reader. Perhaps it was a rather dangerous statement to make, even for such an eminently respected gentleman.

Schoolchildren taking part in the Pageant of 1985 with members of the Sealed Knot Society

Appendix 1

DEVON SUBSIDY ROLL
1524 – 1527
Shebbear Hundred
LANGTRE PARISH (Langtree)

John Brown	G 20		Ann Smale exec. Will	G 3	
John Stapledon	L 5		John Smale		
Richard Martyn	G...		William Yoldon	G 10	
Richard Waterman	....		Richard Prodham	W 1	
John Waterman	....		John Mason of Withecote	G 8	
Hugh John	G...		William Martyn	G 3	
William John	....		Henry Babcombe	G 10	
John Kene	G...		Jane Eyre exec. Will	G 6	
Richard Wyll	....		Of John Eyre		
Miles Boyn	....		Jane Prodham exec Will	G 2	
John Boyn	W 1		Of Jn. Prodham sen.		
Jn. Parson of Birchall	G 2		Walter Batchelor	G 6	
Stephen Toker	W 1		William Hammont	W 1	
John Waterman of	W 1		John Holamore	G 8	
Estlake			Thomas Bronnd	G 4	
John Greneway	W 1		John Olyver	G 1	
Stephen Jose	W 1		Robert Excetter	G 4	
Richard Jose	W 1		John Taylour	G 4	
Jn. Parson mason	G 3		Thomas Erle	W 1	
Walter Colman	G 3		John Prodham of	G 8	
William	W 1		Watertown		
John	G 3		Thomas Prodham	G 4	
....	G 2		Walter Prodham	W 1	
Walter Smyth	G 6		William Boger	W 1	
Richard Dyer	G 6		Davey Crosseman	W 1	
John Whitelock Sen.	G 8		Thomas Preste	W 1	
John Meryfyld	G 6		John Martyn	W 1	
William Pytte	W 1		Richard Whitelocke	W 1	
Jn. Whitelocke Jun.	G 4		John Colman	W 1	
John Kelond	G 3		Richard Toly	W 1	
William Prodham	G 3		Walter Smale	G 2	
John Toly	G 3		Thomas Drewaye	W 1	
John Lytherynt	G 2		Henry Willyam	W 1	
Robert Chepman	W 1		Philip Stephyn	W 1	
John Boberygge	G 10				
(64 Names)			Total £7. 5s. 4d.		

Note the names Toker (Tucker) and Eyre (Ayre). The names of Brown, Stapledon, and Holamore are now local place names. Martyn, Smyth, Dyer, Whitelock, Meryfyld (Merrifield), Prodham, Excetter (later Exeter) and Smale are all long standing local surnames.

Appendix 2

DEVON MUSTER ROLL
1569
LANGTREE PARRISHE (Langtree)

Presenters sworn: Thomas Browne, Robert Chaple, Nicholas Stapledon Richard Prudham, John Skynner.

Who do presente as aforesaide

Thomas Browne gent.	L 8		John Skynner	L10
Richard Prudham	L10		John Hunte	G 7
+ 1 caliver			Richard Stapledon	G 7
Alexander Frayne	L10		John Waterman	G 6
Richard Collacott	G 7		John Smytham	G 7
John Prudham	G 7		Robert Fugars	G 7
Thomas Crocker	G 7		John Meryfilde	G 7
Nicholas Stapledon	L10		Richard Martyn	G 7

The inhabitants not particlarlie chardged by the statute are acessed to fynde etc.
2 corselets, 2 pikes, 2 caliviers and 2 murrions.

The names of all thabell menne within the saide parish of Langtree mustered as aforesaid etc.

Archers

John Prudham   William Hodge

Harquebusiers

John Skyre	John Rawe	John Risedon
John Beaple	William Dyer	Henry Jorye
Richard Stapledon	John Howe	John Stephen Jun.
John Martyn	William Pitte	William Prudham
Richard Tom	Peter Clyverdon	

Pikemen

John Waterman   William Stapledon   Nicholas Rawe

Billmen

Robert Froste	William Downe	Roger Hutchyns
Amys Whitlock	Richard Downe	Thomas Crocker
Richard Hunte	Thomas Dyer	John Morishe
	John Boucher	

Appendix 3

DEVON PROTESTATION RETURN
1641-1642
LANGTREE RETURN

Signed by all men over the age of 16 years.

Ackland, Nicholas	Futts, Humphrey	Rew, William
Addam, Hervard	Futts, John	Scott, Elias
Allyn, Roger	Gilbert, John	Scott, John Sen.
Amery, Nicholas	Glawen, John	Scott, John
Arnold, John	Griffyn, Henry	Scott, William
Avery, Francis	Harrys, William	Scott, Thomas
Bartram, Roger	Hayman, Roger	Slade, Michael
Bate, William	Heddon, William	Sloman, Bartholomew
Berryman, John	Hethemore, Thomas	Smale, Thomas
Berryman, Valentine	Hogg, Roger	Southwood, Henry
Blatchford, Ezekiel	Hollamore, Thomas	Squire, John
Bowden, John	Hopper, Leonard	Stevens, Richard
Bowman, George	Hutchings, Nicholas	Sticke, William
Bowman, Richard	Hutchins, John	Tandy, Richard
Bowman, Roger	Judd, Geoffrey	Tayler, Barnabus
Bragg, John	Judd, Richard	Tidhill, Geoffrey
Bragg, Josiah	Judd, William	Tome, Richard
Bragg, Samuel Sen.	Keene, William	Tomas, John Sen.
Bragg, Samuel Jun.	Lamprey, Thomas	Tone, John of Suddon
Bray, Nicholas	Langdon, Thomas	Toner, Thomas
Brocke, Richard	Levie, Thomas	Trenden, John
Brocke, Samuel	Mackley, John	Trills, Richard
Budd, William	Mannsey, William	Tucker, Arthur
Budd, John	Mayne, John	Tucker, Walter
Cleeve, George	Merrifield, John	Tucker. William
Dunn, John	Mounsey, John	Turner, Tobias
Durden, William	Moyse, Benjamin	White, William
Eames, Henry	Mug, Lewis	Whitelocke, Thomas.
Earel, Thomas	Nylman, John	Wilkey, John
Earell, William	Nanskewe, Robert Sen.	Williams, Chris
Earle, Henry	Nanskewe, Robert Jun.	Williams, Edward
Earle, John	Nethaway, Henry	Williams, Humphry
Eyre, Anthony	Palmer, Christopher	Williams, John
Eyre, Edward	Palmer, Humphrey	Williams, Mark
Eyre, Richard	Palmer, John Sen.	Williams, Richard
Eyre, Samuel	Petherick, Elnaehem	Williams, Thomas
Frayne, John Sen.	Pradham, John	Wilman, Richard
Frayne, John Jun.	Reeve, John	Worden, Timothy
Fray, James	Rocke, William	Yolland, Henry
Fray, Thomas	Rew, John	Yollans, Matthew

(all written in the same hand)
The following seven signatures:

John Badcock	Minister	John Palmer	Church warden
Joseph Welsh	Constable	Peter Netherway	Church warden
Samuel Bragg	Constable	John Judd	Overseer
Thomas Scott	Overseer		

Mr. Thomas Bayliese did not take the Protestation.

Appendix 4　　　　　CHARITIES

Details from endowed charities (Devon 1905) and the Charity Commissioners Report for Devon pulished 1909.

Phipp's Gift
Robert Phipp's (will dated 2nd Oct. 1676) gave to the parish of Langtree £60, to be bestowed in lands of inheritance, the rents and profits thereof to be employed to buy linen cloth at Easter for old men and women such of the said parish as had none or little relief from the said parish, the said linen cloth to be dowlas of 10d. a yard and each poor man and woman to have 3 yards apiece. He directed that his executors, William Sumpter, John Edye and Thomas Cole, should nominate as many Trustees as they should think fit.

In 1681 the Executors purchased land called Little Close, Middle Close and North Close (part of a tenement called East Hole), in Black Torrington, from John Webber. By 1818, these lands brought in an annual rent of £13.

Church and Poor Lands
In 1713 a further tenement called Middle Stibb was purchased (about 13 acres) and by 1818 rent from this land was £11 per year.

Gilbert's Gift
Genson Gilbert gave £10 to the poor of the parish in about 1766. The interest from that was to go to Church repairs.

Futt's Gift
Humphrey Futts in 1784, gave, by his will, £20 to the poor of the parish producing an interest of £1 per year for distribution to the poor. This was first held by the Rector but later seemed to have passed into the general Churchwardens Account.

William Bayly
Also gave £10 for the Church Charities but no further details of this exists and the amount appears to have been written off.

By the end of the 19th century these charities were administered as one – the Phipps Charity – and a body of Trustees (9) were appointed to oversee it.

One third of the income was used for the repair and maintenance of the Church and was paid into another charity, The Loveland Charity. Two thirds of the income was used for the benefit and advantage of the poor of the parish and was distributed on Good Friday. The distribution of cloth was discontinued in 1863 because of the shortage of cotton owing to the American Civil War. Money had since been given.

Three classes of recipients were listed in 1909:
a) Labourers in regular work (boundmen)
b) Labourers not in regular work (job workmen) and widows and widowers
c) Cottagers who keep live stock.

All must have lived in the parish for one year. All amounts were given at the discretion of the Trustees, the Churchwardens and the Overseers of the poor.

Churchlands or Lovelands Charity
Other small amounts of land were also held in charities by the Church. By 1823 they were as follows:

1. An Estate called Lovelands, made up of:
a) Two houses with orchards, gardens and a meadow.
b) Two copses called Hill and Sandy Park.
c) Two closes called Middle Close and Little Meadow.
d) A field called Common Close and another called Moor Meadow.
e) Three small dwellings with gardens.
2. A small annuity of 3s.4d. paid by John Slade of Stowford
3. A small rent paid (and often disputed) by the parish of Gt. Torrington of 1s.0d.

By 1909 the Churchlands and Lovelands Charity was administered by a body of three appointed trustees, usually the Rector and two Churchwardens. The interest from the charity was to be used for "... charges lawfully incurred by the Churchwardens in maintenance and repair of the Church". The residue in any one year was to be invested for future projects and improvements or alterations to the Church.

Receipts from these two charities were about equal in 1907:

Phipps Charity	£30. 10. 0d.
Lovelands Charity	£31. 7.10d.
	£61. 17.10d

Appendix 5   DEVONSHIRE DIRECTORIES ENTRIES 1850–1939

Much Mentioned Farmers (listed here alphabetically)

Name		Farm	Dates Mentioned
Adams	Jas. Hy	Lake	Followed Tuckers 1939
Andrews	John	West Browns	1850
	Daniel		1856–1890
	Philip		1890 – 1933
	John		1910–1919
	Bros.		1939
Ashton	Lawrence	Lambert	1866 – 1878
Bale	Charles	H. Stowford	1926–1939
Balkwill	James	Lambert	1883–1926
	Arthur	Lambert	1926–1939
Balsdon	Thomas	Muffrey	1902–1939
Bamberry	Richard	Berry	1856-1857
Beer	Thomas	Doggaport	1926–1939
	William	E. & W. Wood	1850-56
Bond	Eli	Stapleton	1906–1939
Brookes	Edmund	Hillashmoor	1856–1893
	John	Ashberry	1889–1902
	Mrs. Anne	Ashberry	1902–1926
	Thomas	Ashberry	1926–1939
	William	Hillashmoor	1910–1939
Chambers	Simon	Ashberry	1866–1873
Clements	John	Berry	1857–1878
	Samuel	Berry	1850–1857
Cole	Philip	Langtree Week	1883–1926
	Samuel Webber	Langtree Week	1926–1939
Copp	Caleb	Little Burston	1857–1870
	Henry	Suddon	1850–1857
	John	Lambert	1850–1866
	John H.	Emmys	1902–1923
	Mrs Annie	Emmys	1926–1939
	John Tanton	H. Mill Clements Week	1866–1914
	Mrs Bessie Ward	H. Mill Clements Week	1919–1933
	William	Badslake	1857–1866
	Wm. Shamburgh	H. Mill	1893–1919
Curtis	John	Chollash	1890–1906
Darch	John	Withecott	1878–1893
Deyman	Samuel	Stibb Cross	1878–1893
Ellias	Fras.	Stibb Cross	1919–1926
	William	Stibb Cross	1889–1914
Facey	Wm. Lionel	H. Thorne	1933–1939
Fishleigh	Leonard	Stibb Cross	1890–1926
Furze	William	Stapleton	1856–1857
Furze	William	Burston	1878–1890
Furze	Samuel	Burston	1902–1939
Goss	George	West Wood/Buda	1866 – 1878
	John	Stowford	1866 – 1893
	John Jun	Buda / Stowford	1878 – 1893
	Mrs. Eliza	Buda / Stowford	1906 – 1926
	Bros.	Buda / Stowford	1933-1939
Guscott	John	L. Collacott	1893 – 1902
		H. Stowford	1902 – 1923

53

Much Mentioned Farmers continued/. . . . (listed here alphabetically)

Name		Farm	Dates Mentioned
Hackwill	George How	E. Collacott	1850–1893
	Wm. Henry	E. Collacott '78	1878–1933
		Stapleton '89	
		Suddon '02	
	William A.	Collacott	1923–1926
Harris	Herbert	Rivaton	1923–1939
Headon	Thomas	Badslake	1883–1893
	William	Badslake	1873–1883
Hearn	George	Putshole	1933–1939
Hutchings	Thos.	Earleswood	1902–1926
Huxtable	James Sen.	Birchill and Smallridge	1866–1893
Huxtable	James Jun.	Doggaport/Withecott	1878–1933
Huxtable	Richard	Doggaport/Withecott	1902–1939
Johns	Thomas	Parnicotts	1850–1870
Jones	Philip	Watertown	1902–1939
Kellaway	William	Little Comfort and	1883–1910
Kellaway	Herbert	Lower Mill	1919–1939
Knapman	Noel	L Collacott	1933–1939
Ley	James	Withecott	1850–1866
	Henry	Withecott	1870–1878
	Charles	Withecott	1902–1919
	Stanley Ge	Withecott	1926–1939
	Percy	Cholash	1933–1939
Madge	John & Walter	Stowford	1850–1857
Mallett	Humph. and Jas.	East Browns	1850–1866
Moore	Charles	Cholash / Ashbury	1910–1926
Moore	John	East Browns	1883–1919
Mrs.	Eliz.	East Browns	1923–1926
Moore	John Thos.	Smallholder	1914–1939
Nancekieville	John	Bearhouse	1857–1878
Netherway	Henry E.	Doggaport	1850–1906
Netherway	Hy. Esekiel	Doggaport	1910–1926
Newcombe	John	Stapleton	1866–1878
Newcombe	William	Putshole	1878–1893
Nicholls	Thos.	Woodwell '70	1870–1919
		Wedlands '93	1870–1919
Osborne	James	L. Mill	1850–1857
Osborne	Robert	L. Mill/Gortlease	1866–1893
Osborne	William	Cholash	1857–1878
Pellew	John	Ammys/BirchillCot.	1878–1926
Pope	James	Thatton	1883–1926
Pope	Thomas	H. Thorne	1889–1926
Short	William	Thorne	1923–1939
Soby	Josiah	Badslake	1906–1926
Soby	Archibald	Badslake	1933–1939
Soby	Alfred	Berry	1933–1939
Tanton	Thos & Saml	Thatton	1856–1866
Thorne	William	Lake	1906–1914
Trewin	Thomas	Collacott	1902–1914
Tucker	Miss Peternel	Riverton / Lake	1856–1883
	John Elias	Riverton	1866–1919
	Arthur John	Lake	1906–1926
	Mrs Lydia Ann	Lake	1933–1939
	Norman	Lake	1933–1939

Much Mentioned Farmers continued/. . . . (listed here alphabetically)

Name		Farm	Dates Mentioned
Vanstone	John	Stowford	1850–1866
	Joshua	Stowford	1870–1878
	James	Thorne 70)	1870–1893
		Stowford 89)	1870–1893
	John	Collacott 19)	
		Wedlands 23)	1919–1939
Wadland	William	Watertown	1873–1893
Ward	Thomas	LittleComfort	1850–1878
Walters	William		1902–1914
Webber	John	Berry	1883–1914
Webber	Francis John	Berry	1919–1926
Wilton	William	Collacott	1933–1939
Whitlock	George	Collacott	1850–1893

Tradesmen and Craftsmen (listed here alphabetically)

<u>Carpenters & Wheelwrights</u>

Name		Place	Dates Mentioned
Adams	George	Berry Cross	1893
Ayre	William		1883–1890
Burrows	William	Watertown	1878–1933
Hadger	Thomas		1850–1856
Hill	Albert	StibbCross	1910–1939
Martin	William		1893
Saunders	John	Stibb Cross	1870–1910
	Thomas		1850
Vanstone	John	New Houses	1850–1857
	Samuel		1856–1878
	William		1856–1883
	Wm. Jun		1889–1923
	(Undertaker and Glazier)		
	Edward Charles		1933–1939

<u>Masons</u>

Name		Place	Dates Mentioned
Balsdon	John	Stibb Cross	1857
Davey	William	Stibb Cross	1870–1923
Knight	James		1856–1883
Mounce	William		1906
Saunders	Stephen	Sandy Lane	1887–1926
			Bld.Contractors,
			Paper Hanger etc.,
Short	Humphrey		1856 – 1870
	Thomas		1870 – 1906
	William		1873–1906

<u>Thatchers</u>

Name		Place	Dates Mentioned
Ford	Charles	Berry Cross	1914–1939
	William	Rose Cottaage	1914–1919
Heale	William		1890
Knight	Henry	Withecott	1893

<u>Carpenter/Machinist</u>

Name		Place	Dates Mentioned
Davie	Philip		1870–1878

Professions & Craftsmen (listed here alphabetically)

Tailors

Name		Place	Dates Mentioned
Bale	William	Backaton	1870–1910
Dark	William	(Clothes Dlr)	1850
Ford	John	Stibb Cross	1850–1870
		(Shopkeeper)	
Gabell	William	(Clothes Dlr)	1850
Lang	William	Clothes Dlr.	1850
Horn	Samuel	Stibb Cross	1893–1906
		(Shopkeeper)	
Squire	Joshua	(also Grocer)	1870–1889
Thorne	John	Shopkeeper	1850–1866
	William		1856–1893

Blacksmiths

Name		Place	Dates Mentioned
Blight	Frank	Stibb Cross	1933–1939
	Humphrey	Sandy Lane	1850–1870
	Isaac	Lake	1873–1893
	John	Stibb Cross	1870–1923
	William	Stibb Cross	1850–1873
Furzeman	Joseph	The Forge	1866–1893 (Baker)
Gerry	Augustus		1914–1939
Thorne	Richard		1870–1910
	William		1850–1866

Boot & Shoemakers

Name		Place	Dates Mentioned
Ayre	John	Berry Cross	1857 and 1873–1910
Cole	James (Cal)		1850–1866
Davey	William	Stibb Cross	1873–1923
	also Mason		
Hobbs	Richard		1850
	Thomas		1857–1873
Martin	James		1870–1919
Palmer	John		1850–1866
	George		1856
Slade	William		1926
Smale	James	Stibb Cross	1890
Vodden	Robert	Green Dragon	1870–1878

Other Trades & Professions

Name		Trade	Place	Dates Mentioned
Harness	William	Sadler	Earleswood	1857
Hill	Samuel	Motor Engineer	Stibb Cross	1923–1939
Holman	John	Machinist	Lang. Week	1870
	Elias	Machinist	Lang. Week	1878–1919
Lockyer	FredWm.	Engineer	Green Dragon	1893
Richards	Samuel	Carrier To Bideford Coal Del. Tue. Thur. Sat.		1878
Babbage	George	Police Sergeant		1878
Kelly	Fred Wm.	Police Sergeant		1910
Nicholas	John	Police Sergeant		1890
Vincent	Edwin	Police Sergeant		1906
Westaway	Arthur	Police Sergeant		1914
Mills	John	First Postmaster/Receiver (also Parish Clerk)		1873–1902
Saunders	Sam J.	Fmr./Overseer/First Clerk to Parish Council		1902–1923

Landlords of Inns

DATE	GREEN DRAGON	UNION INN	NEW INN
1850	(Two 'Beerhouses' in Langtree)	Mr. Kievill and John Parnicott	
1850	John Clements		William Clerdon
1856	John Blake	John Clements	William Hutchings
1866	John Blake	Henry Kelly	William Warmington
1870	Robert Vodden	Henry Kelly	
1883	Robert Vodden	Robert Philp	
1889	William Vodden	George Bond	
1893	Willliam Lockyer	George Bond	
1902	Henry Gribble	John Bromell	
1910	Thomas Jenkins	James Hocking	
1919	Percy Cannon	Thomas Jenkins	
1926	Richard Vanstone	Thomas Jenkins	
1939	Richard Vanstone	Mrs Eliz. Jenkins	

Shops and Shopkeepers

DATE	NAME	PLACE	DETAIL
1906–1914	Arduino Emma		Shopkeeper
1914–1939	Bale Frederick	Berry Cross	Shopkeeper
1878–1906	Blight William	Stibb Cross	Baker
1919–1926	Blight William	Stibb Cross	Baker
1850–1866	Cole James		Shoemaker/Shopkeeper
1919–1926	Curtis Mrs J.		Shopkeeper
1883–1893	Deyman Samuel	Stibb Cross	Shopkeeper
1923–1939	Down Herbert	Langtree	Post Office Shopkeeper
1850–1873	Ford John	Stibb Cross	Tailor/Shopkeeper
1878–1883	Furzeman Jos.	The Forge	Blacksmith/Baker/Shopkeeper
1939	Gerry Reginald		Shopkeeper
1906	Horn Samuel	Stibb Cross	Tailor / Shopkeeper
1910–1923	Mrs	Stibb Cross	Tailor / Shopkeeper
1926–1939	Bros	Stibb Cross	Flour Dealers
1870–1890	Nicholls Thos.	Woodwell	Butcher/Baker
1893–1914		Wedlands	Fmr. / Shopkeeper
1890	Nichols John		Shopkeeper
1939	Scott James	Stibb Cross	Baker
1873 – 1890	Squires Josh.		Grocer / Draper
1910 – 1914	Stoneman Thos.	Stibb Cross	Shopkeeper
1850 – 1866	Thorne John		Tailor / Draper
1893 – 1906	Trigger Wm.	Langtree	P.O. Shopkeeper
1910–1919	Mrs E	Langtree	P.O. Shopkeeper
1890 – 1893	Walters Wm.		Grocer/Baker/Draper/Farmer/Threshing Machine Prop.
1870	Ward Thos.		Shopkeeper

Schoolteachers and Assistant Teachers

Date	Head Teachers	Assistant Teachers
1850 – 1857	John Bassett	Mrs. Eliz. Short
1857	Mrs. Kievill (Siloam)	
1866	John Cole	Mrs. Sophia Cole
1870 – 1873	John Mills	Mrs. Mary Mills
1878	C.G. Bradley	
1879 – 1883	Richard Smith	
1889 – 1890	Jonathan Snow	Mrs. Emma Vodden
1893	Albert Rich. Broderick	Miss E. Squire
1902	Arthur Austerberry	Miss Mary Anne Huxtable
1906	Arthur Farrow	Mrs. Lucy Lusmore
1910 – 1914	Samuel H. Kelly	Mrs. Emily Kelly
		Miss Bessie Newberry '10
		Miss Edith Hooper '14
1923 – 1939	Walter Westcott	Miss Mary Pratt '23
		Miss Cath. Jenkins '26
		Mrs. Katherine Down '26
1944	Mrs. L. Fishleigh	Mrs. G. Mills
1952	Mrs. Soby	Mrs. J. Gibby
1958	Mr. R. A. Yeo Jenn	A.C. Edgcombe '59
		Miss B. Lees
		Mrs. L. Stone '60
		Mrs. D. Metherell '66
		Mr. J. Allison '69
		Mr. H. Cornish '73
1974	A.C. Edgcombe	Mrs. T. Insull '74
		Mrs. A. Bunney '75
		Mrs. M. Clayton '77
1991	Mr Ellis	Mrs M Roe
		Miss Matthews
		Miss Mellody
		Mr Adams
		Mr Barnes
1995	Mrs Marshall	Mrs Ferguson
		Mr M Barnes
2002	Miss Mellody	Mrs Crocker

Details taken from directories and school records.

Appendix 6   THE RECTORS OF LANGTREE

1285	Elias De Forde
1317	Sir Simon
1336	Reginald De Dunnyngtone
1339	Sir Henry Graistoke
1348	Sir John De Tuvertone
1348	Sir William De Prestone
1351	Sir John De Tuvertone
1356	Sir John Cornewaylle
1411	Walter Cook
1424	Sir Richard Bele
1451	Sir John Lawry
1460	Sir William Nelme
	Sir John Wylle (No date recorded)
1507	Master Halnothene (Alnetheus) Arscott
1536	Sir John Browne
1549	Master Gabriel Donne
1559	Sir John Muoye
1565	Robert Brayle
1565	Thomas Washington
1573	Samuel Beck
1585	William Earthe
	Eustace Marshall (No date recorded)
1594	Master William Baylie
1624	Thomas Baylis
1640	Nicholas Monck
1662	Theophilus Powell
1667	John Elston
1705	Elston Whitlocke
1731	Adam Flaxman
1758	Thomas Morrison
1778	Charles Hammett
1795	Peter Glubb
1810	John Moore
1822	Joseph Prust
1839	John Guard
1873	Herbert Barnes
1890	Edward John Hall
1911	Charles Esdaile Burkitt
1914	Bernard Hallowes
1945	Thomas Rees Gibby
1959	Harry Leslie Neville
1964	Richard A. Wellington

Appendix 7   GLOSSARY OF LOCAL PLACE NAMES

Glossary of Local Place Names

HILLASH or Hillashmoor	(1238)	spelt Illeryss. Means ash on a hill Later spelt Yllers and Illeherashe.
CHOLASH	(1244)	spelt Chaldhasse. Means cold ash tree. Later spelt Coldeaisshe.
LAMBERT	(1269)	spelt Lampford. Means lamb ford. Later spelt Lamberd.
BUDA	(1287)	spelt Bowode. Means curved wood.
MUFFWORTHY	(1244)	spelt Mokewrthe. Worthy means a clearing on the moor. Later spelt Moggewurthi by the 19th century Muffery and Muggery.
THATTON	(1288)	Means roof of thatch.
STAPLETON	(1291)	mentioned at Galhille (the area was later known as Goat Hill) when it come into possession of the de Stapledon family. It is first mentioned as Stapledon in 1314.
DOGGAPORT	(1330)	spelt Thokirport. 'Port' means gap or gate and the first part means vagabond or tramp. Possibly a reference to the poorer dwellings in the parish.
STIBB	(1330)	spelt Stybbe or Stibbe. Means stump of a tree.
WITHECOTT	(1330)	spelt Wydicott means withy or willow.
SUDDON	(1333)	spelt Sodden means south down or south of the hill.
STOWFORD	(1330)	spelt Stouford and later Stauford could mean safe place by the ford
RIVATON	(1314)	was Revetone and probably means Reeve's Farm.
BROWNS	(1330)	named after the Brown family who lived there.
BERRY	(1333)	The home of Philip de Byry
WEEK	(1333)	was named after Richard de Wyke
SMALLRIDGE	(1333)	the house of William de Smalerugge
WATERTOWN	(1333)	the farm of Richard atte Watere
BEARA	(1390)	spelt Bearehouse or Berehouse
BURSTONE		spelt without the 'e' until recently, was named after Burton Wood or Beartown Wood.
PUTSHOLE	(1555)	spelt Pyottsale, perhaps meaning priest's cell. It is probably the oldest surviving building in the village.
BADSLAKE		possibly once called Estlake when it was the home of John Waterman in 1524. Lake means stream or river.
BIRCHILL		mentioned as Birchall the home of John Parsons in 1524
COLLACOTT		Probably named after Richard Collacott (1569)

Appendix 8

LORDS OF THE MANOR OF LANGTREE
AND OTHER NOTED LANDOWNERS

This list has been compiled with the aid of several sources including the list of Church Patrons. It would appear that a number of places in the parish have been held separately from the main manor from time to time and it is often difficult to distinquish these landowners from the overlords. However, the general picture is as follows:

Pre	1066	Earls of Gloucester
In	1066	Queen Matilda wife of William I.
By	1285	Gilbert de Clare, Earl of Gloucester (Note: 1290 Galhille, now Stapleton, Purchased by Walter and Richard de Stapleton from Robert de Bulkaworth.
In	1295	The de Spencer family
By	1339	Sir Hugh de Spencer, Lord of Glamorgan
By	1366	Edmond la de Spencer, Lord of Glamorgan
By	1411	Constance de Spencer Thomas Lord Spencer (his daughter, Isobel married Richard Beauchamp, Earl of Worcester and Earl of Warwick) (Note: by 1419 Rivaton and Hillash were held from the Earls of Warwick by Richard Hankford of Annery. Upon his death by Sir William Hankford who died in 1423).
By	1424	Richard Beauchamp, Earl of Warwick, (Rivaton and Hillash were held by Elizabeth, the daughter of Richard Hankford). (By 1433 those lands were held by the Duchess of Eartes, wife of Richard Hankford).
By	1457	Thomas Boteler (Butler), Earl of Ormond (through his marriage to Richard Hankford's other daughter)
By	1461	Richard Neville, Knight, of Earl of Warwick died 1471, Anne, the daughter of Thomas Boteler, married James St.Leger. The land then passed to the St. Legers.
In	1484	Earl St. Leger (and Thomas Browne of Langtree) executed by Richard III
By	1507	Giles Dawbeney, Lord of Dawbeney
By	1536	John Browne, Gentleman, was listed as Church Patron (it was about this time that the Brownes purchased some lands from the St. Legers).
By	1549	Sir Thomas Dennys of Orleigh Court. (Note: other lands in the parish were held by the Brownes. Week was held by Sackvilles).
By	1559	Sir Edmund Dennys
By	1565	Sir Robert Dennys
1565		William Dennys
By	1594	Sir Thomas Dennys
By	1602	Henry Rolle of Stevenstone (Note: Richard Copplestone of Woodland held Week. Other lands were still held by the Brownes). Note: 1613, the last of the Brownes, Sir Thomas, died, leaving his estates to the Harris family of Peters Marland. They owned Rivaton for many years.
By	1617	Dennys Rolle
In	1638	Henry Rolle of Beam
By	1640	Sir John Rolle (Knighted 1660) he owned 45 manors in Devon, and others in Somerset and Northampton.
By	1731	Henry Lord Rolle (later Baron Stevenstone)
In	1750	Dennys Rolle of Stevenstone
By	1758	John Rolle Walter of Bicton and Stevenstone
In	1796	John Rolle became a Peer, Baron Rolle of Stevenstone, John Lord Rolle.
By	1842	Hon. Mark Kerr Rolle (nephew of John Rolle)
By	1910	Lord Clinton (Note: the Clinton Estates in Langtree were sold off in the 1950s)

*Langtree Parish photograph
taken on Monday 3rd June 2002
to celebrate the Golden Jubilee of Queen Elizabeth the Second*

By kind permission Evanda Hill

Langtree Parish
History and Memories
Part Two

Langtree, June 1963

As you begin to read on into the second half of this book, you will find that there is some overlap of subject matter but hopefully not of information. The larger section of Part One deals with the history of Langtree up until about 1940. Chapter 8 'The Twentieth Century' has touched briefly on many things of that era which I have also written about. I make no apology for this as many people have shared memories about these things, which are important to record; also I have been able to develop some of the stories more intensively. Working to a fairly tight timescale of less than six months for research and writing up, it has not been possible to blend these two sections together in a seamless story. I trust this will not distract from the readers enjoyment of the whole, and that any apparent duplication will be forgiven.

Chapter Nine PUBLIC FACILITIES

Langtree School

There was a school in Langtree in 1818 for about 40 children. The fee for having your children taught there was three-shillings per quarter for reading and five shillings and three pence for writing and arithmetic.

A day school was held in the rear of the church prior to the old school being built. This may be the one mentioned above.

In 1832 there was a meeting place and day school at Siloam – Ben Copp's father went to Siloam School. Ben thinks the chapel was probably built onto it later.

Mrs Alma Carter (née Daniel) remembers being told of a small class of children being taught by her grandmother in their home at Thorne House, in the room on the left as you enter the front door where the porch is. She is not sure what date that would have been.

Elementary Education became compulsory for children in 1880, and was made free to all in 1891. Before that time many children would have had little or no teaching in the three 'Rs', though no doubt they were skilled and wise in other ways, such as how to survive in a tough environment, and making the most of what there was around them to feed, clothe, and occupy themselves usefully.

Langtree's first purpose built school was provided for the community in 1840 at the instigation of the Rev John Guard. This is referred to in the first section of the book

Ben Copp, who attended that school remembers one of the teachers, she was a Miss Hooper from Peters Marland: "I remember her being courted by Bill Brownscombe. They married and lived in the cottage opposite the Old School at Rose Vale". Ben continues, "In 1923 Mr Westcott and Miss Major were teaching there. The children played in the street from the Church gates to the Clubroom and along the road to the end of the Churchyard wall. There was no running water at the school. There were four ash bucket toilets. In the winter, water would be carried from neighbours and heated in a pan on one of the three open grates, and

School group c1920 courtesy of Ruth Wood. Ben Copp remembers only a few of the names, as follows:
l to r Back row 1st Fred Dymond, 10th Eddie Underhill; 2nd back row 5th Muriel Furse, 3rd back row 11th Iris Copp, 4th row from back, 3rd Dolly Copp, 6th Ben Copp, 7th Fred Adams, 15th Fred Slade, 16th, Norman Brooks, Front row, 2nd Elsie Withycombe.

School group courtesy of H. Daniel. Back five, L-R;
Philip Beer, Dudley Cox, Bob Harris, Norman Cole, William Daniel. Next row: Mr Westcott, Alice Cox, Jack Berryman.
Middle row. Raymond Sanders, Harold Daniel, Olive Underhill, Verona Hackwell, Ethel Wheeler, Frances Westcott,
Alma Daniel, Muriel Sanders, Gwen Moore, Will Johns, John Beer.
Front row. Edwin Brownscome, Arthur Harris, Verna Sanders, Olive Daniel, Barbara Furse, Hedley Nichols, John Webber.

milk and cocoa were added, but no sugar. The children played marbles, hopscotch and iron hoops; no football and no swearing!"

Ben also remembers his Granny Kellaway (his mother's mother) telling him that as children at the old school, they would "go up and down the Tower for a pastime".

There are a number of photos available of the children in this school but mostly from the early 1900s, nothing from the 1800s. Not many of the names of the children from these photos are known.

Mr Walter Westcott, who is still clearly remembered by many, was headmaster in the closing years of the old school and the beginning of the new, providing some sense of continuity. It must have seemed wonderful for the children to have their own special play area. School was deemed to be closed in-between the end of morning lessons and the start of the afternoon session. While village children went home for dinner, those who brought their food from home seemed to have to look out for themselves and often walked about the village. Sybil Budd (née Balsdon) remembers buying sherbert and sweets from Mr Burrows' shop on the corner where the garden is now, then sitting on the grass bank outside the church wall and eating them.

There was a growing concern as the years passed by, that having the school next to the graveyard was not a good environment for the children, for they were often witness to the many funerals that took place.

Langtree's new school was opened on Jan 20th 1930, building having been completed the previous year as the date of 1929 on the building declares. The official opening was performed by J. W. Squance C.C, with Mr W Westcott as Head teacher, Miss K M Dawn as Infant Mistress and Miss C Leach as Monitor. 61 children enrolled, though only 57 attended on that first day. Two were absent because of scarlet fever. At that time the school consisted of the main building divided into two classrooms, with a toilet block across an alleyway. Over the years the school has been enlarged and many additional facilities added.

Much of the following is taken from the new school log book:

Oct 23rd 1944. The dining centre began today. Meals are brought by van from Holsworthy. Sometimes, in bad weather, the deliveries were unable to get through. [Emergency rations consisting of tins of soups, and tins of chopped ham and pork were kept in stock for such occasions.]

Dec 21th 1955. On account of the building operations, teaching has been at great disadvantage for

Langtree school in the 1930s

New Temporary Classroom c1997

the whole term. Only part of the junior classroom has been available, to accommodate 39 scholars and all the furniture. Some have been facing sideways; others seated behind the teacher's desk, close under the blackboard – no access to some desks with removal of others. The same applies to cupboards and drawers, all of which are stacked to utmost capacity, the original store cupboard having been demolished in the building extension. In addition, only a cardboard partition separates workmen from children. Consequently the noise and disturbances have made both teaching and attention very difficult indeed.

Jan 12th 1956. Re-opened today – building operations complete and classrooms nicely decorated. Junior classroom now much longer and we are using the new kitchen for plate warming and washing up.

Apr 19th 1956. Cooking on the premises, in the new kitchen begins. In charge are Mrs Bichnell, and Mrs Huxtable

Mar 1965. Swimming pool delivered, along with paving slabs.

May 1974. Swimming pool was extended.

Sept 1967. Secure fence put around parts of the field and garden, there has been occasional trespassing there for years.

Sept 1969. PE shed erected.

1976. New toilet block. [On Jan 20th it was recorded what work was necessary by a Mr Bowen – no record of when it was completed.]

Previous toilets have been very bad for past 4-5yrs.

Sept 1992. Special opening of new entrance area, new temporary classrooms and transfer of nursery unit from chapel room to the bottom classroom.

School Acquisitions and Landmark Occasions

Sept 1939. Older children first transported to Torrington Secondary Modern School.

April 11th 1940. Headmaster attends official opening of Torrington Secondary Modern School at 2pm.

During the 1930s and 1940s there were regular tests for religious knowledge. The Rector usually

New Nursery Unit next to the Swimming Pool. Photo taken September 2003.

undertook this, though occasionally the Headmaster of Shebbear College conducted the exam. It consisted of the examiner listening to the children sing their hymns and read the scriptures, then they where questioned about what they had been reading. Usually the examiner was very impressed, not only with the children's enthusiasm and answers, but also with the whole tone of the school. In 1934 the comment was made by the examiner, Rev R James of Shebbear, "On the whole I would say that this school is the best I have visited in this district. They knew, they understood and they were really all eager to answer". On another occasion however, the examiner felt the children had learnt the right answers without understanding what it was really about.

April 5th 1944. Long-time headmaster Walter Westcott leaves. He wrote in the log book: "This is my last day of leading in this school and I take the opportunity to thank the School Managers, and inhabitants of Langtree for their numerous acts of kindness and assistance they have given me during my twenty three years at Langtree."

February 2nd 1945. First mention of "The Preliminary Entrance Test to Secondary School" (11+). It was held under the observation of the Head Teacher. The Rev B Hallowes, chairman of the managers acted as supervisor. The following children born in 1934 took the test. Doreen Hutchings, Esther Balsdon, Audrey Daniel, Trevor Wood, Thomas Curtice, Roy Daniel, and Elaine Hayes. Some of the evacuees had taken exams set by their own school boards from their hometown. Scholarship exams had been taking place before this time for schools such as Shebbear and Edgehill Colleges.

Nov 1946. Electric boiler used first time.

Sept 1950. School wired for radio.

June 1953. TV installed for 1 day for children to watch the Coronation of Queen Elizabeth II.

Dec 1953. First Christmas concert in the school, 40 parents much enjoyed it.

Nov 1956. Mains water connected. School Well now defunct.

May 3rd 1957. Infants are to use Church Hall again.

Feb 12th 1958. Recorder group started.

Summer 1961. Mrs Mitchell bottling fruit, making jam for the school store cupboard.

Summer 1963. New temporary classroom fitted (eventually removed in the early 1990s).

Oct 14 1966. Telephone connected to the school.

Jan 1972. School acquires a kiln, Mr Alison teaches pottery.

Feb 1972. First mention of a parents committee, also first mention of parents' evening to discuss pupils' progress.

Sept 1972. First mention of serious traffic concerns.

Dec 17th 1973. Mr R.A. Yeo Jenn is ill at home. He returned to teach for a while from 16th May 1974 then became seriously ill on Nov 12 that same year. He tendered his resignation in the spring of 1975. Having taught at the school since 1958, the logbook records "this is a sad ending to an exiting chapter of the history of the school". A fund was opened whereby past and present pupils could contribute to a thank you and farewell gift for him.

March 10th 1977. School entered Torrington Music Festival. Came 2nd.

Sept 1980. Rising-5s start coming Thursday afternoons to get used to school environment.

June 1983. School took delivery of computer.

1984 Colour TV stolen, it had been bought by hard-earned parents' committee funds.

March 12th 1987. County needlework organiser was so impressed with the girls' needlework, she asks permission to show it to the Langtree WI where she was due to speak the following week.

June 28th 1988. School do a pageant of village history and Exhibition.

July 1988. Juniors have a trip to Lundy.

Nov 1988. School burgled. £92 missing, Savings Books also taken, but were recovered intact!

December 1990 Mr Allan Edgcombe takes early retirement on health grounds. His entry in the log-book reads: "I would like to express my sincere thanks to all the staff, governors and parents for their support during my headship. I was first appointed to Langtree School in 1959 as a probationary teacher and have been either closely connected, or teaching here ever since that time. I leave with great sadness but many happy memories.

March 1992. The school holds a Thank You and Farewell event for Allan Edgcombe. The children prepared the food, with the help of school cook Mrs June Cann. Then they entertained him with two plays, recorder pieces and a song especially composed for him by a former pupil, Laura Insull. He was presented with a 'Book of Reminiscences". The following evening there was a farewell party for him at Little Torrington Hall attended by pupils and parents, past and present.

After the retirement of Mr Edgcombe, the school was overseen for one term by Mr J Palk as acting Head, whilst a more permanent Head was found. Mr David Ellis from Huddersfield was then appointed, beginning his Headship at Langtree on 15th April 1991. One of his biggest achievements while here was to ensure that two temporary Elliot classrooms were erected, and that the nursery was moved into the old 'Devon Lady' building. He left, following a much-appreciated farewell assembly, to take up duties as headmaster at Bickington, near Barnstaple on 7th April 1995.

Later that month Mrs Rebekah Marshall was appointed Head. During her tenure the County Council built a new Nursery/Key Stage One Unit (see picture on the previous page).

Following a period as Acting Head, Miss Mellody was appointed Head in 2002. During this

*School Girls Sewing.
Left to Right:
Judy Fisher,
Margaret Sutton,
Pam Curtice,
Pat Gerry,
Maureen Harris.*

time she has overseen the building of a computer suite, a new entrance from the school into the Parish Hall car park; the establishment of a new Reception Class to cater for the extra children attending the school, and she is now starting the process to get the Elliott rooms replaced with permanent buildings.

Summer 2003. Jill Mitchell was nominated by the school for the Teaching Assistant of the Year Award and received a special commendation. Jill is part of a large number of people who help in many ways to make the school what it is today, and are extra to the official teachers in the sense that we used to know them. School has moved on from what many of us remember and is now seriously involved in helping today's children to grow up and be able to cope with an increasingly complex and demanding world – no easy task.

On two occasions in the earlier years of the school, a single member of staff managed the whole school by themselves. In 1945 the following is recorded:

27th June. School closed. Mrs E. R. Kirby away, husband on leave.

28th June. School re-opened and Mrs C .M. Mills carried on the School by herself.

5th July. School closed to be used as Polling Station.

9th July. Mrs Kirby resumes duties.

It would appear that Mrs Mills taught and supervised the school single-handed from June 28th to July 8th, though there may have been a weekend involved.

The second incident, for just one day, was on Oct 24th 1956. Mrs Gibby (who is temporariy in charge due to Mrs Fishleigh being off sick) writes: "Mrs Thorpe is absent today so I have to cope with 66 children on my own."

Oct 25 1956. Mrs Thorpe arrived 11a.m. Half Term holiday begins tomorrow.

We are given no reason for Mrs Thorpe's absence, but it was probably not illness.

This photograph and those on the following two pages show the children who are now attending the school involved in various lessons or play during September 2003.

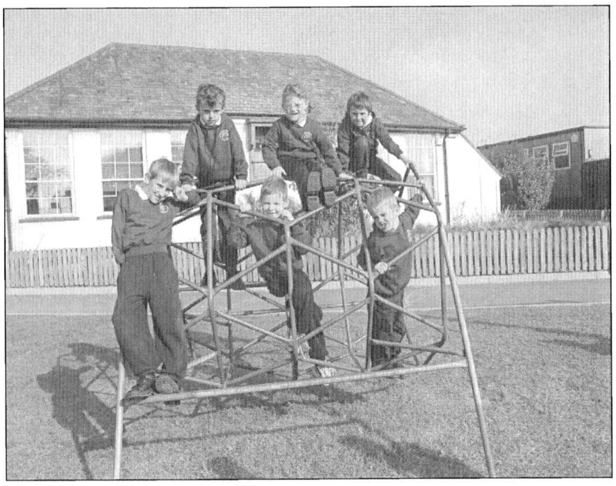
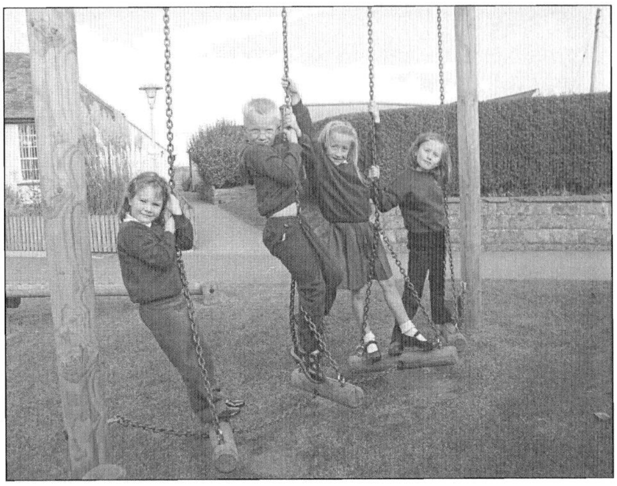
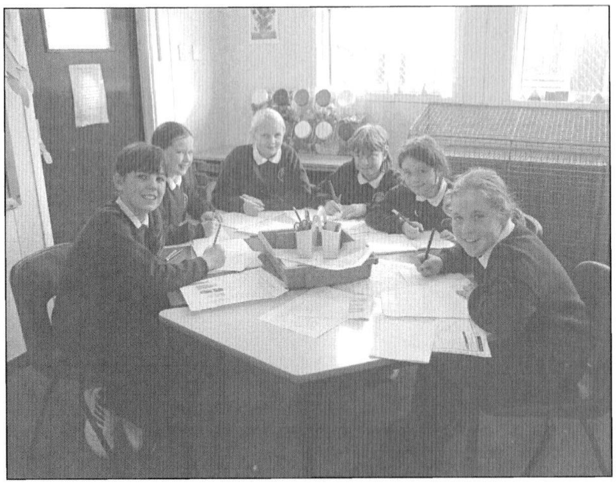
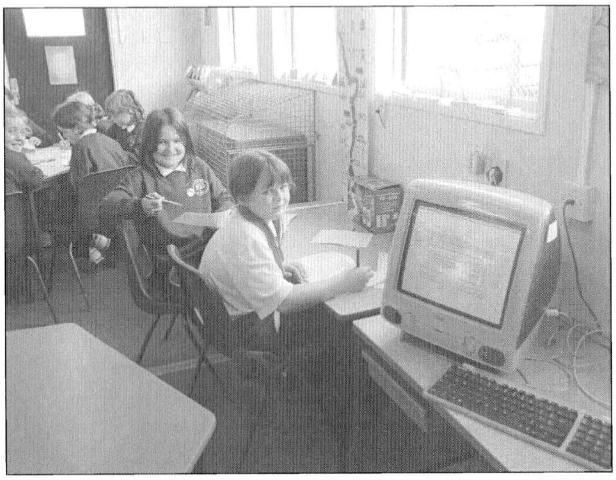
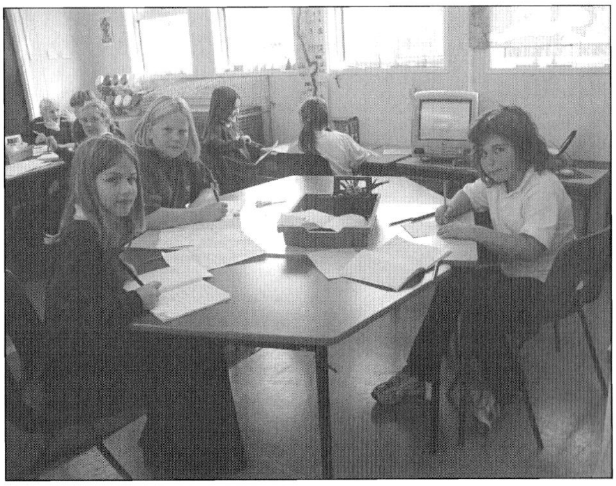
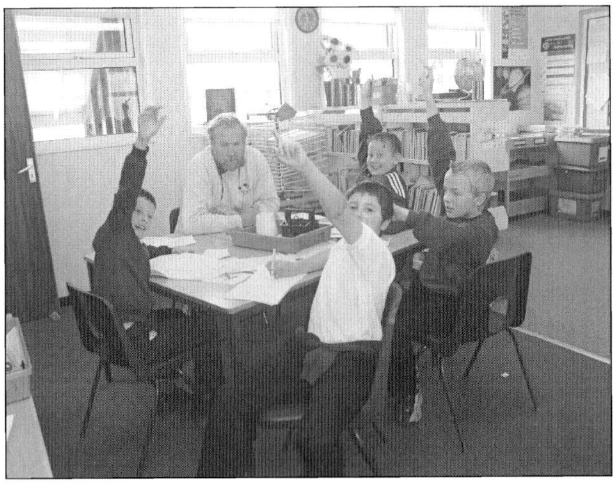

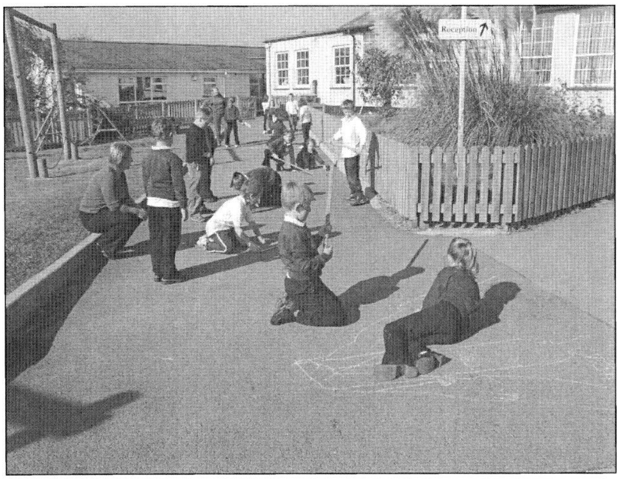
Reception

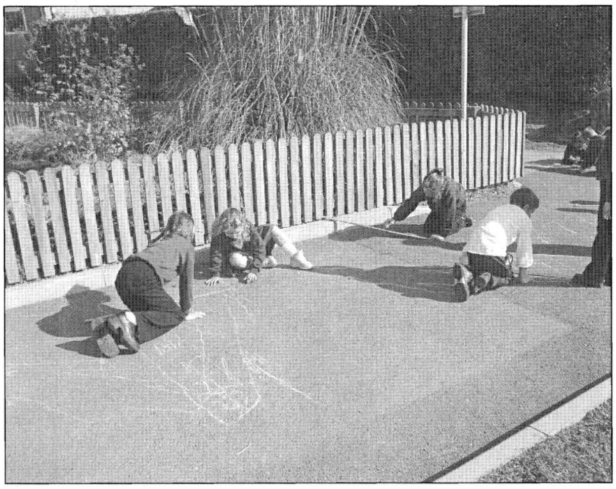

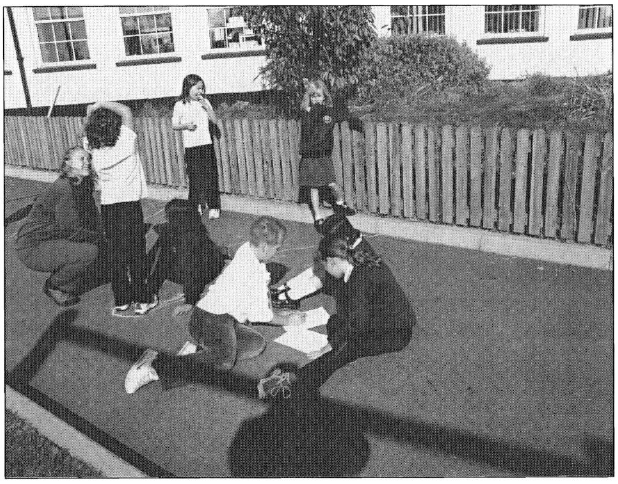

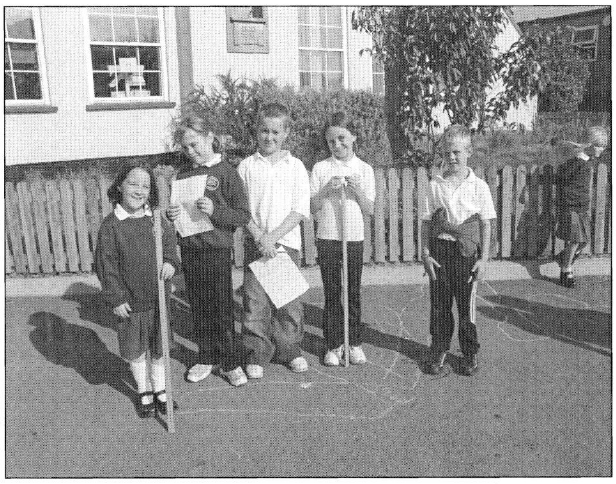

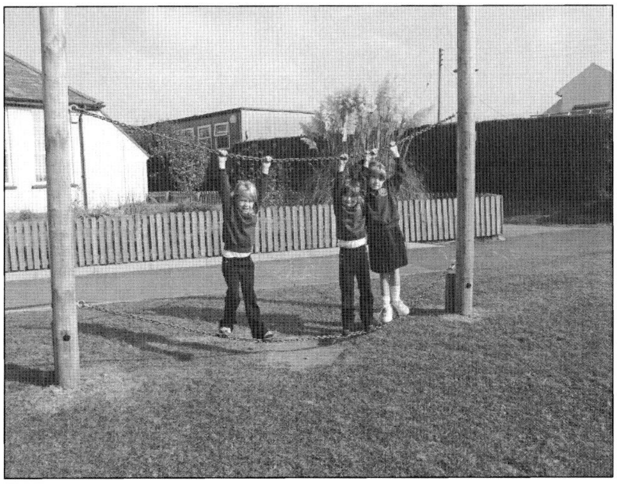

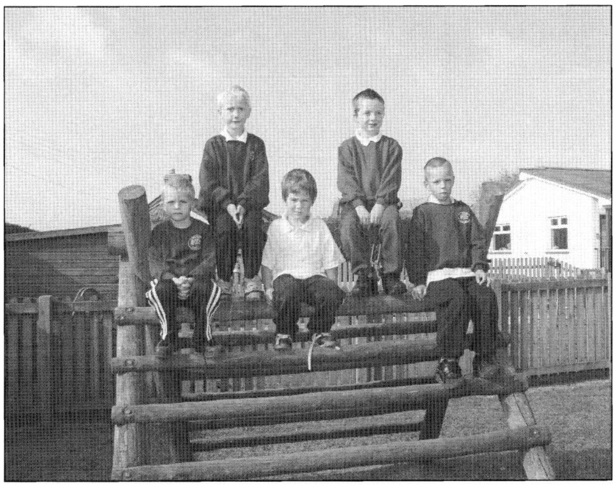

The Parish Hall

The possibility of a Parish Hall for Langtree had long been a dream. Bernard Hill remembers a parish meeting in the mid-1940s when the subject was discussed. Some felt strongly that there was a need; others felt the existing buildings, the Social Club room and the Church Hall, were adequate. The proposal was out-voted and the idea dropped at that time, yet did not really go away.

Our Parish Hall beginning to take shape, Summer 2002

By the 1980s, the need was becoming more urgent. Many more people were celebrating special birthdays and anniversaries with a party and having to go outside the community to other Parish Halls. The existing facilities were no longer adequate for the kind of community events now being organised, so a decision was taken and serious fund raising began. In the summer of 1985 a new committee consisting of representatives from all the organisations in the parish was formed.

A number of possible sites were considered, but North Park was felt to be by far the best. This was because it would also solve the nightmare traffic problem and great potential danger to school children each day at 9.00 am and 3.30 pm as they arrived and left the school by its only entrance directly onto a very busy road. It was also near to the other public facilities – church, chapel, public house and playing field.

In February 1992 it was agreed, in principle, that Mrs Squires and family would donate a site at North Park for a Parish Hall and car park area, in exchange for planning permission for three building sites that would otherwise have been deemed outside the Development Plan.

By October 1996 the Hall site was pegged out. A bid for Lottery funding was submitted in February 1999 and in June that year the village was awarded funding of £264,000 for the building of the new Hall. Final signing over of the land took place in May 2000 and building began in Winter 2001.

Over fifteen years of serious fundraising has involved a vast and fascinating list of events and ideas. Enormous credit is due to the ingenuity and dedication of a very hard-working committee who never lost the vision of a Hall for Langtree. A great deal of discussion took place as to what size hall we should have, and what facilities should be supplied. The finished hall is bigger than we would have dared to dream of at first. No-one could have visualised being able to raise the amount of capital needed; yet it has happened and we are well on the way to clearing outstanding debts.

Gradually we saw our Hall take shape and, in spite of various hold-ups, eventually reach completion.

September 12th 2002 saw the builders officially hand the Hall over to the committee, although the water supply was still not connected. The first group to use the Hall was the women's skittle team, and the first event to be organised was a Wine and Wisdom evening for Hall funds on 16th November. How fitting that one of its first meals to be organised there was a Christmas lunch for two local firms, Bridgmans and Horns.

The finished Hall, though car park and grounds still have much work to be done

Committee Members and helpers L-R: Geoff Bond, Pet Cole, Julie Bond, Trish & Pete Crofts, Jill & Pat Mitchell, Debbie Langmead, Sue Folland, Sue Lee, Geoff Folland, Terry Atwell, Linda Westall, with the tables laid for the first parish meal in the hall.

The variety of fundraising events has been enormous – some of them are covered elsewhere in this book. Let me give a taster of what the people of Langtree, with much support from others outside the Parish, have been up to these past eighteen years. Pride of place must go to the Fun-day, which grew into a whole weekend of events and happened for more than ten years; The annual Collective Sale on Farm has also been a great success. Safari Suppers, Village Midday Meals, Big Breakfasts, Sheep Scheme, Open Gardens and many other things have been part of the fund-raising efforts.

Now the Hall is up and running it is being enjoyed by a wide range of people from across the community and further afield.

One of the highlights are the Parish Lunches, held twice a year, with much of the work being done by committee members and helpers. First course is a roast with choice of two meats, and a wide selection of vegetables, with all the trimmings. Desserts are contributed by many in the Parish and have become a real feature of the event. Then there's the cheese and biscuits, another wide variety and chosen from the many in the westcountry. A meal to savour, and to be enjoyed with friends.

Something is happening at the Hall on most days and the car park is in regular use as the school children, staff and parents enter school by the new and safe gate directly from the car park. The School is also able to make use of the Hall for various activities.

During its first year the Hall has hosted various concerts, including Barnstaple Male Voice Choir, and The Old Scorpion Band, as well as Morris Dancing, Photo Exhibitions and a Film Show by Beaford Arts Centre. Many fund raising events for various organisations within the community have taken place within this spacious and pleasant setting. A growing number of people are using it to celebrate special family occasions such as wedding anniversaries, birthdays and even for wedding receptions, with the committee sometimes providing the catering service.

As we move into autumn, 2003, work is continuing on the car park, which is proving to be a real blessing to the community. No more having to park on the road in a very busy street. This is particularly relevant for the parents who no longer have to arrive half-an-hour early to get a parking space. Hedges of beech and thorn have been planted, grass seeds tilled and soon attractive shrubs will be planted to enhance what is already a pleasant site with a wonderful view of surrounding countryside.

Short Mat Bowls

Work begins on the new car park area in September 2003 with Michael 'Jimmy' Daniel & Pat Mitchell

The Hall has its own IT centre, which is in great demand now that more and more people want to become computer literate. Keep Fit, Short Mat Bowls, Skittles, Badminton and Snooker are some of the things that are now happening on a regular basis in our new Parish Hall. Children's out-of-school activities also take place here regularly: providing a focus for youthful energy and imagination.

Langtree Post Office
Dates and details from Kelly's Directories

1855-6 & 1866–70. Letters through Torrington, which is nearest money order office.

1873. Letters through Exeter via Torrington.

1873. First mention of Post Office. Letters received at 10.35 am and despatched at 3.15 pm. John Mills, Sub-postmaster. There is also a John Mills who was Parish Clerk and John and Mary Mills were schoolteachers at Langtree – probably the same person. John Mills continued as sub-postmaster until sometime between 1893 and 1902.

1878. Postal times had changed a little: 9.40 a.m. & 4.30 p.m. weekdays only. There was a walled letterbox at Stibb Cross from this time, cleared 10.30 am, weekdays only.

1889. Stibb Cross letterbox now cleared at 12.40 am weekdays only. Also from this time there was a walled letterbox at Berry Cross cleared 3.45 pm daily.

1902. Postmaster was William Trigger. Postal Orders could now be issued here, but not paid. There is now no link between Postmaster and Schoolmaster. William Trigger was Postmaster until 1910 when a Mrs Elizabeth Trigger took it on. Possibly William has died and his widow is continuing to run the Post Office.

1906. Postal Orders can now be paid out as well as issued at Langtree.

1910. Mentions no Sunday deliveries, this would suggest deliveries on all other days, so Saturday deliveries have begun sometime since 1906.

1914. First mention of a letterbox at Week. All three letterboxes have weekday collections only. Stibb Cross cleared at 3.45 pm, Berry at 4 pm and Week at 8.15 am and 5.05 pm. The Post Office receiving times were now 8.30 am and despatched at 4.30 pm.

1919. Postmistress was still Mrs E Trigger, but by 1923 it had changed to Mr Herbert Down. Mrs Trigger probably remarried and became Mrs Huxtable. She sold the property to Mr Down in 1928, but he had taken over as Postmaster sometime before 1923.

1930. Listed as T & T E D Office and also in 1935.

1939. Listed as M O & T Office.

From approximately 1939 to 1946, Langtree's postal address was Brandis Corner (as listed in Kelly's Directories).

1901. First public telephone was opened in North Devon at Barnstaple Post Office, but Langtree would have had its first public telephone in the 1930s. It was inside the Post Office in what is now the sitting room. There was a wooden sectioned-off area on the right of the room for the phone.

Brandis Corner Postal Area

Post Office Owners

1928. Mrs E M Huxtable owned it before selling it to H Down.

1935. H Down sold it to G G D Watkins.

1936. G Watkins sold it to E J R Jones.

1958. E Jones sold it to Mr and Mrs Somerset-Wilson.

1959. The Somerset-Wilsons sold it to Mr & Mrs S J Fovargue.

1967. S Fovargue sold it to Mr & Mrs Wm. Harold Dyas. Sadly Mrs Dyas died shortly after coming to Langtree.

The old postman's hut near the top of Beara Hill

1980 (September). W. Dyas sold it to J. Pollard.

1998. John Pollard sold it to D. Shaw.

First mention of telephone numbers in Kelly's Directory is 1935. At that time, there were telephones at the Post Office; Rivaton (Harris); Hills Motors, Stibb Cross; Horn Brothers, Flour Dealers; Watertown (PB Jones); E Vanstone, Carpenter; – six telephones in all. By 1946 telephones had also been acquired at Lower Lake (J Adams); Wayside Motor Engineers (R Bray); Suddon (N Brooks); East Browns (W Brooks); Langtree Week (Cole); Stowford (Goss); – a further six telephones!

11. 12. 58. Telegraph facility removed.

18. 2. 72. Request for all houses to be clearly numbered or named to help Postman.

30. 7. 80. First suggestion of pensions being paid straight into bank accounts. Parish Council sent letter of protest to Member of Parliament.

21. 1. 82. First mention of stamps to pay bills by instalments (in this case electricity!).

21. 9. 92. BT mast erected in Langtree village.

There are also post boxes at Rivaton and Lake, as well as one at Langtree Week which is Victorian.

Bryan Ley remembers there was a Postman's hut on Beara Hill (on the left hand side near the top as you begin to go down at the place where it's a bit wider). It was painted a brownish red. The postman came out from Torrington and delivered his mail then went to his hut and boiled up a kettle to make tea and eat his lunch. "I remember being at school and in the dinner hour we walked about the village and would come to Beara Hill and see the smoke coming out of the chimney. He waited there until another postman from Newton St Petrock arrived with letters that needed sending on. He gave them to the Langtree postman who then took them back to Torrington".

Parish Church

You will have read some information about the Parish Church in section one, and also the profile of some of the Rectors. I want to build on that information and enlarge the picture, particularly including some of the more recent happenings at Langtree Parish Church.

One Rector who oversaw changes in Langtree Church, and is briefly mentioned previously, was the Rev Edward John Hall. He was Rector of Langtree from 1890–1911. The organ was installed and dedicated soon after his arrival. It was dedicated in 1891 during a service at which the Rev Herbert Barnes, the previous Rector of Langtree who had become the Archdeacon of Barnstaple, preached the sermon. Also during his incumbency an addition to the churchyard was made (1896) and the bells were re-hung (1905).

Rev. Edward John Hall

Rev Bernard Hallowes was another of Langtree's longer-serving vicars and is still fondly remembered by many today. As well as his role in the church, he was very much involved with the Men's Club and in 1945 was its President. He was a school governor and also presided over the regular examination of the children in religious knowledge. His daughter Rachel was the main instigator of the gymkhana held in the 1930s and when she was married, in 1935, the children were invited to the rectory for tea the afternoon before the wedding – school finishing early to enable this to happen. Many still remember that it snowed the day of the wedding, May 17th, but it didn't settle.

Rev T. R. Gibby also saw changes in the church. There were panels near the altar with the 10 commandments inscribed on them, – these were plastered over in the early 1950s. Also the seats, which had been a natural pine, were coated in dark varnish and some embellishments on the "preachers pew" were removed. Not everyone was happy about this.

1964 saw the arrival of Rev Richard Wallington. No stranger to the area, he had previously been headmaster at Buckland House boarding school, Buckland Filleigh. He was to be Langtree's last resident Rector, although that was not realised at the time of his arrival.

He, like many before him, was much involved in the community, through Parish and District Council amongst other things.

One of the things for which he and his wife, St Clair, became well known was their annual Nativity plays. Drawing in people from all parts of the community they continued for about 20 years and involved people of all age groups.

There was a complete overhaul of the organ in early 1966 and new oil heating was installed later that year at a cost of £270. Sadly in the autumn of 1972 a number of stones were thrown, smashing the 100 year old west window, which had been dedicated to Martin Guard, son of the previously mentioned Rev Guard. This was repaired by two art students, who were working under the direction of their Principal James Paterson. Stained glass work was part of their course and this would have been good experience for them.

Nativity Play

Back row: Nan Fovargue, Dick Wallington, unknown, John Folland, Patricia Soby, unknown both behind, and to her right , Chris Daniel.
Middle row: Barbara Channing-Pierce, St Clair Wallington, Sylvia Smith, May Gerry, Iris Andrew.
Front row:
Adrian Folland, Jason Ford, Neil Folland, Julie Langmead, Cathy Gerry, Helen Westerman.

In Feb 1973 the coat of arms was repainted. There are hundreds of coats of arms throughout the country but George II ones are very rare. Langtree's version is George II. It dates from about 1727 and is made of Barnstaple plaster and lath. Mr Bill Hudson, late student at Bideford School of Art, who also made mouldings for the rose and thistle emblems, previously painted flat on the background, did the painting. Mr Bill Daniel did the plaster repair. At the same time the roof bosses were gilded for the first time in history – the idea of Mr George Heath, churchwarden.

Dennis Pengilly and James Saunders built the steps near the church gates leading up into the graveyard in 1977, and Dennis's young daughter, Katrina officially opened them in September of that year. Memorials to Richard and St Clair were added to them in 1986 and 1999.

The following year (1978) brass candlesticks, which had long been lost, were found. They were in a poor state, but with careful restoration were able to be restored to their original position on the pulpit. An old photo had brought to light the fact of their previous existence, then the search was on to see if they could be found. They were discovered in the vestry wrapped in a piece of old carpet in a box.

Langtree held the first of a number of flower festivals in the Church in 1982, with arrangements being beautifully done by the Atlantic Flower Club. The following year saw the visit of Dudley Savage who gave a concert of organ music. He was well known and enjoyed for years through his weekly Sunday programme on the radio of live organ music and requests.

A welcoming and beautiful entrance at the 1991 Flower Festival

Rev and Mrs Wallington at their Golden Wedding celebration in the Parish.

1985 saw the celebration of there having being a church in Langtree for 700 years. There was a flower festival, a special Sunday lunch at Hillash Farm hosted by Colin and Mary Nicholls, and a pageant. The pageant began with the school but also involved many other adult members of the community. It was while researching for this pageant that Mr Allan Edgcombe, then Headmaster, put together the information which became his book 'A Short History of Langtree' that is reproduced as the early part of this publication.

At the end of 1984 Rev Wallington retired, though he, his wife St. Clair and sister Barbara Channing-Pierce continued to live in the Rectory for a while. He died on Christmas Day 1986. Having taken a service in the church and had his Christmas dinner, he then quietly slipped into the realms of eternity.

His retirement marked an historic moment for the village as it brought to an end Langtree having its own Vicar. The Parish joined with Shebbear, and their Rector, Rev Nigel Mead became ours. During reorganisation in 1988 Langtree, for a short time, came under the jurisdiction of the Petrockstowe area and Rev Chris Hanson, followed by Rev John Adams became our vicar. We reverted back to Shebbear in 2000 under the ministry of Rev Ronnie Mechanic, followed by our present vicar Rev Martin Warren.

1989-90 was a very tough time for Langtree Parish Church and it came very close to closing. The tower was found to be unsafe and the main beam supporting the bells was rotting away – the bells could no longer be rung. The estimated cost of all these repairs was £150,000 – far too big for the small congregation then actively involved to be able to raise themselves. There seemed no other way out but closure. Then an anonymous donation of £30,000, which became £35,000 when the donor was revealed to be Mr Bill Balsdon and tax was reclaimed, gave new hope. English Heritage took up the cause, which realised another £65,000, and suddenly people saw light at the end of what had seemed a long dark tunnel. The tower was repaired and bells re-hung in 1992-3.

Work well under way to restore the tower and bells

In the early 1990s Peter Vardy lead a series of Monthly Family Services which were very popular, with about 40 people attending, but he was unable to continue this indefinitely as pressure of work as a lecturer in Theology in London made it impractical.

In the 1970s Lord Clinton visited Langtree Church, attending a service on an annual basis and acknowledging his links with the village.

In 1994 it was discovered by a Professor at Exeter University that Langtree Parish Church did have a dedication and name; that of 'All Saints'. He had set himself the task of finding out why only a few parish churches in the whole country had no name. It was found that in fact a number of them, including Langtree, did have names which had somehow been lost. He was researching abroad (I'm not sure in which country) when the information concerning the name and dedication of our Parish Church came to light.

Langtree Church's newly hung and reconditioned peal of bells are now considered to be amongst the finest in the south of England. Ringers come from many areas to enjoy ringing the bells. Sadly we do not have our own team of ringers at this present time.

All Saints' latest acquisition is a state of the art 'niche' gas heating system.

The second Sunday of each month is a united service, with the Chapel congregation joining us, with the compliment returned the following week.

Zion Chapel

William O'Bryan, a travelling preacher from Luxillian in Cornwall, and converted under John Wesley's preaching, came to Langtree and preached on the Green. He went on to Shebbear and formed a group called 'The Bible Christians'. On 9th October 1815 there were 22 signatories to the newly formed Society. William O'Bryan lived for a while in Langtree,

January 30th 1817. James Thorne, a Bible Christian preacher of the Shebbear Society, preached at Berry Cross. 13 were present. He and his wife Catherine also resided here from 1829–1835. Thorne House in Fore Street is named after the family, as so often used to happen in those days. Until recently their descendants, members of the Daniel family, were still living in the house.

The old Zion old chapel was built in either 1821 or 1825 to seat 130. In a religious census at the Records Office in Barnstaple it states that the average attendance at this time was 125, and that William Nancekivell was Chapel Steward. This remained the same in the 1851 record. There was a Sunday School at the Chapel in 1826 with 32 boys and 50 girls attending. In the years 1834, 1837, 1839, 1840, & 1841 the annual Bible Christian Conference was held at Langtree.

A Teetotal Males Friendly Society was formed at Langtree and on May 23rd 1871 they met for the annual festival. Rev Guard presided, the band played, and they went to the Green Dragon for a meal. There was also a Temperance Society in the Parish formed by Mr James Thorne in 1837 and also a 'Band of Hope' at each of the Bible Christian chapels in the village, Hope and Siloam. In 1882 there was a heated debate as to which of these two Temperance organisations had the biggest impact on the parish, and which had been there first. There were letters in the local paper from the two main participants, Rev H Barnes and Thomas Ruddle BA of Shebbear College.

All Saints Church, Langtree.

Possibly a Bible Christian Conference, held at Langtree Chapel with the marquee likely to have been sited in the field where the Crescent Houses now are.

The old Chapel was rebuilt in 1871 at a cost of £200, when the seating was increased to 150. Twenty years later this was deemed too small as plans were made to build a new and bigger Chapel while the old one became the Sunday school room. A new Chapel was built and it was opened on October 6th 1904. The celebrations involved special services and a meal in the old chapel. The celebrations continued for several weeks with special speakers each Sunday. A Rev E Hortop gave part of the ground on which the Chapel was built, and the rest was bought from Mr Copp. The ground was called Bearhouse, and a ruined shippon, linhay and pigsty had to be cleared before the building could begin. The cost of the ground and of building was £700. Mr Bowden of Torrington was the builder, and the new Chapel seated 170.

An event in the old Chapel round about 1900, The little girl on the pulpit, who is probably singing or reciting is believed to be Doris Moore, later to become Mrs S Ley, & mother of Eileen and Bryan.

The Bible Christian movement became part of the United Methodist Church in 1907 when three branches of the Christian Church came together. Bible Christian, Methodist New Connexion and United Methodist Free churches, became The United Methodist Church. Later, in 1932, there was a further joining together with the Primitive Methodists and the Wesleyans. making the Methodist Church as we know it today.

Re-opening of the chapel after re-decorating in 1954. Mrs Johns had been presented with flowers by a young Pam Daniel. The Minister was Rev A Olds, accompanied by the Minister from Hatherliegh. On the right is Pastor Capener. Those looking on are: back two Mrs Glover, Evelyn Hill, Muriel Furse, Audrey Kellaway, Marion Hill, Alma Carter née Daniel, Next lady unknown though possibly she is the wife of the Hatherleigh Minister.
I've not been able to find out the name of the little boy.
Front row Daisy Ley, unknown, M Sanders, E Millman.

Meanwhile, back at Langtree, new toilets and a cloakroom were added to the old Sunday school room in 1930 and in 1941 the electricity supply was connected to both buildings at a cost of £2.6s.10d. In 1954 Mrs Johns, the first bride to be married in the Chapel, performed a reopening ceremony after redecorating.

This coincided with the Chapel's Golden Jubilee. Mr Francis Moore was the organist at this time, he had started this task at the early age of

Opening of the schoolroom by Mrs Dorothy Huxtable Marion Goaman presented her with flowers.

eleven and continued until he was sixty, only giving up then because of arthritis in his hands. In more recent years Jean Kellaway became organist at the young age of nine, continuing until the birth of her daughter more than twenty years later. David and Cathy Ley, two of our present organists, have also undertaken the task for over twenty years each, and both sometimes play at All Saints Church. There would often be concerts at the chapel given by various choirs over the years, some local and some from further afield.

The Caretaker's cottage was sold in 1965, then in 1969 toilets were built onto the Chapel. In the same year a new electric organ was installed, the previous one had to be hand blown. There was a lever at the side, which had to be continuously and evenly pumped up and down while the organ was played. Over the years many took a turn at this, sitting quietly beside the organist and keeping a steady rhythm going. The last two teenage lads to do this job were Charles Ley and David Goaman.

In 1977 land was bought from Mr Dyas at the Post Office and the new Sunday School room and kitchen were built at the back of the chapel. This was opened on March 8th 1978 by Mrs Dorothy Huxtable, a former Sunday School superintendent, and the preacher was Rev Amos Cresswell, Chairman of the District. Bringing children from the chapel to the Sunday school room and having to cross two roads had become increasingly dangerous, so it was a great relief to have a room adjoining which could be used for the children and many other activities. With the closing of the Church Hall and the Social Club in the late 1990s, this room became the main functions room for the use of village committees until the new Hall became available.

In 1982 the choir seats were removed from the front of the chapel and the raised platform area was built, the work having been done by local builder Ron Neal. This was much more practical for modern forms of worship involving drama and music groups

Four years later a large chunk of plaster from the ceiling fell on the organ seat a few moments after the organist Angela Ley had left it. How thankful we all were that it had not fallen whilst the service was still taking place. It was decided to renew the whole ceiling. A specialist firm from Crediton was employed to do the job at a cost of £3,531; then in the 1990s double-glazed windows were installed.

During the 1900s two sets of modern Hymnbooks "Hymns and Psalms" and "Mission Praise" were purchased. Since 1994, *Challenge*, the Good News newspaper has been distributed each month in the two villages, and two Alpha courses were run during the winter of 1998-9 in conjunction with the Church.

An Alpha course during the winter of 1998–99.

There has always been a Sunday school at the Chapel, and each year the young people have a range of special activities to be involved in. Over the years these have included youth services, nativity plays, sponsored walks for charities, outings, barbeques, toy service and nativity plays. The older youths have had barn services at Withacott and Burstone, as well as leading the worship with singing and instruments at open-air services in the playing field and in the marquee used at the fun day for a number of years. During the war years the Sunday school numbers were greatly increased by the evacuees who came along with their host families.

The saddest incident of the Sunday School was on July 25th 1946. It was the occasion of the annual outing and the venue that year was Bude. Some of the older teenagers had been allowed to go without their parents. Whilst some of the boys were enjoying themselves in the water, one of them, 15 year old Leonard Mills, got caught in the undercurrent near the canal mouth and was swept off his feet. He was pulled from the water fairly quickly but was unable to be resuscitated. His

Stibb Cross Chapel while still in use for worship.

death was a great loss on what should have been a happy occasion and a memorial tablet was placed in the Chapel by the Sunday School.

Stibb Cross

The 1851 census states that there was a Bible Christian meeting in Stibb Cross from the 1825. It was held in a home, but it is not known which one. Twenty people attended meetings which were held fortnightly, and Mr W Osborne of Cholash was the Steward. In 1896 the Chapel was built at a cost of £120. Mr Leonard Fishleigh gave the land for the Chapel and a Mr Parsons was the Architect. The builders were Short and Sanders, and Miss Gilbert of Binworthy laid the stone on 24th June 1896. Three hundred sat down to tea in a coach house lent by Mr Bromwell. Langtree Brass Band played, conducted by Mr Sanders. The evening meeting was held in Mr Blight's field and Langtree Choir sang at the service.

A Schoolroom was added in 1903. Mr W Ellis was the architect and the building cost £200. It was opened on 12th November with three services. Morning preacher Rev J.B. Stedeford; afternoon Rev W.B.Lark; and the evening Chairman Mr W Goaman of Bideford. Miss Julia Ley played the harmonium. There was a luncheon and tea, when the helpers were Mesdames E Brooks, W Ellis, F Blight, S Horn, J Ellis, M Squires, and Misses E Gilbert, S Blight, B & M Cleverdon.

Back row, Charlie Ley, Rev Sidney Quick, Nathaniel Gilbert, Ashmead Vanstone. Front row, Albert Hill, Rev Sandercock, A.B.Shorney, T.Squire.

The two Miss Balsdons who were part of Stibb Chapel for many years and who became Mrs Capener and Mrs Moore. Mrs Moore was a long time organist at the Chapel. Her husband Eddie is standing behind,

Stibb Cross also had a Sunday School and in 1925 there were 44 scholars, reducing to 24 by 1935. These are large numbers when you remember there were also Sunday Schools at Langtree and Siloam Chapels; and the Parish Church. In addition Rowden, Thornhillhead and Newton were only short distances away. Mrs Daisy Watkins has a record of the names of children in attendance, covering a number of those years. Teachers involved at that time were John Blight, Nathaniel Gilbert, Ethel Andrew and Mary Ellis. A few years later Winnie Andrews and Ida Blight had replaced the two women.

After a lapse of some years a Sunday School was again instigated, when Maurice Adams, followed by Betty Breeze, then Brenda Prentice, Jill Earley and Margaret Hill took on the work. Another worker at the chapel was Mrs Moore who was an organist at Stibb Cross chapel for many years.

In 1921 there was a visit of the Delabole Choir to Stibb Cross at the invitation of the Chapel. The event was held in a marquee in a field near the village. It was a very big event for the Chapel and was talked about for many years afterward.

In 1953 renovations took place at the Chapel, and on 24th September that year there was a special celebration to mark the occasion. It included an afternoon service and a tea, then an evening concert with the Beaford concert party. The expenses account for that time, which includes repairs to the organ and provision of two electric stoves, was £509.

The first wedding at Stibb Cross was that of Miss Nancy Hearn and Mr Godfrey Larkworthy

In 1962 a new Methodist Manse was built at Stibb Cross next to the Chapel, and housed the Assistant Minister of the Shebbear Circuit until the late 1990s.

Stibb Cross Chapel closed for worship in 1993, when it was revealed that major repair work was needed. The worshippers have since joined three other nearby chapels. Planning permission was applied for and the chapel was sold.

Siloam after it had been closed for worship

Siloam

The 1851 census declares that Siloam was erected in 1828, and that the average attendance was 77 in the afternoons and 48 in the evenings. The steward was Mr Thomas Tucker of Lake, Langtree.

The 1832 census states that at Siloam there is a meeting place and a day school. Mr Ben Copp remembers being told that his father attended this school.

There is a reference in 1841 of a Mr John Whitlock of North Collacott being the owner of the Meeting House, and the existence of a lease, the rent being one peppercorn per year. The Signatories and Trustees at that time are listed as James Thorne, Langtree, dissenting minister; Messrs Henry Copp, George How Hackwill, Thomas Tucker, John Whitlock jnr., Richard Whitlock, James Nancekivell, all described as Yeomen; William Ayre, Cordwainer, and Richard Sanders, Carpenter. There was a clause in the document regarding the release of the land to the Bible Christians stating that "preachers shall adhere to the doctrine contained in the late John Wesley's notes on the New Testament, and the sermons by him". Names are on record of the Trustees for the years 1851, 1873, 1898 & 1938.

In 1903 extra ground was bought to enlarge the burial ground for the price of £3. Electricity was installed at the chapel in 1964 at a cost of £30. In 1955 a re-opening was held and the only picture of Chapel events at Siloam we have is from this time.

The re-opening of Siloam in 1955. The little boy is Peter Ley and his mother, Audrey Ley, sister of Grenville Bond, is close at hand. The opening is being performed by Mrs Bale. Dolly Copp, sister of Ben, is on the right at the back

Siloam closed for worship, and was sold shortly afterwards in 1973, but its graveyard remains open for burials. There was probably a Sunday School at Siloam for many years, with the children who attended day school also having gone to Sunday School there. We know that this was the case in the 1830s and 40s as it is referred to in a little book called 'Memoir of Mary Richards'. Mary was murdered and her grave is at Siloam (her story is covered elsewhere in this book). She was sent to the Sunday School at Siloam from the age of four years old, where a Mr Tucker who later bore testimony to her faith and character taught her. For the last four years of her life she was a Sunday School teacher, and was described as a young lady of clear conviction and strong faith. She taught her scholars well. At the time of her attack she had been training the children for the Sunday School Anniversary services.

Alma Bond remembers being told by her parents-in-law that when the family came to Rivaton to farm in 1938, fairly soon after their arrival, Mr Ford of Berry Cross visited them and invited them to attend Siloam Chapel (perhaps he already knew they were a Chapel-going family). He said numbers were quite low and there was some concern about it closing. The family soon became regular attendees:

"I remember people being involved in redecorating the place and there was a special re-opening in 1955. Our nephew, Peter Ley, presented a bouquet to the person re-opening the Chapel. That was Mrs Bale of Newton St Petrock. Peter was a young boy of 5 at the time.

There was a Sunday School outing; I can't remember which year or where we went. Mr Charlie Hill was driving the bus and a leak developed in a pipe – possibly a petrol pipe. To repair it, so we could finish our journey, Mr Hill sealed the crack with soap – it worked, and we had a good trip".

After Siloam closed it was sold to a local resident, Mr John Scudder. He stored furniture etc in it, to be sold in Scudders Emporium at the top of Bridge Street, Bideford. The building was sold again and planning permission granted but never used. Sadly it is now in a poor state of repair.

Union Inn – Stibb Cross

In 1901 this property was owned by the brewery – Starkey Knight and Ford Ltd.

Maureen Richards remembers that she moved to Stibb Cross with her family in 1950, and her father Mr Dick Harris became the licensee of The Union Inn. Then in 1957 he purchased the Inn, and later the cottage next door where a Mrs Johns used to live. The property was then made into one

"I remember that the first door into the pub led into a small lobby from where a staircase led originally to the bedroom above. To the left was a small room; this was the 'snug' with a piano. The right hand door led into the main bar which had a very big fireplace and the door just to the left of the window led up to the kitchen. Here there was a Rayburn, and the stairs leading up to the bedrooms. Downstairs a door led out into the scullery and backyard. There was an outside toilet. A door from the kitchen led to another small lobby, and into a small sitting room. Dad had the place altered and the stairs were moved to the small lobby. When he bought the next-door cottage another room was entered via the sitting room. This was used as a dining room and on Mondays as an Office for Kivells. There was now also a very large bedroom which was the family room for visitors. This was above what was the cottage, then there was a smaller room, and I had the room above the kitchen, so it was nice and warm in the winter. I still remember there could be ice on the inside of the window, and I dressed in bed to keep warm. There was a long landing and another two bedrooms (above the bar), a bathroom and toilet extension. There was a large garden and an orchard, which was later made into the car park.

In the autumn there was always a Harvest Festival

Harvest Festival at the Union Inn in the late 1950s/early 1960s. L – R: Johnie Cole, Charlie Walters, Joe Cole, Dick Harris. The rest are unknown except the vicar, Rev Wade, and the taller man by the bar on the right is Mr Gilbert of Venn Farm, Newton St Petrock where the scout party used to stay

at the Inn, led by a vicar from London who used to come down with a group of Scouts camping on a farm at Newton St Petrock. Mrs Popham from Torrington would play the piano, and there would be supper afterwards".

"I remember some really happy times with the visitors in the holiday season, singing and dancing in the bar, a good time. Christmas was always a lively time also, with everyone going outside at midnight and singing carols. Dad and Mum were kept very busy all the time, because Dad also had the cows, pigs and sheep to look after and the milking to do. There was also hay-making time. The hay was kept above the shippen and in the garage. Lightning struck the side of the barn one night and everyone had to go and help clear the road."

In the late 1800s the Bond family lived in the Union Inn. They were one of the families that had diphtheria and all survived. At that time there were two Doctors who had different methods of treating their patients. The Bond family Doctor kept all the affected members isolated and in one room, and they all recovered. Many others were not so fortunate.

Perhaps one of the biggest changes in 'pub' life has been the move into regular provision of food at most times of the day. The Union Inn has been a place for 'eating out' for many years.

For a short period of time the name of the Inn was changed to 'The Snooty Fox' but fairly soon reverted to its original name again. The Beer Garden became a building site in the 1990s.

The Green Dragon

There is a document hanging in the Green Dragon which gives some of it long history and the Inn is referred to in Part One of this book on pages 29, 34, 35, 40, 41, 46 & 47. Some of the licensees during the 19th century were also the village Bookmakers. As already mentioned, the Inn was burnt down in 1924 and rebuilt. During a later reconstruction, the drawing room of the cottage was made into the present games room and has sometimes been used as a small restaurant. The adjoining stables still have the original cobbled floor

The Green Dragon Inn prior to the 1924 fire.

Over the years, some of the Green Dragon garden has been taken up in two building sites, and during the summer of 2003 the old plaster on the outer walls was stripped away to reveal the stonework beneath. Meals are not served at the Green Dragon at this present time, although there have been periods when they were. As well as being able to enjoy a pint, patrons can also play Pool, Skittles, Darts, and take part in the quizzes held occasionally. Sometimes special charity events are held.

Following on from the list of Landlords at the end of Section One of this book, the more recent

The Green Dragon Inn as a result of the fire in 1924

The Green Dragon Inn after being re-built following the fire.

licensees have been Mrs Dick Vanstone, Alf Jones, Dougie Bond, Cyril and Margorie Dyer, Major and Mrs Law, John and Barbara Law, Ron and Gwen Gent, Laurie and Diane Isaac, John Corby, Tony and Margaret Binloss, Bernard and Eve Piggott, Chris Brown, John and Patricia Soby, Rick Myra, Mr Barnfield, and to bring us up to this present time, Mr Taylor.

The Green Dragon Inn 1954

Jubilee Playing Area

This field was purchased by the Parish Council for a village playing area and to mark the Silver Jubilee of Queen Elizabeth II. A committee was formed consisting of the following people: Mrs E Ford and Mrs E Huxtable, J Folland, A. Mills, W Dowson, L Knapman, P Langmead and M Richards.

Linda Mitchell about to enter the water in the 'ducking stool' game at one of the fun events in the play area

They held their first meeting on July 12th 1978 and the immediate priority was to clear the site of some old poultry sheds and to improve the entrance into Latch Lane, setting the gate back from the road for safety reasons. Two dates were set for these tasks to be done with J Coles helping with the digger work. The next priority was to raise some funds. Having to "start from scratch" the committee set to work and had the field cleaned up enough to hold their first function on 12th August that year. An afternoon and evening of fun was arranged with a Five-a-Side Football Tournament, Skittles, Slippery Pole, and Buried Treasure; also a bonfire with a Bangers and Bean Feast in the evening. A lively and enjoyable start had been made to fundraising.

There were still many problems to be faced. What to do about the fast growing grass and how to get some play equipment became the next priorities. In 1979 a sandpit was made for the very young with a load of sand being donated by Bryan Ley. Jack Walters' sheep were used periodically to eat off the grass. He also rolled the field with his heavy farm roller to even up the ground, and at times cut the grass with his field mower. At some point the field was ploughed and re-seeded by Geoff Bond.

November 5th saw the first Parish bonfire evening in the field, with people donating either fireworks or money to contribute to one large display. This was to become a popular, annual event until well into the 1990s when increasing safety consciousness made it no longer viable in a children's play area. Hot food was always part of bonfire night. Jacket potatoes and soup in the early years, and sometimes a lamb roast in the late 1980s. Tinky Mills, Geoff Bond and Les Knapman were responsible for putting on the firework display and setting them off. Some years there was a competition for the 'Best Guy'. One year there was a sing-song around the fire lead by Ron Neale. Bonfire night was always a non-profit making event put on simply to draw the community together, though sometimes it did create a surplus of funds, which went to the play area account.

In the spring of 1980 an entrance was made from the school directly into the play area; this was jointly funded by the committee and the school. Nine years later a concrete path was laid from this new school entrance, travelling across the play area, to the entrance into the Chapel ground, so that the nursery children, who were using the Chapel room for their activities, could easily and safely access the school without using the busy road.

A concert was organised, with school children and local talent taking part, to finance this new development. The concert was successful and the idea was repeated the next year. A special song was written for this concert and sung by one of the singing groups of teenagers. It is printed overleaf.

The fun afternoon, which had been the committee's first fundraiser, became an annual event with slight variations to format. In 1984 the Eaglescott Sky-Divers came, drawing a large crowd, and the following year there was a radio-controlled aeroplane display in the adjoining field.

From 1984-1992 a sponsored cross-country race was held each spring. There were three classes: under elevens; eleven to sixteens; and over sixteens. It was held in either March or April, starting in the play area. The race took a path up Latch Lane, across Trathens field towards Bibbear, then along the road to Southcott and up the back lane past Wooda to the top corner then across the fields to the top of Latch Lane and back into the play area for the finish. A tiring but enjoyable afternoon.

The Eaglescott skydivers land in the play area.

In 1989, and for a few years after, a farmhouse supper was held each August Bank-holiday Monday at the home of Geoff and Julie Bond, or at David and Cathy Ley's, with people contributing home-made plate pasties of every sort with apple pies, fruit salad and junkets to follow. All this was enjoyed in the open air with competitions in the nearby barn. Sometimes these evenings incorporated a car treasure hunt and a pig roast.

Acquiring play equipment was difficult. There weren't as many grants for leisure activities then, so funding was the greatest difficulty. It soon became necessary to pay for regular grass cutting from the Council. But slowly the committee were able to begin putting things in place. Some of the equipment they made and erected themselves.

A section of a three-seat wide slide, became redundant at Westward Ho when they dismantled their Big Dipper Slide over the pebble ridge. This became available, and after a lot of work, was erected in the playing field. There was also a swing, a see-saw and a climbing frame. These were enjoyed for some years.

A Song for Langtree   Tune: Marching to Georgia

'Lizabeth our Queen, one day a Jubilee did share
Calling people everywhere to show they really care.
Do something constructive;
  see just how your neighbours fare
If you are living in Langtree.

Chorus
  Hurrah! Hurrah! We'll make a playing field
  Hurrah! Hurrah! The kids can come to play
  So we'll work together through
    each sunny happy day
  Building a future for Langtree.

So we bought a field you know, with people working well
Picked up all the rubbish,
  then Geoff ploughed the field, heard tell
Then they planted grass seeds, now it looks real swell
For all who're living in Langtree.

Now we've got a fine new swing
  on which the kids can ride
Got some football goal posts just for playing '5 a-side'
Going to have a sandpit and a lot more things beside
For all the children of Langtree.

Come good people everywhere, we need your help today
For all new things that are bought,
  someone must surely pay
If we want amenities we all must find a way
Working together for Langtree.

Final Chorus
  Come on, come on,
    lets have some interest shown
  Come on, come on,
    till all our plans have grown
  Pulling all together with a song of Jubilee
  Building a future for Langtree.

      Margaret Knapman 1980

As time passed and fundraising for a new Hall began, it became even more difficult to keep support for all the various activities, so the committee merged with the Hall Committee for a while, yet an incredible lot had been done by a small group with many fun events and activities provided for the children and youth of the Parish. A worthy effort and one to be proud of.

In 1999, a separate committee was again established but as this was jointly a Millennium committee it is covered in another section. Suffice to say that new and safe equipment was purchased bringing the play area right up-to-date. Now the search is on for a similar facility for Stibb Cross, where the growing number of children will also have a safe place to play, which is near to home for parental supervision.

Parish Newsletter

In the 1960s, and through to the mid 1980s, there was a village news-sheet that went out each month with the Parish Church Deanery magazine. This was a useful source of news and information and was produced by Rev and Mrs Wallington, but only reached those who bought the church magazine. During the 1980s George Heath produced a folded A4 page of historical bits and pieces called 'Langtree Jottings'. This also was available alongside the Deanery magazine.

Between 1992-4 Langtree saw its first multi-paged Newsletter come into being, simply called 'Langtree News'. It was printed and produced by Jeremy Horn at P.H.C, three or four times a year, according to how much information he had gathered. The organisations within the Parish were invited to contribute news and updates on their activities, there were some special interest features and various other items, as well as advertisements. The newsletter was distributed by Geoff and Sue Folland on their milk round and about 200 copies of each issue were printed. Having got the thing started and established, a number of appeals were made for someone to take over as editor. When no-one was found, Jeremy had to reluctantly relinquish the task through pressure of work and it ceased publication.

In 2000, with the start of the new Millennium, Langtree Parish Newsletter was reborn in a slightly different format and more pages, when Tom Bond offered to print and produce it if an editor could be found. Eventually Pat Dowson took up the challenge. It continued to rely on the community for information and articles. Tom produced the newsletter until he left home for university, with photocopying being done at the home of his friends Stephen and Linda Saywell, three hundred copies being printed.

Our present Newsletter Editors Trish Shaw with son Ben, and Pat Dowson

These newsletters were delivered around the villages, with extra copies left in strategic places for people to help themselves – ie Post Office, Pubs, Church and Chapel.

After this Trish Shaw took on the role of Producer. Pat Dowson continues to gather the items and Trish produces each Master copy. Then it is back to Pat again to get it photocopied. Once the material is gathered it takes about a week to sort and print up the first copy (remember this is a spare time activity for people who already live busy lives).

There are now 4 issues a year – 360 copies each issue and at least 12 or 14 sides per copy. To get the Master photocopied has always been a mammoth task and can take up to 40 hours for each issue. The photocopier can get 'red hot' with the volume of output, which can be in the region of 4,500 and 5,000, sides of paper. It has to be done in batches to let the copier rest and cool. Then each copy has to be stapled together. Sometimes Pat's family help her out. At the moment it is 'copied' at Bridgmans of Newton St Petrock. Then it is hand delivered free to every home by Mike and Pat Cole, Mary Goaman, Kay Galvin and Geoff Heaton. Not bad going for voluntary tasks. Fifteen copies are posted and there is a constant search for that article that's a little different, someone's unusual job or adventure perhaps?

The newsletter is funded by voluntary contributions and adverts. There had been a hope of purchasing an adequate photocopier for the Parish but this will be an expensive item having to cope with such a volume of work over a short period and has not yet become possible. Something for the future perhaps.

Stibb Cross Market

We cannot be sure when Stibb Cross Market really started. As stated in Part One, Kelly's Directory first lists it in 1930, yet listening to the farmers of the Parish it becomes apparent this was not really the beginning of marketing at Stibb Cross. Perhaps this was the time when the buildings or pens, as they were latterly remembered, were put up, or maybe the point of some official recognition. There are those who remember the marketing of livestock happening earlier than that date. Cattle Market facilities are recorded as existing in Bideford and Torrington in the 1890s so maybe something less official was happening at Stibb Cross also. In the early days of the officially-recorded market the auctioneers were Hannaford, Ward and Southcombe but it was in the hands of Kivells at the time of its closure

Aerial view of Stibb Cross Market

Joe Bond remembers that his father brought stone to the village to rebuild the Green Dragon in 1924, when the fine rubble and anything not suitable for building was taken to Stibb Cross and used as hardcore in the Market, which up until then was, at times, a very muddy place. Ben Copp believes there was some form of marketing going on there before the First World War. Whatever the date of its beginning it was a very important Market, and played a central part for the farmers of this and other parishes.

Jack Beer remembers Stibb Cross market when Walter Slee was the auctioneer, in 1919 and the Bankers were Fox and Fowler: "My father's account book records that Lloyds took over the banking from 19th April 1921. I remember walking cows to Taddiport from Withacott. Stibb Cross was a very important market in those days; one of the most important in Devon."

Mr Arch Soby with his prize Devon in 1963

A special sale of 300 store and fat cattle was recorded in the Bideford Gazette in 1938, and there is a photo (opposite) of a special sheep sale in 1957 when Mr Bill Cousins of Kivells was the Auctioneer.

Joe Bond also remembers that at one period, Mr Nath Gilbert of Binworthy regularly won prizes with his Devon cattle and Devon long-wool sheep: "No-one else could touch him for quality of animals at that time". Over the years many others would also have won prizes as the above picture of Mr A Soby shows.

Bryan Ley remembers Stibb Cross Market was a collecting centre during the war. Finished stock ready for slaughter was brought there and bought by the Ministry of Food on behalf of the Government. Everything was controlled; there was a representative for the Ministry and a representative for the farmers. They would decide on the grade of each animal, which governed the set price that would be paid. This went on probably into the mid 1950s. Stibb Cross Market was one of the largest Collecting Centres in Devon. Mr Slee from Torrington was an auctioneer at some point.

Sheep sale at Stibb Cross.

Joe Bond remembers that sometimes cattle were sold, brought home till another day, then taken to Torrington Station to be transported by train to the London butchers

Les Knapman remembers that store bullocks also were sold, then brought home again perhaps for as long as a fortnight, to be looked after until cattle dealer Fred Cook had bought enough to charter a train from Torrington station. On the appointed day the farmers took their cattle on foot to the station, sometimes meeting up with others doing the same thing. Les recalls that from Collacott where they lived at that time, the cattle were taken down the road to Gortlege, up Frizenham Hill, on through Taddiport then along the track by the milk factory which came out more or less opposite the station. It would take much of the day to accomplish this. Sometimes they would meet up with other farmers engaged in the same task.

Pair of Porkers Prize Certificate

Jack Folland remembers the Cattle Market was a good day out and a chance to meet up with neighbours and fellow farmers. A time to exchange news and views, discuss prices and stock, and make a break from the daily work of the farm. Many farmers went into the Union Inn for their dinner; it was a real day out.

Edward Ley recalls that Mrs Maud Mills used to milk the cows after they had been sold.

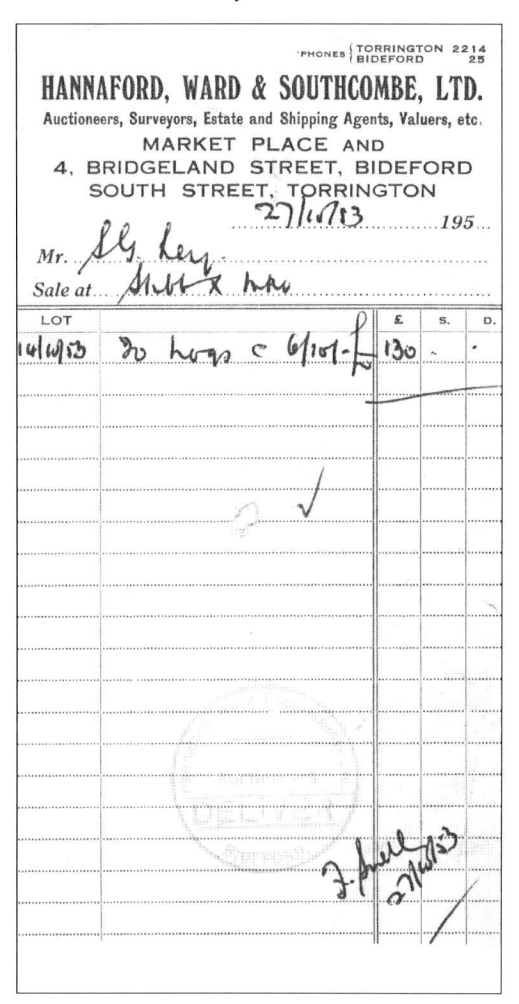

S Ley Receipt 1953

Sandra Juniper remembers being told by her father that Darch's of Torrington built Stibb Cross Market. "My Grandfather and Uncle, Stanley and Harold Bowden, worked for Darch's, and their nephew Richard Bowden, who recalls they were carpenters, told me that on one occasion he travelled with them to help with the work."

Maureen Richards (née Harris) remembers her dad purchased the Cattle Market a few years after its closure. The Market had been held on Mondays and it was a very busy and lively one: "Mum used to serve roast lunches at the Pub for the farmers. Kivells used the top rooms as their offices for that day. There was also a branch of a Bank that would come for this day, and I think this was across in Miss Blight's. There was a very big shed with a big weighing pen for the animals, and lots of little pens around the area. There were several little wooden sheds at the far end, where the two bungalows stand, next to Whitegates. These were for the different firms to use as offices. I seem to remember these were always green.

The cattle market made an excellent place to play at other times of the week for all of us children in the village, and later we all used to meet there on a Sunday night. We were most likely very rowdy at times. On fireworks night everyone used to come and bring their fireworks there and it would be quite a noisy place. I hated fireworks and used to stand on the barn steps well out of the way. The area was a useful parking place for the Pub as well."

Watergate Halt

Marland Clay Works Industrial line was built in 1887, and Watergate Halt was built for passengers in 1926. In the late 1940s Watergate was used as a milk collection point from where milk was sent to London via Torrington. The line closed to passengers in 1965.

Ethel Huxtable used the train regularly in the early 1950s to go back to Meeth and visit her parents. Her husband Albert would take her and their daughter to catch the train at 9.10 am. Young Jo was in the pushchair. They travelled in the guard van so Jo could stay in her chair and sleep if she wanted to, with Mum keeping watch. The return trip left Meeth at 7.20 pm. Sometimes if there had been a heavy downpour the line would flood at Watergate. The guard would get out and carry Jo in her chair to the safety of the platform and Ethel waded through the water – almost up to her knees sometimes.

Ethel travelled on the train from Watergate Halt to Meeth on the day it made its final passenger journey and has kept the ticket – a copy is reproduced overleaf.

Les Knapman remembers hearing people say when he was a young lad, that they could get off the train, pick themselves a bunch of wild flowers and easily catch it up and board again, because of the slow speed it did. Of course it was acceptable to pick wild flowers in those days and people did so freely.

Edna Daniel remembers going to Bideford and Barnstaple on the train, catching it at Watergate Halt.

John Upfold remembers his childhood trips on the Tarka line and holidays in Devon: "It was a great adventure when as a child, I travelled with my family from our home in Surrey to spend a summer holiday with our relations in Devonshire.

This was the era immediately after the Second World War when annual holidays were becoming within the reach of many more families. However, trips abroad were still uncommon and beyond most domestic budgets. Car ownership for most people was still something for the future and travel was mainly by coach or train.

I vividly recall making the journey westward by steam train, which left Waterloo Station in London. Carriages were detached along the way at Exeter and Barnstaple for various seaside destinations and after many hours we arrived at Torrington late in the afternoon. However, our journey to Langtree was still not over as we transferred to the little train which left Torrington for Hallwill Junction just twice daily. This consisted of only a single carriage, pulled by a small tank engine. After a couple of miles our day-long railway experience ended when we reached Watergate Halt. Then for me came the best part of the entire journey as we were met by my Uncle Joe Bond, with the horse and cart from the farm. We loaded the luggage onto the cart and jumped up ourselves, to sit swinging our legs as Dolly plodded her way along Southcott Lane to West Wooda Farm. Our wonderful holiday had begun at last."

On a later trip in 1961, when John came with his new wife to Langtree, he took a photo of the train at Watergate Halt, providing us with the only picture we have of our own local train service in action.

Linda Westall remembers that for Langtree under-5s one very memorable trip was to the

The train at Watergate Holt

Pottery at Watergate, which Nick Chapman had set up. His two children both came to the playgroup sessions: "It was an early spring morning round about 1981, with a slight frost still in the air. We parked the cars at the bottom of the drive and as we walked up to the Pottery, the Marland Clay train came past. The children were thrilled to see it, particularly as the men waved to them and blew the whistle for the crossing. After our trip around the Pottery, and making their own small pots, we walked back and sat on the railway platform to drink our milk and eat biscuits. The last clay train ran in August 1982, so we were really glad the children had had this opportunity to see the train so near to home." Watergate platform is actually just across the border onto Frithelstock land, but is listed in Kelly's Directory as belonging to Langtree. Part of the line is definitely in Langtree parish.

Meals on wheels

This facility was available in Langtree for a time in the late 1980s and into the 1990s. Co-ordinator was Sonia Ovenall, and various people delivered the meals. They were cooked at the primary school along with the childrens' dinners, and were collected from there at twelve noon two days each week; Tuesday and Thursday. Packed individually in aluminium covered containers and stacked in a cool-box they were taken out to those who lived alone or who needed the provision of a ready-cooked hot meal. First delivery was next door to the school for Queenie Harding, then on to the other areas at Southcott, Berry Cross and Langtree Week, Stibb Cross and Newton St Petrock. This facility ceased, as many of those needing the meals were elderly and unwell, and when they died there was no further take up of the facility.

One of the last tickets to be issued

*Above:
Sunday Best, Langtree
c1900*

Left: John Elias Tucker and his wife (great-grandparents of Ruth Wood) at Rivaton c1880

*Right:
Bert Ayre
during World War One.*

*Below Left:
Corn harvest at Smallridge c1940. With the horse is Mr Bill Huxtable, and by the binder is Barbara Babbs' Grandad Jim Huxtable, with her aunty Emily Richards, and Margery Underhill*

*Below Right:
Jim Adams with his stone-crushing machine at Langtree Quarry in the 1950s*

Above:
Girls from Langtree School who put on a special display in 1914 for Lady Gertrude Rolle on the occasion of the opening of the Social Club

Left:
Joe Bond sowing grass seeds with a fiddle in 1945

Right:
Maud Walters and Charlie Stevens at Langtree Parish Church on their wedding day around the time of World War One

Left: Members of the Order of Rechabites pose outside the Men's Social Clubroom in Langtree c 1920. Standing: members are believed to be L-R, Mrs Daniel, ? , Mr Burrows, Mr Palmer, ? , Seated: Miss Gertrude Palmer, ?, Mrs Burrows ? , ? .

Chapter Ten CLUBS & ORGANISATIONS

Parish Council

Not many people get an opportunity to read through Parish Council minutes books, but having done so it becomes apparent that many of the benefits the Parish enjoys are often hard fought for, sometimes over a number of years before the results are seen and established in the Parish.

Social Club minutes remind us that in March 1940 the Parish Council hired their room for meetings for 6d.

For many years up to 1971, the Parish Council met in the school, then rising hire rates caused them to move to the Church Hall. When this closed they met in the Chapel room, until the new Hall was completed. With the opening of the Hall they took great pleasure in moving into the purpose-built committee room.

In the early days the Parish Council met as and when the need arose, usually three or four times a year. As the years passed the number of meetings per year slowly increased until it became a monthly event, settling to a fixed date in 1993.

The Parish Council have had responsibility over the years for things like street lighting, footpaths and bridleways, notice boards, litter bins, recycling pavilion, traffic needs, sewage and planning applications. Their responsibilities have always been subject to, and somewhat limited by, District and County Council and other Authorities over them.

They also undertake to keep the Church tower clock in good repair, as it is the village War Memorial. In the 1950s there were only two or three streetlights in the Parish. These were gradually increased, sometimes one or two at a time, untill we have our present number. At first they were only on in the evenings. This was extended to include mornings in 1969 particularly to help the children walking to school on dark winter days. In 1990 all night lighting was proposed, and was instigated soon afterwards. Autumn 2003 will see lights placed along Dragon Hill.

Here are some of the things they have worked to establish in our parish:

In the 1960s public notice-boards and the first public litterbin were put in place.

In the late 1960s and early 1970s the Parish had two official Council rubbish tips, one at Sandy Lane, and the other at Watertown Cross. This one is now a beautiful garden, created and tended by Alfie and Dianne Daniel, Catherine and Heather.

A Preservation Order was placed on the old Beech tree at the Green Dragon in 1974. Footpaths were first signposted in 1985.

The playing field was bought for the community in 1977, and was called the Jubilee Playing Field in honour of the Queen's Silver Jubilee that year. The field was previously called Judd's and was part of the estate of Mr Ned Vanstone who had died earlier in the year. £800 was paid for the ground, the price being fixed by the District Valuer. A special meeting was called to discuss ways of financing the project; Rev Wallington reported that the Parochial Council was willing to lend the money from the Churchyard fund. It was unanimously agreed to accept the offer at an interest rate of 6%.

In 1978 tree planting took place at Withacott Corner, Buda Corners, at the entrance to the

Gerald (Jock) Mills receives a farewell presentation on retiring as Parish Clerk. The presentation is being made by Mr A Soby, as Chairman. The other Councillors are: J Walters, J Folland, L Mills, Rev Wallington, B Ley, A Mill, L Knapman and S Roberts.

Planting the Chestnut Trees at Doggaport end of the village in 1977. L-R: J Mills, B Ley, P Soby, W Soby ,A Mills, and J Corby Also involved with the planting was L Knapman who was taking the photo

village from Stibb Cross side, where the Chestnut trees have made good growth, and on the Thornhillhead road at Stibb Cross. The trees at Buda did not do so well and the original Thorn had to be replaced by Silver Birch in 1994.

In the autumn of 1999 the corner garden was created from what had been a dull area of old tarmac. It was planted up in August 2000. The old thatched building that had stood there for many years had been demolished in June 1966 and the site tarmaced and fenced around for child safety. Many remember that old building as the shop of Mr Alf Burrows, where sweets could be bought.

In 1978 a new scheme of grants was put in place by whereby organisations within the Parish could apply to their Parish council for grants. The Social Club was the only group to apply in the first year, and received £15. Other groups soon followed on. Last year's grants, up to the sum of £50, were allocated to six organisations. For several years, now, Torridge District Council have matched these grants by giving an equal amount to each organisation that applies.

Through the 1980s plans were put in place to erect bus shelters, particularly for the use of the children who have to catch school buses each day. Langtree shelter was built in 1986 with no difficulty, and then was altered to remove the front in 1997. Stibb Cross shelter was finally built in 1994 after tremendous efforts to secure a site.

Improvement works were carried out at the Langtree sewerage works in 1985.

Langtree parish precept for 1959 was £20. In 1970 it was £200. By 1986 it had risen to £500, then ten years later in 1996 it was £1000. At the beginning of the new Millennium it had become £3000. For 2003 it has been £4000.

Men's Social Club and Reading Room

Kelly's Directory for 1914 is the first reference stating that a 'Men's Club' was built in 1912 and consisted of a Reading & Billiards Room and mini Rifle Range. "It is vested in the hands of the Rector and Church Wardens." It was officially opened at a village fete by Lady Gertrude Rolle.

Langtree Social Club Opening

The first Minute Book of the Club was lost; searches and enquiries were made for it in the mid 30s but nothing was found, so our earliest records are from 1924. The bank account was opened in 1924 with Lloyds at Torrington with a deposit of £20.

In February 1926, a public meeting was held to consider plans for a proposed extension to house a skittle alley. I understand this was, at that time, a wooden structure. (The skittle alley walls were bricked up in 1950 with just enough white Marland bricks available to make the front section match the rest of the building. It was also re-roofed, all this work being done by Tinky Mills and Reg Glover. The money raised to enable the work to be done was raised by public subscription). Mrs Vincent of Torrington had opened a

The Parish Council meets for the first time in the new Parish Hall. L-R they are: G Bond, A Glover (Chairman) S Hawker (Clerk), P Dowson, F Takkin, J Allin, R Hancock, C Ley, and B Ley

new cement skittle alley on 11th October 1929. This was almost certainly the one housed in the new extension proposed in 1926.

The Club was closed from June 1940 to January 8th, 1945 because of the war, but it was slow to get going again after, so closed from August to October to give people time to consider and join up for the winter. (It was however still in use as a base for the Home Guard).

Social Club 1930s. Back row, L-R: S Nicholls, E Mills, C Tucker, S Hellings, E Underhill, F Dymond jnr, W Wilton, W Mills, F.J Mills. Middle row: G.F Mills, R Stoneman, H Furse, R.B Jones, Rev Hallowes, W Huxtable, F Wadron, C Ayre, H Harris, F Dymond snr. Front row: A Dymond, F Moore, C Squires, C Walters.

In 1926, it was decided, after some discussion, to take the *Daily News* – it seems that, up to this point, a paper had been loaned from the Caretaker. Six months later, they also took the *Daily Herald*. At some point, maybe years later, they must have been cancelled again, because in January 1950 it was decided to once more purchase papers for the Club, namely *Daily Herald*, *Daily Express* and *Picture Post*.

Dances were held in the room. In March 1925 admission cost 1/- (5p now!) including refreshments, with a pianist and violinist, as well as a 'Spot Dance' competition (the Rector chose "the spot" and the couple stopping closest to it at a given time won the prize). During the following winter, dancing classes were held weekly – Fridays 7.30 pm – 10.45 pm. Miss Thorne played the piano and it cost 6d entrance. Jock Mills remembers these events were referred to as "6 penny hops". In 1926 Mrs Brownscombe played the piano for the dances.

In the 1920s to about 1947 members needed transporting to various skittles matches and related events, because very few would have had their own cars. Tenders were requested from rival companies, Hills of Stibb Cross and Hearns of Frithelstock to supply a car, or charabanc as needed. Sometimes the difference would only be 1d a journey, but pennies mattered in those days. The privilege of transporting the players sometimes went to Hearns, and at other times to Hills, there was really very little to choose between them.

Other games mentioned that were played in the Club over the years were darts (a board was given by the Rector, Rev. Bernard Hallowes), table skittles (given by Reg Jones), cards (no gambling!) and a set of skittles made by Mr J Vanstone. Membership fee in 1929 was 1 shilling and there were 43 members. In 1994, membership cost £6.00.

At the beginning, boys over 13 could join if the Committee agreed; this was raised to 15 on 3rd March 1955 in line with the raising of the school leaving age.

In June 1976, a letter was received from the Clinton Estate offering the Club to purchase the freehold of the property. This was taken up and members made loans of £50 to enable the purchase at £500. Later that year, Miss Karen Gerry made a request that ladies be allowed to officially join the Club (it would seem that they had been attending in a non-member capacity). It was agreed that women could join and in 1982, with seven ladies present at the AGM, three joined the committee, being Mesdames S Smith, M Martin and R Hancock. There was a separate cup for the Ladies Section Skittles. In 1983 the instigation of a new name – Langtree Social Club, though not officially changed until April 1992. Mrs P Roberts was the first female office holder – Secretary in September 1992.

Austin (Tinky) Mills, who did much to keep the clubroom in good repair

Of course, the main business of the Club has been its sporting activities and in more recent years skittles has been the main attraction, with both men and women's teams, but with some snooker interest also.

1978 Langtree Prize-winners in Skittles, Geoff Huxtable, Alf Bailey, Henry Box, Jock Mills, John Soby, Bill Soby, Barry Dymond

There were 54 members at the time the vote was taken to sell the clubroom, on 19th October 1992. The Social Club building closed in Spring 2002 and its events were transferred to the new Parish Hall.

Looking through the Minutes, I have selected a few of the things that happened to make the Club the enjoyable and friendly Society it was.

Skittles, Darts, Billiards tournament – 5th, November to the 19th, November, 1938.

The Snooker Cup was won in 1970 by D. Pearce and in 1972 by A.R. Mills. J. Soby won it outright winter of 1976/77, then donated it.

1990/91 Winners. Langtree Dragons Skittles Team L-R: Janet Beer, Margarita Fisher, Rose Issac Sheila Roberts Captain, Eileen Beer, Pauline Goaman, Ros Hancock.

12 hour Snooker Marathon – fundraising September 25th 1979. Organised by G Huxtable.

Dave Beer won Bideford & District Skittles Individual Title. Also Langtree Dragons and Langtree Lions won their divisions.

Club enters for Devon County Championship Cup, August 9th, 1953.

Westlake Cup given to Club by Mr G Westlake on January 6th, 1931.

Discussion on full size Billiards table in 1931.

July 18th 1936, the Club met to discuss fixing electric light – agreed. Fixed up but not connected until April 30th 1937.

E Vanstone & H Taylor gave table tennis for youth September 1949.

Rev. Wallington give table tennis for youth December 1983.

Supported war effort £3. 3s 0d – then closed until after the war.

Ladies Skittles team bought electric boiler, cups and saucers – October 7th 1969.

In 1970, ladies prizes were half of what men's were!

"Have nothing to do with a Rifle Club" was a comment made in April 1927. Again in December 1945 a request was refused for this activity.

Women's Institute

The first record that we have of a Women's Institute meeting in Langtree speaks of a business meeting being held at Siloam Chapel on Thursday 27th December 1917. The names of the people attending are Mesdames Squance, Vanstone, Fowstone, Isaac, Ford, Cocks, Wilton, and the Misses Moore, Pope, and Cleverdon. A Mrs E Vanstone was the President with Miss Cleverdon as 'Secretaria'. The main business was:

1. To elect officers for the coming year (President Mrs Cocks, Secretaria Mrs Wilton and Mrs Cleverdon)

2. To plan the Anniversary of the branch which was to be held as usual on Easter Monday at either Rowden, Putford or Sutcombe

3. To express sympathy to the relatives of the late Miss Nellie Moore, Mrs Tanton, Pte. Goss and parents of R and W Ayers.

This was not Langtree WI as this was not formed until much later, but it would appear that people from the Parish may well have been involved, especially from the Berry Cross area.

A meeting was held in the primary school on 2nd Feb 1949 to discuss the possibility of the formation of a Women's Institute in Langtree. 58 people attended the meeting and Mrs Smyth-Richards, a Voluntary County Organiser spoke about the aims and objectives of the movement.

W.I. Members 1963/64. L-R Back row: Gladys Mitchell, Ethel Huxtable, Joyce Sutton, Patricia Soby, Dolly Copp, Mary Adams, Rose Sutton, Sylvia Curtis, Margaret Hill, Dorothy Huxtable. Middle row: Mrs K Hill, unknown, Vera Fisher, Mahala Boundy, Hilda Mills, Iris Andrew, Florrie Johns, May Andrew. Front row: Nell Harris, Annie Hearn, Mrs Balman, Doris Ley, Mrs Scott, Eleanor Folland, A. (Polly) Dymond

The decision was taken to start a W.I. in Langtree and a small committee was appointed (someone was heard to comment "it will never last" but time has proved them wrong).

An inaugural meeting was fixed for the following week, the 8th Feb when 68 members were enrolled. Subscriptions were 3s/6d, and the minimum age 14 years. New members to be "proposed" and then "seconded", then approved by the Committee before acceptance. How times have changed – I hope no one was turned away.

The first year's programme included demonstrations on the making of string mats, slippers and useful gifts. The competition for November that first year was a 'hankie made from a flour bag'. For those who can't remember such times, flour came in cloth sacks and as nothing was wasted, the sack material was put to good use making household items.

Membership had risen to 73 by May 1949, with meetings held in the school. Over the years the WI have met in the School, Church Hall, the old Chapel, the new Chapel room, and now the new Parish Hall. For many years the WI organised the "Miss Langtree" Dance, the winner going on to compete for the role of Torrington Carnival Queen. They also entered a float sometimes in the Carnival during the 1950s. In past years the WI have organised outings to many places and held various events, including summer fetes, run jointly with the men's Social Club.

A flowering crab tree was planted in the school grounds to celebrate the National Federation of WI's Golden Jubilee on December 20th 1965, and daffodil bulbs were planted in 1998 at each entrance into Langtree and Stibb Cross to mark the Millennium. Plans are also in hand to plant a commemorative tree near the new Parish Hall.

In 1994 it was decided to join in the project to mark 75 years of Devon Federation of WI's and make a Parish map. The map, which is made of calico, and measures 6ft by 4ft now hangs in the entrance hall of the new Parish Hall. Although it was a WI initiative, it became a community project as different organisations made representative panels to stitch onto it. It is pictured on the front cover of this book. Those helping with the Parish map were; Ethel Huxtable, Margaret Tabor, Shelagh Carey, Esmé Coulson, Margaret Knapman, Sylvia Smith, Pat Soby, Rita Deacon, Barbara Svenstone, Sarah Folland and Sheila Johnstone. It was framed by Mr Charles Folland.

In 1998 a photographic project funded by Devon and Cornwall Arts and entitled "Langtree by Langtree people" was completed. It covered all aspects and ages of our community life and its people, and was undertaken with the guidance of Mr Keith Duncan who set the whole thing up and acquired the Award for us.

The WI has also organised events to help others raise funds by doing sponsored walks, knit-ins and coffee mornings for hospices, the local hospital and Macmillan Nurses etc. It has long since lost its Jam & Jerusalem image, now reflecting a wide range of interests for all age-groups and has, of course, become famous in recent years for its slow handclap as a sign of disapproval.

Golden Jubilee, and launch of the Photo Book, February 1999. Back row: Pauline Goaman, Angela Ley, Lynne Blenkinsop, Diane Heard, Julie Bond, Sue Folland, Pet Coles, Carol Ley. Front row. Mary Goaman, Ethel Huxtable, Margaret Knapman

For the past few years, the Institute has entered Torrington Horticultural Show, winning in their class a couple of times. Each spring a Group meeting is held, when a competition is set and entertainment provided by each of the institutes of the Group in turn. Langtree's last entertainment six years ago included music, drama and line dancing. It is our turn again in April 2004, the competition is set "a Summer Cruise" and the entertainment is being prepared but kept top secret until the night.

During the first 20 years, the WI celebrated its birthday each February with a party. This was changed to an annual dinner in 1960. In 1999 the Golden Jubilee dinner was held at The Royal Hotel, Bideford, with husbands and past members invited. The cake, which was iced by former member Carol Ley, was cut by founder member Ethel Huxtable assisted by the youngest member, Julie Bond. Sometimes a 'Christmas Meal' takes place and one we remember well was when, after a candlelit meal, we were exchanging cards and lucky dip presents when somehow a serviette caught fire; it was very quickly extinguished so no harm done and we soon saw the funny side, whilst also seeing the serious possibilities.

Over 60s club

The inaugural meeting for this Club took place on Tuesday 5th March 1974. The formation of the Club was one of the suggestions put forward at a recently held public meeting, chaired by Mr Allison (acting Head) at Langtree Primary School, to discuss activities which the Community College could usefully promote in the locality. Rev Wallington distributed notices to see what interest there was. A large number turned up on the appointed date. Others helping to get the Club going were Rev B Earley, Mrs Wallington, Mrs Patricia Soby and Brian Hughes, the Community Tutor from Holsworthy. Harold Ford was the first Chairman, Nell Colley the first Secretary, and Patricia Soby was both Treasurer and also main organiser. The Club met fortnightly.

There was a 50p membership fee, 10p for the draw and 10p for tea. Draw prizes and food for the tea was contributed by members. A member's comment was: "there's so much food it's well worth coming for the tea alone, not that the rest wasn't good also."

Meetings were held at first in the Church Hall, free of charge, then later in the Chapel room.

Members played cards, nap and whist (nap is the name of an old established card game in the area). Sometimes they just had a good old natter together. Mrs Moore, Dolly Copp, Mrs Florrie Johns and Mrs Gertie Slade loved to play whist together, and Alfred Soby, Fred Slade, Claude Fishleigh, Charlie Britton, Marwood Adams, Dippity Johns, and Charlie Walters would stay in the dining room and play nap. Sometimes Bryan and Daisy Ley brought their record player and we had a dance. Another much enjoyed afternoon was slide shows.

Among those in this photograph are : Mrs F Hill, Mrs N Larkwothy, Mrs R Goaman, Mrs H Mills, Miss Andrew, Mrs Gent, Mr P Kellaway, Mr R Morrish, Mr J Goaman, Mr W Gent, Mr R Curtis, Mr M Adams, Miss Andrews, Mrs Adams, Miss D Copp, Rev Wallington, Mrs F Moor, Mr C Ayre, Mr W Andrew, Mr N Colley, Mr F Adams, Mrs Northam, Mrs Jons, Mrs Box, Mr N Johns, Mrs M Mills, Mr & Mrs E Moore, Mr C Walters, Mr Langmead Mrs Nell Colley, Mrs Morrish.

Having started in the Spring, by Autumn enough funds had accumulated to take a subsidised outing, with members having to pay only 50p each. For the first Christmas a dinner was enjoyed at the Beaford House Hotel. The Club became so popular in the early days that there were soon enough funds to enjoy two outings as well as their Christmas dinner each year.

One well-remembered trip was to Exmoor and 'Lorna Doone Country'. One of the older gentlemen needed regular stops for 'the call of nature'. The bus had to stop on a narrow stretch of road in Doone valley because his need had suddenly became urgent. Whilst the desperate gentleman found a quiet place, traffic came to a standstill behind the waiting bus until quite a long queue had formed. Did I hear a loud cheer when the now relieved gentleman returned to the coach and traffic could again move on? Later, as they reached Oare Farm, a lady desperately wanted to buy a particular gift to bring home. After a twenty minute wait she climbed aboard the bus clutching the gift: and what was this very special item? A doormat. They moved on to Oare Church and when it was time to leave, a quick count was made, 'Everybody here?'– a resounding "Yes!"

and the coach moved off. Some way down the road it was realised someone was missing. A turning place had to be found – not easy for this size vehicle on those narrow roads – then back to the Church they went and the missing passenger was quickly found, much to that person's relief.

Another outing was to Polzeath. On the outward journey a stop was made at Weybridge for people to stretch their legs, have a cuppa or visit the toilets. Many of the men got back to the coach with bundles of bamboo cane, to stake their beans with, cheaper here than at home. One person was missing, it was realised this time before the coach moved off -twenty minutes after everyone else was seated she arrived, having decided to pay a quick visit to a relative in the town.

After a pleasant day in Polzeath a stop was planned on the homeward journey at Launceston for fish and chips. The driver made a wrong turning on the roundabout and ended up in the hospital forecourt. Seeing a bus load of elderly people arrive at a hospital led to hasty (and wrong) conclusions, and staff appeared with oxygen, etc to deal with the supposed sick passenger only to be told "thank you very much, we're all ok just hungry and looking for our supper".

Membership dwindled as members died and around 1984 it drew to a natural end. One of the last events was an 80th birthday tea for Mrs Alice Box, which was held on June 21st, 1984 in the Chapel room, organised by her neighbour Rose Isaac and helpers.

Supervisor Linda Westall with, L-R: children David Mitchell, Naomi Horn, Linda Mitchell with sister Claire on her lap, Robert Ovenall, unknown wearing hat and half hidden by Santa played by Mike Garman. Two back views smallest Jessica Horn, other unknown. Early 1980s.

The 80th birthday of Alice Box. L-R: Mr L Mills, Mrs E Daniel, Mrs A Box, Mrs M Mills, Mr C Ayre, Mr H Ford

Pre-School & Out of School Activities
Linda Westall on Under 5s

In Early 1979 Government funding was made available for communities to put in place some form of activities for under 5s. Mr A. Edgcombe, as Headmaster of the Primary School, called a meeting on 12th March to find out how much interest there was in Langtree for such a scheme – from that meeting, Langtree Under 5s came into being. It commenced on 6th June 1979 as a toddler group with Linda Westall as supervisor, Libby Volkk as secretary and Sonia Ovenal as Treasurer.

At first it was held just on Thursday afternoons in the Chapel room. In October a playgroup also began for one morning a week. The toddler group later became 3 sessions a week: Monday, Wednesday and Friday. Libby was a qualified leader from the start, and Linda qualified soon after. The sessions often revolved around a set theme, and the aim was "learning through play". Linda continued for 10 years. When she gave up, Jenny Cole and Jill Mitchell kept it going for a term (Sept-Dec 89); Cathy Ley and Nicky Sanders were also involved. Throughout this time the group had been affiliated to the National Pre-school Playgroup Association.

Playgroup finished at the end of 1989 as no new qualified leader could be found. At that point Devon County Council took over and it became a nursery class attached to the school. It was staffed by a nursery teacher (Val Curtis) and a nursery nurse (Sarah Pike). It was still held in the Chapel schoolroom at this point.

Nursery Unit

The Nursery Unit moved up to the old infant classroom at the School whilst Allan Edgcombe was still headmaster in 1989.

That classroom was later condemned and a new purpose-built nursery unit erected.

Children of 3 & 4 years old are in the nursery class, while rising 5s go to reception in September or January. The nursery unit is following Early Learning goals with curriculum guidance for foundation stage (nursery/reception) set by government. There is a maximum of 26 children to 2 adults in the nursery class, with an average of 18. Classes are held half-days on Monday, Wednesday, Thursday 9.05–11.45; as well as Tuesday, and Friday 1.30–3.30.

Initially the nursery only had three sessions as staffing was shared between three schools. Now there are five sessions, with the staff being shared between 2 schools.

Nursery Group

Little Acorns
Jackie Daniel remembers, "I knew the group as Langtree Under 5s Mother and Toddler Group. In 1993 there were between 10-12 parents and lots of children, approx 16, under three years old. We used to meet on Tuesday afternoons behind the Methodist Chapel in their back room. In 1995 I took over as Treasurer. We moved the group to Langtree Community School Hall in October 1999 and renamed it 'Little Acorns' changing the sessions to Thursday mornings."

Sam Mills now runs the Little Acorn Toddler Group, which continues to meet on a Thursday morning, during term time, in the Parish Hall. She tells us, "Prior to the Hall being built we met in the School Hall. The children that attend the group with their mums range from newborn babies to 3 years. On reaching 3, they then move on to the Nursery Unit.

We are a small friendly group. At the time of writing we have approximately 15 children on our register. We purchase our toys through grants and fund raising. Our weekly charges are £1 for mum and first child – siblings are an additional 50p. This covers the cost of the hall and the refreshments. We usually take the children on a summer outing to a local attraction and we have a Christmas Party where the children receive a small gift. The Toddler Group allows the children to make friends, encourages play and helps the child to have confidence in joining Nursery. The mums find it a place where they can share experiences or problems and enjoy some adult company."

Out of school activities for older children
"Tearaways" Play Scheme
Jackie Daniel was approached by a Development Worker from Torridge District Play Council called Joanne Tennets to see if there was a need for a Play Scheme in the village for the children, where the children could come, be safe, cared for, become socially aware and interact with others. Here their time could be taken up constructively with activities and projects.

Helpers after serving an Italian meal at a fund-raising evening for 'Tearaways', Summer 2003

Jackie gives the following information:
"We started a pilot scheme in October 2001 at Langtree Community School. It was well attended with 20 children. We had more pilots until we were sure it would be worth starting up. We now run 1 day every school holiday and a whole week in the summer holidays. We moved to Frithelstock Village Hall for a year doing other pilot schemes. Then, when our new Parish Hall was built and opened in October 2002, we set up

Nursery Group

home there. In the summer holidays we run for a whole week when we put on activities including pottery and large projects, which the children get involved with. We also go on trips, this year to Skern Lodge Adventure Centre at Appledore. We do lots of cooking and craft activities plus we have play equipment. Since starting the Play Scheme we know it's what is wanted by the parents and children, they get so much out of it and this Play Scheme is always well attended."

Saturday Club

Jackie Daniel continues, "We started this club up after listening to parents and children who said that just running the 'Tearaways' play scheme in the summer holidays was not enough, so with that information we got a grant from 'Better Play Plus 0-14' to pilot this club.

We opened in February 2003 at Langtree Parish Hall and ran the club on the 1st and 3rd Saturday of every month. It has gone from strength to strength with 10–15 children attending most sessions. The age-range of the children who attend is between 4 and 15 years old. We also have children come from other villages and towns. At the moment we're the only village that offers this facility of a Saturday club, at this present time, even Torrington does not have one."

Snack and Chat Club

"This club was started up in June 2003 for year Six and above (10 to 18 year olds). Some parents thought there was a need for this club, because the young people needed somewhere to go, time out, and space for themselves. As a parent of a year Seven, I wanted a safe place for my son to go to mix with other young people from different schools and cultures. Also to learn some life skills such as cooking, learn and use computers which is part of the future, be able to play more grown up games "together" i.e. badminton, snooker and use the football table. By offering this they can all interact with each other. We have professional people come and talk to them, advice about jobs, life etc. We've been able to start these Clubs by being given grants from 0–14 Plus, Better Pay, Torridge District Council, & Langtree Parish Council. We also have to do a lot of fund raising."

The people that organise these clubs are:
Jackie Daniel	Play Leader	NVQ 3 Coordinator
Jane Beaumont	Play Worker	NVQ 2
Jill Bewes	Play Worker	NVQ 2
Lisa Copp	Play Worker	NVQ 2
Rita Burgess	Play Assistant	
Kate Taylor	Play Assistant	

There is a fee to attend these clubs

Youth Club

Through the 1970s and into the 1980s a youth club was in operation in connection with the two Methodist Chapels open in the Parish at that time. It was called 'The Shell Club', a shell being the symbol of the Methodist Association of Youth Clubs. It ran jointly for the teenagers of Stibb Cross, Langtree, Milton Damerel and Putford, and was under the leadership of Rev Brian Earley who lived in the manse at Stibb Cross. Many activities took place in the various Chapel schoolrooms during the winter, and the Club met fortnightly. In the summer there were sports and games as well as trips out. Visits were made to Greencliff at Abbotsham, and Northam Burrows for sausage-sizzles, also visits to the countryside museums of Philip Jenkinson at Petersmarland, and Mr and Mrs Luxton of Chilsworthy. They also held an annual 'Sports and Fun' open evening at the home of Mr and Mrs Glover of Putford to raise funds for the club. The Club met on Friday evenings, on a rota-system at each of the chapels. There were adult helpers from each of the villages. It continued for quite a few years and latterly had connections with Bradford Youth Club. It was very well supported.

In 1985 through to 1998 some Langtree teenagers attended a Youth Club based at Thornhillhead, and run by Stuart and Rosemary Falkner, who had lived for a short time in Langtree Village.

This was a mixed Youth Club for the 8–16yr olds, meeting fortnightly on a Friday evening. Average attendance was 18–21 per meeting, 70% of which came from Langtree Parish

During the winter period events centred on the schoolroom at Thornhillhead Chapel and included various games, and crafts of many kinds. Sometimes they cooked their own cakes and sweets. Visiting speakers included a local Vet, the R.S.P.B. a Police-dog handler and specialists in sugar-craft, paper folding, and pottery. During

Brian and Jill Earley who started the first Youth Club for Langtree in the 1970s.

They are pictured here on Brian's retirement in July 2003

Youth Club Group

In the later 1980s a Youth Club began again in Langtree village. Seeing a need for young people to have somewhere to meet, Edgar Pett, who was part of the Chapel Fellowship let it be known that on a certain evening he would be in the Chapel room and if any young people wanted a Youth Club, would they please come and tell him. A considerable number of young people came to meet him and a Youth Club was set in motion. It began meeting in the Church Hall and various helpers became involved. Cathy Ley became Treasurer for a while and was followed by Tony Hagan. Other helpers were: Jim Allan, Jan Garman, Mike Smith, Donna Hagan, Rose Isaac and Jill Mitchell. Some of the children also came along to the Committee meetings so they could have a say in how the Club was run.

the summer the Club played outdoor games on the Moor and had lots of trips out to places of interest. They did many adventurous things such as rowing at Bideford, abseiling at Hartland, archery with Colin Smithers, beach trips and barbeques. There were also outings to Butlins at Minehead, and to Paignton Zoo, as well as local swimming pools and pantomimes. A fund raising dance was held at Buda, Langtree the home of Brian and Eileen Mills. At first it was just Stuart and Rosemary who ran the Club, but eventually many parents became involved. Langtree parents who helped include: Eileen Mills, Sonia Ovenall and Joyce Tucker, and the last two helpers were Jill Mitchell and Hazel Parnell.

Youth Club Fancy Dress Walk

Jan Garman takes up the story, and tells us that the club was run on a Friday evening, and that the children who attended were from eight years old upwards. The children would come to socialise, play their music, and enjoy different team games together. " In the summer we would go out on trips. There was also a tuck shop, which the children looked after. Any profit from it helped with Club funds.

"We did a lot of fund-raising, we also had a grant from the Parish Council each year. We raised money in many different ways. We had Jumble Sales, and a Fashion Show, We put on a show called 'The Langtree Follies' when the children danced, sang, played their guitars and put on a little sketch. They made all the scenery themselves by painting pictures on cardboard, and it all looked very good.

Each year we held a cream tea afternoon at Higher Lake (Home of the Garman Family). The children would come beforehand and help with the cooking of cakes and scones, then on the day they would wait on tables for the guests. After they had gone, they brought all the tables together and enjoyed their own cream tea.

Youth Club Dance Team

We entered several dance competitions. The first one we entered we came third, with the help of Rita Falmer. Following on from this the children came first in a solo dance and a team dance, then went on to win the South West Finals, but because of insufficient funds we couldn't go on any further in the competition.

Some of our trips out to various places included Flambards, Killarny Springs, Ice-Skating, Swimming, Roller-Skating, and trips on the Tarka Trail which ended with a meal at The Puffing Billy. In the holidays we stayed at a school on Exmoor and did camping at Higher Lake.

The club entered Torrington Carnival, and for this we borrowed a flat-bed lorry from PHC and the children decorated it. One year we did 'The Flintstones', another year 'The Movies' when we had a 'Junk Band' made up by the children and played as they travelled along on their float.

Each year we would walk from Langtree to Stibb Cross and back in Fancy Dress to raise money for 'Children in Need'. One year we delivered the money personally to Radio Devon, and were also able to visit the Studio.

At one point we won an Annual Award from the Devon Youth Association as one of the top six Youth Clubs in Devon. Unfortunately, owing to the deterioration of the Church Hall, and there being nowhere else we could meet, there came a point where we felt it was in the best interest of the children to close the Youth Club. Over the years I think we all, children and adults, enjoyed the Youth Club in many ways."

Langtree players

Patricia Soby and Sylvia Smith formed Langtree Players, both having enjoyed being involved in drama previously through W.I. etc. The first recorded concert that the players were involved in was held on the 12th July 1982, from which they raised £84. The performances were all held in the Church Hall. It became obvious from the first performance that stage curtains would enhance the proceeding; in fact they were an urgent necessity.

Sylvia Smith tells us, "We held a progressive dinner (later these were known as Safari dinners), the first to be held in the village, and with the proceeds from these two events the curtains were bought in December 1982 for £118.69."

A series of various concerts, plays and pantomimes followed. The performers were all local people, including many members of the Langtree W.I. The final pantomime was 'Mother Goose' in 1987, where we finished with 36 cast members on stage at the finale! With so many people taking part, it was hard to find a local family that was not involved in some way.

Ethel Huxtable and Mary Goaman as 'Aggie and Maggie'

All the events were well attended, and donations were made to village organisations including £451 to the Church Hall fund (later to become the Langtree Parish Hall fund).

Donations also went to the: Over 60s Club, the Mum's and Toddlers, the Play area, Social Club and the School. Unfortunately, the Church Hall had to close and the venue was lost. However, the Langtree Players had tremendous success during its reign, and remains a very happy memory

Sylvia Smith and Steve Taylor pull the strings for Paul and Katie Langmead.

for the performers, the costume makers, scenery makers and shifters, the people behind the scenes and of course all the audiences. Now we have a new Hall, with plans to purchase staging in the near future, who knows, maybe we shall see the Langtree Players back in action again, and continuing to thrill their audiences with laughter and skill.

Royal British Legion

Langtree along with Milton Dameral belonged to the Newton St Petrock branch of the Legion, which celebrated its fiftieth anniversary (a few months late) in May 1981 with a special service at Langtree Parish Church. The branch had been founded on 6th June 1930. Unfortunately it closed on 30th June 1988 when there was again a special service in Langtree Church for the laying up of the banner where it continues to rest. Langtree is now a part of the Mid-Torridge Branch, which along with Holswothy, belongs to the Tamar group. This group once had 6 or 7 branches, now there are only the two, yet the work remains. There hasn't been a single year since World War II when our service people haven't been involved in action somewhere, so the need for the British Legion is as strong as ever. The Legion has full members who are ex-service men, and associated members who are those with a special interest, perhaps through family connections. Those involved in the Langtree part of the Legion include the following; Mr Reg Glover, Mr Fred Beck, Mr Dick Harris and Mr Owen Cook, Bob Clements, David Hill, Stan Mitchell, Tony Glover and Peter Roberts. Poppy sellers have included: Iris Andrew, Diane Daniel, Edna & Helen Westerman, Lesley Willey, Tom & Rose Shelly, Tinky Mills, David and Margaret Hill and Jock Mills.

Each year a Service of Remembrance is held in the Parish, usually in the Church but has occasionally been in the Chapel.

Part of the work of the British Legion includes facilities for rehabilitation, training and employment, welfare and benevolence, specifically for the care of ex-service personnel and their dependants. Over the years the following have been some of the ways that help has been made available: A Rehabilitation Centre at Preston Hall in Maidstone linked to an industrial unit where most of the county's road signs are made (in fact signs of many kinds are made there); homes and sheltered accommodation for the frail or elderly, and a factory in Wales making clothes and rugs.

The homes for this area are Somerset Legion House on the sea-front at Weston Super Mare (for holidays); and Dunkirk House near Taunton (residential). So when we buy our poppies and stand silently to remember on the Sunday nearest the 11th November each year, we are identifying with a vast number of people, nationwide, who work hard to help themselves but urgently need our support as well. Not an unreasonable request for the dangers they have faced (photo page 143).

Young Farmers

Langtree had its own Young Farmers Club for a few years. It began in 1938. Joyce Hambly (nee May) remembers its beginning. She was the first Secretary and fulfilled that role for 5 years. Eric Bond was Treasurer for its duration. Joe Bond remembers that Mr Jones from Watertown had a lot to do with it in an advisory capacity. No one remembers who was Chairman and there are no longer any written records. "There were no animals or cattle judging and such like in our Club – none of the competition they have today," says Eric Bond. "It only lasted for the war years or thereabouts." They all remember that YFC dances were often held to raise money for the Red Cross. These were really enjoyed. Joyce May remembers that Mrs Gertie Mills and Mrs Cox, with other helpers, did refreshments for the dance evening and this was very much appreciated. Many of the young people who would have joined the Club were away at the war – others commented: "I didn't have time to join; I was expected to be at home to work". When the Club closed there was £13 left in the funds. The Treasurer held it for a while, and then passed it on to a neighbouring Club. Unfortunately, there are no photos of the Club's events.

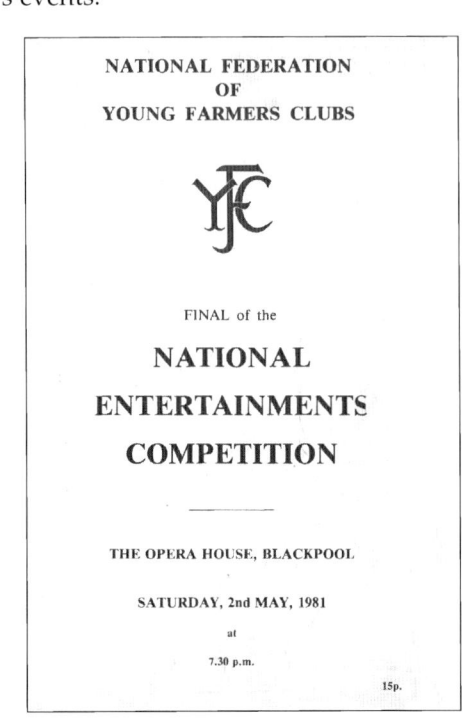

NATIONAL FEDERATION
OF
YOUNG FARMERS CLUBS

YFC

FINAL of the

NATIONAL
ENTERTAINMENTS
COMPETITION

THE OPERA HOUSE, BLACKPOOL

SATURDAY, 2nd MAY, 1981

at

7.30 p.m.

15p.

Programme of Y.F.C. Entertainments Final

In more recent years the young people amongst Langtree's farming families have become members of the Young Farmers Club at Shebbear, or one of the other nearby villages. On May 2nd 1981 the Shebbear Club did well in the national YFC. drama competition which is held bi-annually, winning through to the final at Blackpool with their production "The Fun of the Fair". Forty two young people were on stage, with a further eleven behind the scenes. A number of Langtree people were involved including Ruth Smale (née Ley) Julia Knapman, Geoff Bond, David Fishleigh, and one of the costume makers Julie Bond. Mike Bridgman took the scenery up for them, and Geoff Bond, who was about to become a dad for the first time 'at any moment' was heard to issue an ultimatum, "If Julie goes into labour I'll be off down the road immediately, regardless of the competition". Thankfully the baby stayed where it was long enough for all to proceed as planned and Tom was born two days after the team returned. There were five Clubs competing in the final at Blackpool, and Shebbear was the last to perform, not going on stage until 10.10 p.m. for their half-hour act. They came third, which was a tremendous achievement.

Another event in which the Langtree members of the Club were involved was a sponsored 'muck spread' as a birthday celebration for the Club in February 1988. Club Chairman at the time was Ian Hawker, and the event took place at East Browns, the home of member Geoff Bond. £4,000 was raised to purchase three electric wheel-chairs for Highfield House at Barnstaple, for the use of special needs children. A grand result since they set out with the aim of buying one chair, the response to the event had exceeded their wildest expectations.

Muck everywhere as the Young Farmers get busy

The Hunt

For many years hunting was part of the life of Langtree. As always, not everyone supported it but a considerable number did. There were regular meets through the winter months and many would turn out to watch in addition to those who rode with the hounds. Meets took place at the Union Inn and the Green Dragon as well as at other places. One regular date at Stibb Cross for some years was the Boxing Day Meet. Both Torrington Harriers and Stevenstone Hunt met at Langtree over the years. There were also Hunt Dances every year held in the Church Hall, as a fundraiser and a social occasion.

The Hunt moves off from the Green Dragon Inn – School children have been allowed to come out and watch

On 7th February 1974 Mr Joseph Bond (father of Joe and Eric) celebrated his 85th birthday with a special Hunt meet held in his honour.

Maureen Richards remembers that when her parents lived at the Union Inn, each year at the start of the Hunting season, there was an opening meeting held at Stibb Cross, and "Mum and Dad used to bring out trays of drink for the huntsmen before they set off."

The Hunt at the Union Inn

Langtree and Stibb Cross Band, probably taken at Langtree. about 1912. The players are Albert Hill Snr, and Jnr, Frank Hill, John Hill, Ken Hill, Sam Sanders (a brother-in law to Mr Hill Snr). Mr Ellings, Mr Davey, (a man believed to be Mr Brooks) and three whose names are not known.

Langtree Band

The first reference we have of a band in Langtree Parish is on 23rd May 1871 when they played at the annual festival of the Teetotal Males Friendly Society. The band was connected to the Chapel, but also used to play at various Parish events.

There was a band, probably a brass band, in the Parish in the early part of the 1900s through to about 1930. Quite a few of its members were either Hills or relatives of the Hill family. Some of the people who played in the band were also in the choir, which existed at the same time. The band may well have played at functions in neighbouring parishes as well as our own, but it is doubtful that they travelled far because of the difficulty of transporting men and instruments at that time, for motor transport was in its early days in this area. We have three photos and the names are known of some of the people pictured in them. The photo not shown, taken about 1917, has many of the same people as the one shown above, with the addition of Bill Fishleigh, Alf Burrows, and a Mr Ley, plus three whose names are not known. The photo not used is believed to have been taken at the old Sunday School Room at Thornhillhead (now a dwelling), where the band are thought to have practiced sometimes. The photo opposite (above) was probably taken by the Old Chapel in Langtree with the band members standing where the notice board now is. Perhaps this was prior to an engagement at the Chapel. Older parishioners remember that the wall and railings in this picture were later replaced by the higher wall that many of us are now familiar with. David Hill, who has supplied the group photo that we have used, and some of this information, thinks that the band probably ceased about 1930 when his uncle Mr Sanders, the conductor moved from the area to Plymouth.

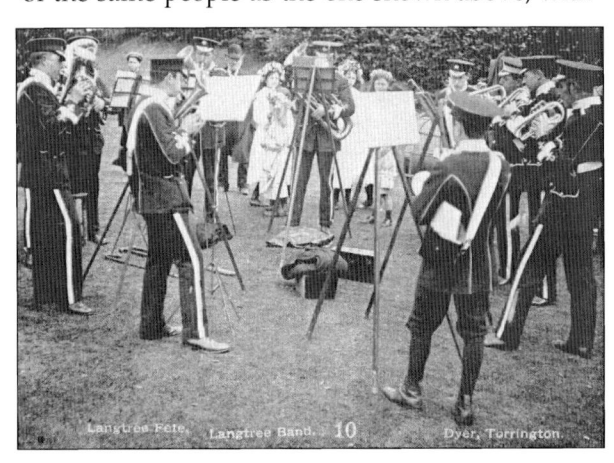

Bottom of previous column we have a photo of Langtree band playing at the Church fete. This is possibly at the Rectory, but we can't be sure and the date is unknown. We do not know who the fete Queen is. The man in the background with the beard and wearing a bowler hat is probably WH (Ginger) Short.

Langtree Choir

Bryan Ley remembers that his uncle, Francis Moore, who was organist at Langtree Chapel from 1910 was also organist for the choir for many years. He also recalls that there had been a Chapel choir at Langtree for a long time, long before the photo shown here was taken, way back when the old Chapel was still in use. There was also a choir on into the 1940s.

Mr Saunders was the conductor in the 1920s, then Mr Noot took it on in the 1930s. They gave

The two players near the front are believed to be: (left) Frank Hill (father of David and Bernard) and to the right, his brother Ken, founder of Hill's Buses.

Langtree Choir 1920s. People pictured are, left-right, back row: F Hill, K. Hill, R Andrew, H Moore, F Moore, P Ley, A Horn, W Fishleigh, A Sanders, N Gilbert; middle row: L Heal, D Moore, I Sanders, S Sanders, F Heal, F Kellaway, E Moore; Front row, P Waters and I Furse.

concerts in many of the Chapels around, perhaps travelling 10 or 15 miles. Mr Kenny Hill would take them in his charabanc. Bryan says, "I remember mother saying they had travelled as far as Dulverton for a concert once and also to Ashreigney. Mother used to sing solos. I think at one time there could have been a male voice choir also."

Mothers' Union

Mothers' Union operated in Langtree for a number of years and was quite a strong organisation in the time of Rev and Mrs Wallington's ministry to the Parish. Meetings were held on the first Wednesday in the month and were usually at the Rectory. The objective of the organisation was to encourage and support family life and social welfare. This was done through practical work and the teaching of the Christian message and standards. There was a missionary link with another Mothers' Union overseas, in Tanzania, and in 1975 a letter was received from them saying that the whole of their village had been moved to an entirely different location, and that as a result they had not received the latest letter from Langtree, an experience completely beyond the comprehension of those of us who have lived a lifetime in one or two places and only moving at our own choice.

Also that year the ladies entertained the residents of Torridge View at a garden party on the vicarage lawn, unfortunately the weather was chilly so they moved into the Church Hall where Dolly Copp 'had them in stitches' with her Devonshire Dialect recitations. Some years earlier (in 1965) the Mothers' Union had held a 'Prayer Wave; when different people committed themselves to pray for 15 minutes consecutively to cover the set period. Those involved with this were; Mrs Wallington, Mrs Tom Vanstone, Mrs J Folland, Mrs Nicolls, Mrs Paddon, Mrs Glover, Mrs Moore, and Miss Boundy.

A Deanery Festival was held each year in the various Churches, and we have various photos of these events when each Church paraded its own banner. There was also a link with underprivileged families in inner cities and at times families from these areas came for a holiday break at the Rectory.

Bellringers

For many years Langtree had its own team of bell ringers and a regular peal on Sunday morning would have been the accepted thing. Joe Bond remembers that at one time there was a whole team of Vanstones, and there were other teams as well. Fred Ford, Harold Ford, and Ned Vanstone were some of the bell ringer Captains that he remembers. "Ned Vanstone was also a judge, when there were ringing competitions with up to fifteen teams taking part. Sometimes the ringing went on all day and well into the evening". Two judges presided over the competition, and sometimes they sat in the upstairs room of Ned's home at Cartref, near to the churchyard, as this was the ideal place to clearly to hear the bells. This practice has continued on into more recent years since Mr and Mrs Bond have lived at Cartref.

Mr Bond remembers a story being told of how Ned bought a set of bell ropes at what he felt was a very good price, though they were not immediately needed. He passed them on to Reg Madge, who passed them to George Nicholls, and from there on to Harold Ford, the succeeding Captains. Eventually the ropes were needed and used, but they didn't last very long as they had 'slept away' or perished; not such a bargain after all.

During the autumn months there would be a Bell-ringers and Choir dinner held in the Church Hall. There would be a large joint of beef carved at one end of the row of tables and an equally large joint of pork at the other end. After the meat course the table would be filled with an array of home-made puddings and desserts, with lashings of home-made scalded or clotted cream. This would have been during the 1920s, in the time of the Rev Hallowes.

There were also ringers' outings, but we have no record of where to.

The scrap-books kept by Mrs Wallington also give us some records of bell ringing activity in Langtree Parish. These are her descriptions of each occasion:

Langtree ladies left to right: Brenda Horn, Jackie Rowe, Joyce Bond, St Clair Wallington, with their banner lead the Mothers' Union Procession from the Rectory to the Church for the Deanery celebration in 1977

Ned Vanstone & his wife with Ringers Shield. Date unknown

October 1964. Ringing practices have started and the experts say there is some very promising material. The ladies are doing well but some wore their fingers not to the bone, but at least to the skin ('Blood on the Bell Ropes' sounds like the clue in a detective story, so says the recorder of the incident at the time).

August 1966. Langtree Belfry was the scene of an historic event last month when the Guild of Devonshire Ringers (Shebbear College Society) rang a peal of 5040 doubles, being 42 extents in 14 methods/variations in 2hrs 38 mins. This is the greatest number of doubles methods yet rung to a peal for the Guild.

August 1969. The Bell-ringers Festival was a tremendous success and I hear that everyone was highly delighted. The magnificent tea contributed to the pleasure of the day, and our thanks are due to Mrs Dora Nicholls and her band of helpers, Many thanks to Mr Mitchell for making all the preparations and to the Men's Club for the use of their room.

Teams taking part were, Alwington A & B, Dolton, Down St Mary, Littleham A & B, Petersmarland, Shebbear, South Tawton, Swimbridge, Torrington, and West Down. The winners were Shebbear 1st Novices, West Down 1st Open, Alwington 'A' 1st Torridge Valley. Langtree was not represented in the competition.

Bell-ringing classes were re-started in 1993, after the bells were re-hung. It was hoped at that time that they would be able to start ringing for services about Christmas time. Unfortunately, for various reasons, this newly formed team was not able to continue long-term, and at the time of writing Langtree does not have its own team of ringers though the bells are frequently rung by visiting teams.

Mary Geary, speaking of her Father who lived at Rivaton until 1939, says "Herbert Harris (junior) was Captain of the Bell-ringers, so I have been told. Dad had told me the names of the team, but this has gone from my memory. Maybe one was Ned Vanstone, who was a good friend of Herbert".

AA Patrol Man

David Hill remembers that when he was a very young boy, 4 years or less, Mr Poole the A.A. man came to their house for the mid-day meal. He brought his own packed lunch but enjoyed sitting in the dry warmth of their home, and no doubt had a fresh, hot cup of tea straight from the pot. Sometimes he had a currant bun and would let the young David pick out the currants and eat them. This would have been in the early 1930s while David's parents lived with Gran and Grandad Hill for a few years at Stibb Cross before moving to their own home in Langtree as their family increased. Mr Poole spent much of his time supervising traffic on the crossway which was even then a dangerous place. The road was much narrower with a hedge where the bungalows now are. Mr Blight's shop was opposite to that and the Cattle Market across from the Union Inn. Mr Poole would hope to catch the interest of farmers and trades people attending the market and thus increase membership of the AA.

There was an AA phone box on the way to Holsworthy, beyond West Park, with a neat, low growing box hedge in half moon shape around the back and sides of it. It is a small lay-by now.

The box was placed there before the war and removed in approximately 1972, the main reason for this being that there were now GPO phone boxes at Stibb Cross and by the junction to Bulkworthy.

Mr Poole (possibly Charlie) also did point duty at Red Post and had an accident there. He probably finished working at Stibb before the Market

Old Stibb Cross

closed down. He was preceded by Mr Freddie Marks, a relative of Florrie Johns, who previously worked at Horrels Ford garage after being in the war. In the early days, Mr Poole would have had a bicycle, which was probably followed by a motorbike.

By the late 1960s, Mr Keith Gibbs, who lived at Marsland, was the AA man in the area, but times had become very different. Now, he travelled up to 100 miles a day; his main area Stibb Cross to Barnstaple, but also included trips to Bideford, Holsworthy, Torrington, and Hatherleigh.

Police

Langtree had its fair share of police cover at one time. Through the 1960s-70s and into the 80s, there were 4 'Specials' in the Parish. Ethel Huxtable, Colin Nicholls and Les Knapman were Special Constables, and Charlie Walters was a Special Sergeant, and for a time was responsible for organising the duty role for the Specials.

Previous to this – in the 1930s and 40s – the following people were also in the Specials – Charlie Walters, Kenny Hill, George Daniel, Fred

*Langtree Special Constables during WW2:
Left to right, Bill May, Reg Baker, Charlie Walters, George Daniel, Horace Furse*

Beck, Horace Furze, Noel Knapman, Reg Baker and Douglas Brock.

"Specials" carried out duties alongside regulars once or twice a month on a Friday or Saturday evening/night. Duty would start at 10pm with signing on at Torrington Police Station and involved doing car patrol alongside a regular who was always the driver. (Specials were not allowed at the controls of police cars). Officially duty finished about 2am the next morning, though if they were involved in a specific 'call out' to a trouble spot, it could be nearer 3 or 4am when they got home. Specials were also called on to do traffic duty for Torrington Mayfair, Carnival, Bonfire Night and various other local events.

Les remembers being on duty for the visit of the Queen to Eggesford and the Duke of Edinburgh to Appledore. On that occasion Les's point of duty was the town end of Bideford's Bridge (old one). One man seemed to be determined to wander into the middle of the road. As the time for the Duke's appearance arrived, Les approached him and asked him to rejoin the crowds at the roadside. He silently put his hand on his jacket to his breast lapel and revealed a very small ID badge. He was a "top notch" plain clothes, Security Officer.

I remember riding to Torrington Carnival with Les one day when he was on duty. We just rounded the corner below our lane on Burstone Hill to be met by a larger vehicle coming up. It immediately went into reverse right to the bottom of the hill to let us through. I was puzzled and surprised. We were far nearer to a passing place and anyway, large vehicles rarely gave way to smaller ones. Then the penny dropped – Les was in full police uniform. I wonder if the same thing would have happened today.

Neighbourhood Watch

Started in the 1980s the following people have been involved over the years: John Pollard, Alfie Daniel, Nicola Sanders, Mr Morrochan, Bob Clements, Andy Mitchell, Claire Allan, Jill Mitchell and the Post Office staff.

Sports Activities

Langtree Re-unites (Netball Club)

The need for this Club became apparent when pupils who had been really keen on netball at Langtree Primary School, and had played competitively for their school for two years or more, found that on moving to a large Comprehensive School, very few had opportunity to be in the school teams (there were so many players to select from, that only the top few were chosen).

Paula Fuller had coached the children at Langtree, and became aware of their frustration and disappointment, as well as their eagerness to still play. Thus the Re-unites were born.

The team was first established in August 1998, for the community of Langtree. It started with one ball, a set of bibs borrowed from school, eighteen enthusiastic netballers and a coach who had no formal training – only self taught through experience – and in the first year they entered the North Devon League as the youngest team ever.

In 1999 the team name was chosen. They found themselves with a new kit sponsored by R & CH Wilson, the Constitution was drawn up, and the Club received a lottery grant of £1740 to purchase much needed equipment and resources.

Re-unites Netball Club A.G.M. Club Trophy Presentation Sept 2001 Left to right: Clair Heard – Players Player. Charlotte Heard – Most Improved Junior. Laura Coles – Most Improved Senior. Paula Fuller – Coach. Grace Hicks – Enthusiasm, Commitment & Effort. Natalie Heard – M.V. Cup. Katie Elston – Outstanding Attendance.

In 2000 Paula passed her AENA (All England Netball Association) Level 1 coaching certificate along with three other members, and the team expanded to offer a separate junior section with trained coaches. The Club received further grant funding to buy equipment for the junior section and they began competing in the newly established North Devon Junior League.

The Club expanded out of the community in 2001 to offer others the opportunity to join and has had in excess of fifty members both male and female. Also in 2001 the senior Club Coach passed her AENA Level 2 coaching certificate. In July 2001, the Club had a visit from Pat Hayden, the AENA Regional Development Officer. Paula says:

"Pat Hayden was very impressed with our achievements, standard of play, overall performance and club structure. We were awarded the Bronze Club Award – only two other clubs have this Award."

Paula continues: "the Club has firm links with Langtree and Torrington Community schools and has been visited by local sports authorities and Heather Crouch who was the England Netball Team Coach. The objective of the club is to encourage the playing of, and interest in the game of netball, and to allow opportunity to participate within the Club, irrelevant of any standard of ability or disability. All Club members are encouraged to learn to umpire the game and are offered the chance to take their Beginner Award when they are sixteen."

Unlike other netball teams and clubs which consist of only 7 players, the Langtree Re-unites allow maximum participation on an inter-change basis, depending on the number of people attending a training session. Everyone will get a chance to play.

Several players have been nominated for awards in the North Devon Netball League and to represent the county. In 2002, the under 12s and under 14s won the League – North Devon Juniors. Aimee Fishleigh was the runner up to the Most Improved Player League Award 2000; Claire Heard Most Improved Umpire from League 2002; Tessa Gorin won runner up Newly Qualified Coach for Devon 2002. In 2003 Rebecca Willis was Under 12s Most Improved Player; and Kevin Weir under 14s Most Improved Player.

Paula says, "In the five years we have been established, many others have achieved similar distinctions. Our action plan for 2004-5 includes our Club running a mixed Netball Tournament to encourage and develop male participation at competition level. Hopefully this will be in February or June 2004.

We are receiving a new kit shortly which is being sponsored by R & CH Wilson and PHC. Apart from grants and sponsorship, the Club also has to hold a variety of fundraising events.

Each year the Club looses members as young people go off to University or leave the area for jobs. Many are using the skills they have learnt through the Club in their new situations, so the influence of Langtree Re-unites is spreading far and wide. Long may it continue.

Football

Mr Bill Gent remembers Langtree had its own football team in 1929, through to 1933, consisting of young men between the ages of 18–26 years approx. With the title of Langtree United Football Club, the team consisted of A Hobbs, Captain; P Jennings, R Jennings, H Nethercott, J Chamberlain, M Chamberlain, S Pett, L Vicary, W Gent, E Vanstone, H Harris, H Larkworthy, J Hearn. The Committee was W Westcott, W Hackwill, C Walters, W Box, S Gerry, A Ayre, R Goss (Treasurer) and F Cox. They entered the Kingley League and did well in it. Other teams in the League were Hatherleigh, Dolton, Merton, Northam, Stratton, Hartland, Appledore, Bideford Old Boys, Bideford AAC, Halwill and Bridgerule, covering quite a wide area! Mr Gent recalls that, although there were plenty of knocks and bruises, no one from the Langtree United team ever suffered any serious injury. The Social Club was sometimes used for a dressing room and Bernard Hill remembers 'home' games were played in the field against Langtree Moor Lane on the village side. It belonged to Mr Hedley Nicholls at the time. Which was the best team? Well, Mr Gent remembers there wasn't much to choose between Hatherleigh, Langtree United, Stratton and Bideford Old Boys. Sadly, we have not been able to track down any photos of the team.

Lions and Magpies football song by W Westcott.

Earlier, Mr Westcott had shown an interest in football as he trained the older lads to play in 1921. Written on Christmas Eve that year, he composed a song about a particular football match between the Magpies and the Lions, two Langtree teams. For many years I had heard talk of this song and copies of Mr Westcott's original writing and drawing have come to light. The song is reproduced above in his own handwriting.

School Sports

27 July 1956 – First reference to Sports Day. Record High Jump by Geoff Folland, aged 11 years 2 months, of 3 ft 11 ins. This stood until June 1987 when Glyn Brown broke it with a 4 ft jump, and then increased it again to 4 ft 1 in. This was equalled in 1988 and 1989 by Robert Ovenell. Also in 1988 Chris Roe set new Long Jump and Hop, Skip, and Jump records, 3.95 metres and 8.70 metres respectively.

24 July 1957 – First reference to School Colours and four teams. At some stage this was reduced to three teams and in July 1967 they had the names of Dolphins, Tigers and Eagles. In 1976, it changed again to Wolves, Hawks, Kestrels and Lions. In 1988 Kestrels had become Falcons.

1958 – Mr Daniel fixed Netball posts. The Junior and Transition girls are to be trained in this game.

*Football team 1985 left to right from back row:
Scott Cockbill, Richard Harding, Chris Roe, Scott Glover,
Duncan Hughs, Glen Brwon, Darren Goaman, David Beer,
Martin Palmer, Stuart Mills, Darren Isaac, John Ovenall*

1961 – R Sutton and A Tucker were selected to play in the Area Football Team.

1988 – Chris Roe and Chris Fallon represented the school in Torridgeside Area Football, as did Robert Ovenell and Chris Fallon in 1989.

Oct 1993 – Daniel Gray, Martin Davey and Jason Fallon represent school in Torridge Area Football team.

Netball and Football area finals have been won some years.

May 1983 – saw the start of Cycling Proficiency course. 26 children gained the award.

By the end of June 1965, the first term with our own swimming pool, fifteen children can swim one length; four can swim two lengths; and two children can swim three lengths.

19th July 1965 – the School's first inter-house swimming sports with separate events for girls and boys.

March 1989 – 5 boys, Nicholas Wyke, Christopher Fallon, Robert Ovenell, Michael Cann and Tom Furness, achieved ASA Gold awards – they are the first to reach such high standards in swimming at Langtree. Later, in 1990 Nicola Roe was the first girl to achieve it.

June 1966 – first reference to school camps. Mr Edgcombe took eleven children to the DCC School Camp at Slapton for the week.

Cricket

For a time in the late 1950s early 1960s cricket was played at Collacott in one of the fields when Mr & Mrs J Folland were living there. Some of the team were Langtree lads but more were from Buckland Filleigh. Allan Edgcome remembers these matches as very enjoyable times and the really special teas that followed the game. Velva Ley (née Tidball) and her sister Peggy helped to serve the teas sometimes, while their brother played in the team. Mrs Eleanor Folland remembers that it was a particular aim of hers to make the refreshments a real feature of the event.

Above is pictured some of the people involved in those cricket events. They are from left to right, back row: J Folland, J Soby, C Davey, W Pett, R Tidball, J Gerry, H Jeffrey, Mrs E Folland, and H Nethacott. Front row: Unknown, Mrs Nethacott, P Tidball, V Tidball.

*Netball team 1991 L-R from back row.
Nicky Row, Rebecca Coles, Charmaine Findly,
Lynette Isaac, Anna Folland, Donna Fallon,
Claire Mitchell, Rebecca Burton*

Women's Institute Office Holders

Date	President	Secretary	Treasurer
1949	Mrs L Rouquette	Mrs C Taylor	Mrs Dymond
1950	"	Mrs Curtis	"
1951	Mrs A Hearn	"	Mrs V J Dymond
1952	"	Mrs Harris	
1957	Mrs V Dymond	Mrs Curtice	Mrs A Dymond
1960	Mrs Curtice	Mrs A Dymond	Mrs J Folland
1961	Mrs P J Dymond	Mrs Curtice	"
1962	Mrs D M Ley	Miss R Adams	"
1963	"	Mrs Dymond	"
1964	"	Mrs Hearn	"
1966	Mrs Balman	"	"
1971	"	Mrs Soby	"
1973	Mrs J Folland	"	Mrs S Folland
1974	"	"	Mrs Jelley
1977	Mrs Soby	Mrs C Ley	"
1978	Mrs S Folland	Mrs M Nicolls	Mrs Soby
1979	Mrs M Nichols	Mrs Soby	Mrs Cook
1982	Mrs C Ley	"	"
1984	Mrs M Cook	"	?
1985	Mrs M Nicholls	"	?
1986	?	?	?
1988	Mrs M Goaman	Mrs E Huxtable	?
1992	Mrs E Coulson	Mrs S Duffy	Mrs E Huxtable
1993	"	Mrs M Knapman	"
1996	"	Mrs M Goaman	"
1997	Mrs M Knapman	"	"
1998	"	"	Mrs P Goaman
2001	Mrs J Bond	Mrs P Cole	"
2002	Mrs S Folland	"	Mrs L Blinkinsop
2003	Mrs Pet Cole	Mrs D Lloyd	"

There is one minute book missing hence the question marks in certain places.

Jubilee Play area committee

Date	Chairman	Secretary	Treasurer
Nov 1997	Mr L Knapman	Mr M Richards	Mr A Mills
1983	"	Mrs S Head	"
1984	"	Mrs L Westall	"
1987	Mr A Carey	"	"
1989	Mr D Ley	"	"
1991	Mr E Pett	Mrs J Mitchell	Mrs L Westall
1993	Joined with the	Parish Hall	Committee

Social Club Office Holders

Date	Chairman	Secretary	Treasurer	President
. .1914				
. .1919		*Mr Samuel Kelly	Mr Samuel Kelly	
. .1923		Rev B Hallowes	Rev B Hallowes	
29.12.24	Rev B Hallowes	Not named	Not named	
30.03.25	Mr P B Jones	Not named	Not named	
28.12.25	Rev B Hallowes	Not named	Not named	
28.06.26	Mr P B Jones	Mr E J R Jones	Mr J Adams	
08.10.27	Rev B Hallowes	"	"	
24.09.28	Mr P B Jones	"	"	
20.07.29	Rev Hallowes	"	"	
05.10.29	"	Mr J Adams	Mr P B Jones	
05.10.30	Mr P B Jones	"	"	
05.04.32	Rev Hallowes	"	"	
13.04.35	"	Mr W Huxtable	"	
25.09.37	"	Mr H Furse	"	
08.01.45	Mr P Jones	"	"	
29.09.46	"	"	Mr P Beer	Rev Gibby
30.12.46	Mr S Squire	"	"	
01.10.48	H Taylor	"	Mr S Hinks	Mr J Scott
15.07.49	"	Mr A Mills	"	
29.09.49	Mr C Walters	"	"	
03.01.50	"	Mr S Hinks	Mr F Moore	Mr J Folland
02.10.51	"	Mr H Furse	"	
20.09.59	Mr S Squire	"	"	
08.10.60	"	Mr L G Mills	"	
08.10.62	"	"	Mr J Soby	
04.10.66	Mr G Mills	"	"	Mr A Soby
14.10.68	"	Mr W Brock	"	
07.10.70	"	Mr A Mills	"	
22.01.74	Mr J Corby	Mr B Dymond	"	
26.09.78	Mr S Balkwill	Mr R Hancock	"	
30.09.81	Mr D Fishleigh	"	Mr D Goaman	
05.10.83	Mr G Huxtable	"	"	Rev Wallington
09.10.85	Mr C Larkworthy	"	"	Mr L Mills
07.10.87	Mr A Mills	"	"	
30.09.92	"	Mrs P Roberts	"	
07.10.94	"	Ms S Lee	"	
09.10.96	"	"	Mr R Hancock	
24.10.01	Mr A Mills	Ms S Lee	Mr R Hancock	

*Prior to 1926 the Office of Secretary and Treasurer was held jointly

Parish Council Chairmen and Clerks

Date	Chairman	Clerk
1897	Mr W Goss	Not Known
1902	Mr W H Hackwill	Mr S J Sanders
1905	Mr Philip Andrew	"
1908	Mr W H Hackwill	"
1909	Mr Philip Andrew	"
1912	Mr Charles H Ley	"
1913	Mr Philip Andrew	"
1914	Mr Charles H Ley	"
1917	Mr P B Jones	"
1922	"	Mr H Down
1925	Mr J Webber	"
1926	Mr W H Short	"
1946	Mr S G Ley	"
1950	"	Mr John Gerry
1952	Mr S W Goss	"
1958	Mr A Soby	Mr G Mills
1973	Mr B G Ley	"
1978	"	Mrs S Roberts
1979	Mr J Walters	"
1987	Mr L S Knapman	"
1992	Mr G Folland	"
1993	"	Mrs S Carey
1995	"	Mrs S Hawker
1996	Mr L S Knapman	"
1999	Mr A Glover	"

Parish Hall Committee

Date	Chairman	Secretary	Treasurer
	Rev N Mead	Mrs M Binloss	Mr L Knapman
Pre 1990	Mr P Mitchell	Mrs R Isaac 7 years	"
Nov 1990	"	"	"
Nov 1991	"	Mr M Smith	"
Sept 1992	"	"	Mr J Horn
Sept 1993	"	Mr J Horn	Mr D Burton
Sept 1995	"	Miss S Dowson	Mr J Horn
Oct 1996	"	"	Mr D Price
Sept 1997	"	Ms S Lee	"
Sept 2001	Mr J Horn	"	Mr M Cole
Sept 2002	Mr P Mitchell	"	"

Chapter Eleven EVENTS

The War Years

Every town and village was affected by each of the two World Wars. I am listing the names of the fallen from both dates. Almost everything else that is written in this section concerns the 1939–1945 conflict as we have very few living memories of the earlier date. That does not mean that one conflict is held as more important to remember than another, for each will hold its own special place in the hearts of those concerned.

There are two plaques in All Saints Church, Langtree. Below are the names inscribed on them:

1914 – 1918

Rodney Ayre	John Goss
William Ayre	Richard Horrel
John T Burrows	John Mills
Thomas Bidway	Edward Moore
Ernest Comer	George Stoneman
Percy Dymond	Fredrick Walters
Wm Henry Froin	Philip Whitlock

1939 – 1945

T E Brabazon Hallowes (Burmese L H)
F W George Mills (DCLI)
F Richard Westcott (RAF)
Ellen L Westcott (WAAF)

Jock Mills, and Harold & Edna Daniels have given me the names of those they remember who were in the War but returned safely. They also will have had some tough experiences and some have carried not only devastating memories, but also physical injuries with them for the rest of their lives. We also owe a debt of gratitude to these people. If any name has been overlooked, I, and the three who have given this information do sincerely apologise. I have not had access to official records on this matter but believe these names are worthy of recording.

Ladies, with maiden names: Alma Daniel, Adeline Flood, Elsie Grey.

Men: Thomas Badge, Douglas Brock mentioned in dispatches three times, Reginald Brock, Norman Cole, Harold Daniel, Harold (Jim) Daniel, Reg Curtice, F Reg Flood, John Gerry, Reg Glover, David Hill, Norman Hill, Sammy Hinks, Albert Huxtable Dispatch Rider, Stanley Lucas, George Jenkins, Philip Mills, Walter Mills, Austin Mills, Raymond Sanders, Harry Sutton, Raymond Sutton, Arthur Slade, Arthur Stevens, Ronald Stoneman (prisoner of war), Cyril Tucker,

There was also many other aspects of service during the war years; Alice Brock (Nee Cox) was a nurse at Torrington Cottage Hospital, and with others nursed the three survivors of a plane crash. Ian Quaife, one of those survivors wrote in the *North Devon Journal* "they were marvellous nurses and we owe a lot to them"

Above left: Reg Curtice, Above Right: Douglas Brock
Below Left: Alma Daniel, Below Right: Norman Hill

*L to R: E Hill, E Folland, Alice Cox
Torrington Hospital 1944*

Langtree's war memorial is the clock in the tower of the Church. It was paid for by local subscription and put in place as a commemoration to those who fell in 1914–1918 War; later the names of the fallen in World War II were added.

Philip Jenkinson of Petersmarland, who has been most helpful with my research concerning the plane crash, also told me that he was a prisoner-of-war in East Prussia, Poland, and Northern Germany for two years. He and his companions were released by the Desert Rats three weeks before the war ended. "Without the Red Cross we would probably not be here today but would have been like the Japanese prisoners-of-war. We were only allowed to receive parcels from our homeland. People from Canada had to send things to our families and they then sent it on to us in an English parcel. We were deeply grateful for the Red Cross. 55,503 aircrew from Bomber Command were lost, including my brother".

Bryan Ley remembers prisoners-of-war – they worked on a number of farms around the parish. A busload would come out from Holsworthy where they had a camp, and be dropped off at various farms, then collected at the end of day. They would bring a hunk of bread and a piece of margarine, which were their rations. Some of the farmers' wives would give them a cooked dinner. They really appreciated that. One, Alfred Teschner, never went back to Germany; he stayed on with Mr and Mrs J Beer at Lower Withacott and is still living with them in Frithelstock. There were German and Italian prisoners. The Germans were a much more serious people but excellent workers. The Italians loved to sing and were very cheerful. The Italians came about 1942-3, and left around 1944-5. The Germans were here around 1945-7. Whilst the war was on, there had to be security. They were kept in camps and the trusted ones were allowed out to work on a daily basis. After the war was finished some of them were allowed to 'live in' on farms, as the security risk was passed (see reference to some of their work in the 'snow section' beginning on page 121)

Bryan also remembers that food became scarcer towards the end of the war. At first, when many acres of land such as Thornhillhead moor were ploughed up for growing potatoes, it was fresh ground for cultivating, and yielded well through 1940-2. Then, because there was no bought-in fertiliser and not a lot of farmyard manure due to there being far fewer animals, by 1947 the ground was very low in nutrients and the crops were much poorer.

Langtree Home Guard

There were 18 men who had the solemn responsibility of keeping things safe on the home front, while others were away in the forces facing the enemy on the battlefront.

They were the members of the Home Guard, which was formed in 1940. The Reading Room, or Men's Social Club as it was sometimes called, served as the headquarters of the Langtree Contingent. The members were responsible for guarding their own parish. It was done in a voluntary capacity with no financial reward, but their uniform was provided and training took place once a week. This often consisted of target shooting at Saunton Sands; they also went to Hartland and Cross House at Little Torrington sometimes.

When on duty there was a hut opposite the Green Dragon from which they operated - there would be someone on guard each night, two or more together. There was also a rounded Nissan-type hut, in the field at the top of Beara Hill, in which supplies of ammunition were kept. The field belongs to W Balsdon now, but P B Jones owned it then. It still goes by the name of Ammunition Field today.

These are the names of the men who belonged to the home guard – information supplied by Mr W Gent.

A Richards, J Stevens, S Beal, N Hill, H Ford, D Kent, T Vanstone, E Moore, P Kellaway, W Gent, E Johns, R Richards, W Wilton, R Madge, W Slade, C Huxtable, S Gerry, A Blight, H Moore, W Daniels.

Mr Norman Hill recalls his time in the Home Guard. He remembers the night two bombs were dropped on Binworthy, beyond Stibb Cross. He was 'on duty' along with Bill Daniel (his future brother-in-law), Harold Ford and Harold Moore. They were near the hut opposite the Green Dragon. The plane was believed to be German and off loading, "we heard the bombs whistling through the air and thought at first they were aimed at us, but soon realised otherwise." They found it a very scary experience. He also remembers there was an open fronted hut with seats near the Post Office. Norman said, "sometimes Bill Daniel and I would be resting in it at night and take turns to sleep with our head on the other's shoulder".

The social clubroom was closed for its usual activities from June 1940 – Jan 1945 because of the war. This would have enabled it to be a convenient and secure base for the men of the Home Guard to use, and its windows easily 'blacked out'.

Sylvia Martin, (Née Richards) remembers that her grandfather, Archie Richards, who had been in the army in World War I, and taken prisoner-of-war by the Germans during 1914–18, was appointed Lieutenant of Langtree Home Guard. Sylvia comments, "A lot of Home Guard activity

Archie Richards leads the Home Guard through Torrington. This could have been the parade when they disbanded at the end of the war. The Langtree contingent is amongst them, Fred Dymond is front centre, next right is Jim Stevens. Reg Richards is by 1st gatepost, and probably Bill Northam by 2nd gatepost with Philip Beer behind him. W Box with white-collar showing, on right of procession, and behind him is Bill Wilton, behind him is Charles Hill

was centred around 'Redlands'. My mother, Ethel Richards, was in charge of WVS and with help from some of the other wives, cooked food for the men on Home Guard duty. Morse Code was tapped out, sending messages from the woods across to 'Redlands' and the village of Langtree".

School War effort

Oct 14th 1940, result of holiday campaign and subsequent effort of scholars:

Sale of cardboard & wood articles made	£1 – 09 – 1
Sale of old iron	£2 – 11 – 6
Sale of 14cwt waste paper collected	£1 – 08 – 0
	£5 – 08 – 7

All monies were handed over to Langtree war Comfort making Association. Knitting of squares sufficient to make 3 blankets from collected old wool and ripped up old garment.

January 4th 1943   17-1/4 cwt waste paper collected by scholars and forwarded to Shelhay Mills Exeter. £4 – 0 – 0 sent to Red Cross realised from paper.

June 30th 1943 1-ton 8cwt of salvage collected by scholars has been sent to Shelhay Paper Mills.

July 2nd 1943 £5 – 10 – 0 has been sent to Red Cross Fund.

March 4th 1944 1-ton 12cwt 3qtrs 16lbs of salvage forwarded to Shelhay Mills Exeter.

National savings first mentioned
December 20 1940   £9 – 6 – 3d

May 12th 1943 Target set for School savings group was £15. Amount raised was £95 – 4 - 6d Cup presented to the school by the Waste Paper Association on October 16th 1942 and again on May 20th 1943 for best collectors in North Devon. Sylvia Martin (née Richards) comments, "Ration books and gas masks were issued to everyone".

Langtree School with the cup for best waste collectors in North Devon They achieved this award twice. Windows are taped to reduce disintegration of glass from any potential nearby explosion and thus minimise damage to the children. Photo is from Peter Johnson, Evacuee.

Evacuees

Listed in alphabetical order, are the evacuees I have found references to or been told about. I do not know where many of them stayed, or for how long:

Mary and Marion Ayers, Sheila Adams, Roy Arscot, Heather Axell, Sheila Burgess, Lewis, Ronald and Joyce Batman, Philip Barrow.

Norman and ? Barham, at Stibb Cross. Cathy and May Burke, with the Gents at Langtree Week.

Iris, June, Joyce, Constance, and Charles Clarke, with the Vanstones.

Iris and Pat Cole. Brian, Myrtle and Mrs Day were at Collacott with the Knapmans. Joyce, Brenda and Eileen Everett, at Wedlands.

Granny Eves, Peter Graham, Donald Gibson (Granny Eves was the mother of Mrs Day and Mrs Sutherland, and was also at Collacott).

Leonard, Irene and Eileen Hanney, with Mrs Tom Vanstone. Eileen Hayes, Marjorie Warner and

Winnie Hazel at Wooda with the Bonds, (Winnie married a local person and now lives in Torrington). Peter, Annette, Joan and Dennis Johnson, at Doggaport with the Mays.

Jean and John Jasper, Leslie Knapp, Geoffrey and Brenda Lutter, Audrey and Edna Lomasney, Marie Landois, R. John Mcloughin.

Joyce and Doris Neal. at Thorne House.

Peter Pomphrey. John Savery at Mrs Burrows.

Betty Stock. Andrew, Christine and Wendy Stone at Putshole. Kenneth Smith. Dorothy, Pat, Carol, and Mrs Sutherland, at Collacott with the Knapmans.

Andrew, Alan and Wendy Stone (this could be the same Wendy Stone as above at Putshole), Alice Thomas, Robert Taylor (died at Langtree, not known if he is buried here), Beryl Usher.

Hazel and Marjorie Warner with the Bonds. Trevor Westbroom, with the Gerry family at the Forge. Mary Weir. Irene Warnier. Joan and Connie Wallinger, who were one week at the rectory, then one week at Collacott, before their parents fetched them.

Adele and Olive ? at Stapleton. George Taylor and Enid Drake with the Walters family at Kenathorpe. John Savage and Dennis Thatcher with the Burrows.

This information has been gathered from an old Sunday school register at the Chapel, the Primary School log book, and from memories people have given me. I have not had access to any official records of where people stayed, so have only been able to mention those told to me.

Back row: Joyce May, Fred Lomansay, Mrs Lonamsay, Mrs Johnson, Peter Johnson, Edna & Audrey Lomansay and Annette Johnson

Sylvia Richards tells us, "we had 6 evacuee girls staying with us at 'Redlands' during the war, one little girl called Jean was so frightened by the bombing in London, when she came to us with her older sister her nerves were so bad she would have shaking fits. The other evacuees at Redlands were Doris Featherstone, Jean & Joan ? (Sisters), Edna Stone, Megan ?"

Dorothy, Pat and Carol Sutherland pictured after they had returned home

Ron Juniper tells us what it was like to be evacuated to an unknown place, from the child's point of view: "I became an evacuee in Sept 1940. I was 5 years old and my brother Harry was 7. I didn't think too much about it at the time but now I realise what a big thing it was for the families in Devon to have all these strange people coming to stay with them for a long period of time. We lived in London (North Kensington) and bombs were falling. Government people came and told us 'you've got to go – families will be provided to look after you.' Some families had already made arrangements for their children to go away and stay in the countryside with friends or relations – these were the unofficial evacuees, as their arrangements had not been done through government officials. We were official, but knew we would be staying with a relative of a relative. I was told three million children were moved in four days.

Some went to Devon, or Wales, and all over, away from the cities. We were moved on day one. The journey seemed to last forever. I remember seeing field after field with cows in as we travelled in the train. We played games and slept, and eventually arrived at Torrington Station. I remember there were lots of people there. We got out of the train and were lined up while people chose which children they would have. We were 'already chosen' and walked up Station Hill to our new home in Well Street, no 42. Next day we were back at the station watching as the next lot of children arrived. It must have been hard for our hosts – they were not used to children. We settled in, though it seemed to me if anything went missing it was always us evacuees who were blamed. It wasn't long before our mother came to join us. This sometimes made for tension – it must have been very hard to have your home invaded by another family. As soon as the war ended and my father was demobbed, he also came to join us and we never went back to London".

"My name is Peter Johnson and I was evacuated from London to Langtree in 1940 at the tender age of 7.

I was delighted to be asked to contribute to the book on Langtree as it gives me the opportunity to record my undying gratitude to the village and the May family in particular for giving me such a safe and happy home during the war.

My two sisters, Joan, and Ann (aged 4), and I arrived complete with gas masks and identifying labels and were taken to the church hall near the Rectory. There, all the evacuees were paired off with villagers prepared to take them in. As Joan's friend Joyce was with us, we were effectively a group of four and not many people were able to take such a large number. Mr & Mrs May of Higher Doggaport however were!

Mrs Elsie May (who became Auntie to us all) took us to Doggaport where we joined her, 'Uncle' Bill May, their two daughters Joyce & Doreen and Ron Harris the farm worker who lived in. Overnight; a family of nine!

We soon settled in and were made to feel welcome. Auntie however was not finished – before long Doggaport residents included (for varying periods) two teachers, Miss Benning & Miss Ford, Mrs Lomasney & her two daughters, a family called Suter and finally my brother Dennis who cycled down from London to escape the Blitz. Doggaport had a big kitchen – just as well as we often had 13 sitting down for a meal!

I was glad of the chance to record my thoughts about Langtree. I have nothing but fond and grateful memories of the village that was such a safe haven for myself, and many others during World War II. As probably the longest evacuee resident in Langtree, I am privileged to say 'THANK YOU' from us all."

Plane Crash

On the night of 27/28th August 1943, at 2200 hrs Halifax Bomber No. DG.412 crashed at Langtree, killing all the crew. The names of these men are recorded on the Roll of Honour for Langtree, and remembered with those lost from our own parish, at our annual Church Remembrance Service each November. The men who died, their rank, family connections and place of burial are listed below.

Pilot
Sgt. John Peter Williams aged 20 RAF.VR. 1387840. Son of John Charles and Mary Frances Williams, Hayward's Heath, Sussex. Buried Heanton Puncharden churchyard, near Chivenor, N. Devon. Row Q – Grave 10

Navigator
Sgt. Raymond Frederick Stainsby, aged 20 RAF. VR. 1528611. Son of Benjamin and Betsy Stainsby of Dormanstown, Redcar, Yorkshire. Buried in Redcar Cemetery, Teeside, Yorkshire. Plot F, Row 36, Grave 4.

Flight Engineer
Sgt. George Rogerson Wheatley aged 18 RAF.VR.1677247. Son of Frederick and Gladys Wheatley of Sunderland, County Durham. Buried in Corsanside Churchyard, Northumberland. Grave in the North West of churchyard.

Bomb Aimer
Flying Officer William Henry Graham aged 28 RAF.VR.151100. Son of William Henry and Jessie Graham of Oldham, Lancashire. Buried in Greenacres Cemetery, Oldham. Section M, Row 11, Grave 253.

Wireless Operator/Air Gunner
Sgt. James Taylor aged 23 RAF.VR. 1655553. Son of William and Agnes Gillespie Taylor of Kirkcaldy, Fife, Scotland. Buried in Hayfield Cemetery, Kirkcaldy, Scotland. Comp 1/2 H, Grave 388.

Mid-Upper Gunner
F/Sgt. Peter Chadwick Bartle Aged 29 RAAF. No. 422103. Son of Mr and Mrs J. A. C. Bartle of Waverley, New South Wales, Australia. Buried in Heanton Puncharden Cemetery, Nr. Chivenor, N. Devon. Row P, Grave 15

Rear Gunner
Sgt. Hugh Patrick Henry Aged 22 RAAF. No. 425158. Son of John and Anne Cecilia Henry of Greenmount, Queensland, Australia. Buried in Heanton Puncharden Cemetery, Nr. Chivenor, N. Devon. Row Q, Grave 11.

All seven deaths were recorded as August 27th 1943.

There had been speculation at the time that bad weather may have been a contributing factor, but the official report makes it clear this was not so. The weather report for the day stated that it was cloudy with a slight mist at first, fair with showers later and fine after dusk. Visibility moderate becoming good. Wind light variable.

The Meteorological Office report stated that rain started at Hartland Point just after midnight, but at 2200 it was still probably dry with the lowest cloud base about 2000ft. The visibility was very good.

The aircraft and its crew were part of 1663 Heavy Commission Unit, based at RAF Marston Moor, Ruffard, Yorkshire. This unit was responsible for the operational training of aircrew and four engine aircraft prior to their posting to one of the main force Halifax Squadrons in No 4 group Bomber Command.

The crew were in the final stages of their training when the crash occurred. The attendant A I B crash report confirms they were engaged in a bulls-eye exercise, the final flight of their training programme, which would include flying in the proximity of enemy territory.

The aircraft was a Halifax B Mk 5 series1, Dg 412. It was built by Rootes Ltd Coventry (as part of a batch of 138, from DG 231 to DG 424) in February 1943. It had taken off from Wyton Hants 2137 hrs and was due back there again between 1550 and 1620. An official report said the Halifax began to break up after being hit by flak on an operation to Brest, then crashed and burnt at Langtree 4 miles South West of Torrington. There was a total loss that night of 33 aircraft.

Men from the Home Guard came to inspect the damage and remove the bodies, placing them in one of the farm outbuildings until they were removed by officials of the RAF.

On January 19th 1944 compensation to the sum of 10 shillings was paid to Mr D Kent, Hillside, Langtree, Brandis Corner, for damage caused by the aircraft on August 27th 1943. The accompanying document was signed on behalf of the Air Commodore, Commanding, and no 41 Base headquarters, RAF Marston Moor.

A Halifax similar to the one that crashed at Langtree

Joe Bond was coming home from a dance at Westford Farm. Cycling at about midnight he hit something in the road. It was a piece of wing off the plane. The plane had crashed in a large plot of land and missed hitting or harming anyone or anything on the ground.

Olive and Alma Daniels (Mrs K Carter and Mrs N Hill) remember that a dance was arranged in the village at the church hall for the Royal Air Force men who came to investigate the crash, collect evidence and clear up.

Les Knapman remembers: "We had just gone to bed; it was dark when we heard a plane roaring around. It was circling. Then it started dropping flares so it could see the landscape and find a place to land. The sky was lit up like daylight. It circled around and came up from the bottom of the meadow behind the Dutch barn probably thinking they could land there but found they were jammed up in a corner confronted by the bull's house (with a Devon Bull in it) and a big fir tree (which is still there). At that stage the fuel tank was torn off as it touched the ground spilling highly inflammable aviation fuel all around. The engine was still running and ammunition started exploding as they were trying to regain height for a fresh attempt. Seconds later as they passed over the small field near Earlswood Lane, one of its engines fell off. The plane managed to rise up over the hill but then crashed at Buda just behind where the farm buildings are now. All on board were killed. We, my brother and I, were quickly out of bed – mother got us up – we weren't sure what was happening but it was very frightening. Father went out and smelt the petrol everywhere – because shells were exploding there was a very real danger of the barn, the bull shed and our home, Collacott farmhouse, going up in flames (one spent shell case landed near the back door. I still have it – made into the nozzle of a pair of bellows that I made at Torrington School woodwork lesson). Father and Bill Wilton went to find out what had happened. Bill Wilton (who lived across the road at Higher Collacott) was in the Home Guard and came out with his rifle and fixed bayonet. They had no idea at this point if it was an enemy plane or one of our own. Officials were fairly quickly on the scene and stayed for approximately a fortnight. After dealing with the immediate crash site and the victims, they searched Collacott grounds and around for debris. No one else was allowed anywhere near where the plane was. They found the fuel tank and other bits of metal in Collacott meadow and the engine halfway down Cleave Hill on the edge of the woods. It had hit with such force it was well embedded in the earth. There was a large hole left when the engine was removed. We could smell petrol for weeks afterwards."

Bad snow falls as recorded in the school Log Book

January 1945   H G Gerry, supply staff
20/21st weekend – 31st school closed, 29th-31st snow fell on 5 consecutive days. School pipe burst with frost.

January 1947   Lucy Fishleigh

29th–Feb 10th Canteen van not come, used emergency rations.

Tues February 4th very severe weather conditions have prevailed over Thursday, Friday, weekend and Monday. School reopened today Tuesday 3rd – staff and 5 scholars present. School kept open but registers not marked.

February 5th Weather and roads are still very bad. School kept open, 12 children present. Canteen van is unable to come. Children from a distance brought their dinners, village children able to go home and then return.

February 6th School remained open again today but attendance is 10. Registers not marked, one fire kept going. Weather remains severe – dismissing scholars at 3pm with instructions to give tomorrow (Friday) a miss and reopen on Monday (weather permitting). Caretaker informs me this morning that on thawing the pump last night it appeared to burst. Correspondent notified of these happenings.

February 10th School reopens, 19 children present (63%). Miss Peate examined children's heads. Cwt coke delivered during weekend.

February 11th 6 tins vegetable soup and 1 tin of meat received as emergency rations.

Wires brought down by ice 1947, at Langtree

January 1963   R A Yoe Jenn

January 8th School reopens with great difficulty on account of weather. (62 on books.)

January 9th continuing under difficulty.

January 10th Complete freeze up of water supply. No water in canteen or toilets. Church hall in similar condition. Closed school for two days.

January 14th Reopened today with water from P.O stored. Only 11 present. Lowest temp recorded 13 F = 19 below freezing.

January 15th Canteen and caretaker staff working under great difficulties (no water).

January 16th Signs of thaw.

January 18th we completed one of the most difficult weeks we have ever experienced. The water supply, apart from one tap, doesn't function. Toilets frozen (flushes). Church hall not useable. We were able to continue only by the whole-hearted co-operation of the staff. Mrs Stone had to share my room. Mr Edgcombe did valiant work with water and heat. Mrs Mitchell and Mrs Huxtable produced meals under great strain. Mr Ford cheerfully coped with flushing the toilets. Mrs Moore did valiant work at Church Hall while they had water. I would like my appreciation of their efforts under most trying conditions to be recorded.

January 21st we began today with frozen pipes in the kitchen – Mr Edgcombe and Mrs Mitchell coped with the thawing and Mr Edgcombe and I tried to lag the pipes more successfully. It should be noted that the main water pipe enters the canteen from an outside wall – about 3ft of pipe exposed! Temp. 13 F during weekend.

January 22nd Temp. 14 F

January 23rd Temp 14 F, mains frozen. N.D.W.B called and reported that as the main is frozen we just have to wait for the thaw.

January 24th Temp 20 F – a little warmer but still no water.

January 28th we have put the juniors in the small room. Transition and Infants in large room divided by cupboards in an attempt to accommodate all children whilst the church hall is out of action. Temp 20 F.

January 30th Temp 30 F

January 31st Temp drops to 22 F last night.

February 1st we have managed (just) to keep going – thanks to the kind cooperation of our neighbours (Mr and Mrs Fovargue at the Post Office)

February 4th Temp at weekend 16 F. To add to our difficulties, Mrs Stone is absent (ill).

February 5th Temp 30 F, Mrs Stone still away.

February 6th Mr Edgcombe, Mrs Stone and I arrived (after exceedingly difficult journey to find only 4 present because of the bad roads and weather.

February 7th many children return today.

February 8th another difficult week ended – still no water.

February 11th WATER! At last we have a supply to the canteen – but not elsewhere. We have been without since Jan 23rd.

February 12th The infants were able to return to the church hall.

February 15th At last the water supply is normal in toilets, cloakroom etc.

February 18th Mr Ford had turned off all the water on Friday, but on Monday, when turned back on, within 20 minutes all pipes were frozen.

February 22nd Half Term.

February 26th Reopens. Temp 19 F over weekend. Toilets again frozen.

February 1978   Allan Edgcombe

February 20th School unable to reopen after half term, owing to blizzards. The staff was unable to get to Langtree and snowdrifts 6ft high were blocking the paths and covering the playground.

February 21st Mr Cornish and I walked from Torrington to Langtree but the school remained closed.

February 22nd Today I dug out paths around the school and from the gates. We will reopen tomorrow but buses will not run.

February 23rd School reopens but only 24 children attend.

February 27th Buses ran today and all children returned to school.

January 1979   Allan Edgcombe

January 17th School closed early owing to heavy snowfalls.

January 18th Meals not served, had to bring packed lunches. T and G W U strike action – no delivery drivers.

Julie Bond walks the dogs on top of the snow Browns Lane, January 1979

January 19th Heavy snow.

January 22nd Industrial action N.U.P.E, caretaker refused to unlock premises. Parents advised not to send children to school. Staff reported to the school gate at 9am and were sent home. Area Office and Chairman of Managers notified.

January 23rd School closed – heavy snowfall

January 25th School reopens. Only 25 children – no buses.

Stibb Cross in the snow

January 1982   Allan Edgcombe

January 8th-13th heavy snowfalls - very icy conditions. Gradual return to normal from 13th.

J Coles clearing snow on Burstone Hill February 1978

There are many other memories of these bad winters, blizzards which blocked roads and made normal life impossible, Milk Tankers that couldn't get through to collect milk, sheep buried under snow drifts and having to be dug out, and medical emergencies where in later years the helicopter was called to the rescue. My husband, Les went down with appendicitis in the 1947 freeze-up, and because neither Doctor nor ambulance could get to Collocott, his appendix ruptured. When they eventually did get through it was almost too late.

He was critically ill and not expected to survive, but praise God he did. It took a whole year off school to recover.

Bryan Ley remembers that in 1947 there was very bad snow. "One evening my mother sent me to visit my grandparents at Bibbear Cottage and take something to them. I stayed and played draughts with Granfer and left about 9pm. When I got up on the top road (Bideford to Stibb Cross) the wind was behind me and blowing the snow past me and along in front. I got to Withacott road and the snow was a foot or so deep there. I eventually got home safely. Next morning I went to Browns Lane and it was blocked solid. I climbed up on top of the snow and walked along it across two fields; it was a bit soft in places but held me up. The lane was blocked for 6 weeks. Eventually a busload of German prisoners came (from Bideford) and using hand shovels they cleared it away, throwing the snow over the hedges. There was probably 30 or more men working on clearing the snow. Withacott road didn't get blocked."

In 1978 Browns Lane was again blocked. Geoff Bond had to make a new gateway to be able to get out across the field (across Horns Fields.) He came with his tractor and loader to try to clear the lane and got stuck. He went back to get a second tractor to pull the first one out, and by the time he got back the first tractor was buried – he had to leave it there. Also in that year the tankers from Torridge Vale couldn't get out to all the farms so the farmers had to take their milk in. The queue at the factory became so bad that a collecting point was set up at Withacott to take some of the pressure off. Farmers in this area brought their milk to the Withacott lay-by and long queues also formed here.

As the tanker became full it took the milk off to the factory and returned for another load. This went on all day.

Tanker and tractors at Withacott collecting depot 1978. Photo reproduced from a slide; many thanks to Bryan and Daisy Ley for making the picture available to us.

Land Riots or Wars

Through the early 1800s, land enclosure became prevalent in rural England and Langtree was no exception.

Farmers and smallholders whose ground adjoined common land started to enclose it as they could turn the ground into pasture. This enraged the villages who would lose land where they had caught rabbits and cut firewood, also pea and bean sticks.

Matters escalated to the extent that the farmers would fence land during the day and the villagers would tear down the fences at night. Tempers flared and reached a climax when Bill Goss of Stowford, who was then the Parish Chairman, was so severely beaten that he was taken to hospital in Plymouth (this was before there was much rail transport in North Devon).

Finally, the whole matter was decided at the High Court in London when it was decreed that land that was enclosed by a certain date should remain in the ownership of the farmers and smallholders and the rest be returned to common land. A copy of the Injunction was to be attached in place of deeds to the enclosed land. This seemed to settle the matter for all time. However, in 1967 the Government decided to nationalise the use and ownership of common land and to do away with such anomalies as; one house in the village having grazing rights for, say, one goose whilst next door had rights for two geese and one pig!

The Parish Council put in a claim that Langtree Moor, Common Moor and Stowford Moor was Common Land and some farmers decreed that they had grazing rights. This was agreed by the Commissioners as follows;-

Mr W Goss and Mr L Facey had rights on Stowford Moor,

Mr J Walters and Mr H Nicholls had rights on Langtree Moor

Mr D Fishleigh and Mr K Duncan had rights on Common Moor.

With regard to Langtree Commons, although the Council said it was Common Land, someone else claimed it. After four years and numerous letters to the Commissioners, the Council was summoned to appear before them.

John Folland and Alfred Soby attended and took as proof the Injunction attached to the deeds belonging to Mrs Elsie Soby.

As soon as the Commissioners saw the Injunction, they agreed that the land was Common Land and no one owned or had rights on it.

This article puts extra 'flesh' onto that which Alan Edgcombe wrote in part one, and was researched by Patricia Soby.

Brave and Faithful Missionary

A memorial service to the Rev. R. H. Goldsworthy, who was killed by bandits on March 6th 1938 at Stone Gateway in South China, where he had been a missionary since 1921, were held at Langtree Methodist Church on Sunday. Mrs. Goldsworthy, formerly Miss Ida Netherway, has been living at her home at Langtree about a year.

Had it not been for health reasons she had hoped to rejoin her husband in the mission field, early this year. Mrs. Goldsworthy is a member of a well-known Langtree family. There is one son, aged ten, who is away at school and a baby girl.

Rev R Goldswothy

The Methodist Memorial service was attended by many friends over a wide area around and was conducted by the Rev. John Ford Reed (Bideford), assisted by the Rev. R. Pyke (Southport) and the Rev. A. Brown (Leeds). Both Rev. J. Ford Reed and Rev. R. Pyke are former presidents of the Conference, and both have ministered at the church at Bristol, which Mr. Goldsworthy attended in his early days and Rev. J. Ford Reed was there when Mr. Goldsworthy actually entered the ministry. Rev. A. Brown was a close personal friend of Mr. Goldsworthy with whom he was a contemporary at college.

Mr F. Moore was at the organ and played special voluntaries. The hymns were "Jesus lives!" "Saviour, quicken many nations," "Hark! The sound of holy voices," and "For all the saints who from their labours rest." The Scripture reading by Rev. J. Ford Reed was from chapter II of the Epistle to the Hebrews, commencing at the 25th verse.

Members of the family and close friends present at the service included: The Widow; Mr. T. Goldsworthy (brother), Mrs. H. Nethaway (sister), Mr. H. Nethaway (father-in-law), Mr. H. Nethaway (brother-in-law) Mrs. T. Goldsworthy (sister-in-law), Mrs. G. Childs (Sister-in-law), Mr. and Mrs. J. Nethaway, and Mr. and Mrs. W. May (brothers-in-law and sisters-in-law), Miss Joyce May, Master John Nethaway and Miss Doreen May (nephew and nieces), Mrs. Daniel and Mrs. May (aunts), Mrs. J. A. Thompson Miss Smith, Messrs. F. Daniel, W. Daniel, W. Routley, and Mrs. F. Daniel (cousins), Mr. and Mrs. Copp, Mr. and Mrs. Whitlock (close friends).

Rev. J. Ford Reed spoke of Mr. Goldsworthy's years of brave and faithful service and of his acquaintance with him in one of his pastorates in Bristol.

Rev. A. Brown, illustrating his zeal as a missionary, quoted from a letter he had from Mr. Goldsworthy about two months ago, in which he said he had journeyed 750 miles on horseback.

Rev. R. Pyke said they wished that night to offer their sympathy, very sincere and tender, to those who most deeply needed it.

In sympathy with the loss of Mr. Goldsworthy, a memorial service was also held at Langtree Parish Church in the morning, special hymns being sung. The Rector and Rural Dean (Rev. B. Hallowes) conducted the service and preached with reference to the martyrdom of St. Stephen, and said although it was a great and sad loss, Mr. Goldsworthy's was a wonderful death in the service of the Master.

This picture was given to Langtree chapel in 1995 by the daughter of Rev and Mrs Goldsworthy, with the following notes: "This is the final resting place of two Methodist missionaries at Stone Gateway, Guizhou Province, S.W.China. The graves of Rev. Samuel Pollard (foreground) 1864-1915, and The Rev. Heber Goldsworthy 1895-1938." Photographed 7th Sept. 1995 by their daughter.

The graves were broken down during the Cultural Revolution by the Red Guards, but by government order, they have been rebuilt and the site made a national memorial – "to be preserved for ever".

A few hours before he was killed by bandits on the night of March 6th 1938, Rev Heber Goldsworthy preached from this text: "I have fought the good fight, I have finished the course, I have kept the faith," 2 Timothy 4.7. The ashes of Mrs Ida Goldsworthy (nèe Nethaway of Doggaport Farm, Langtree) were sprinkled on her husband's grave on September 7th 1995."

Langtree Rector's Daughter Marries

On 24th May, 1935 the wedding of Rachel Hallowes and Etienne Henry Tudor Boileau was reported in the *Western Times*: "The church was full, and many lined the sides of the canopy leading from the church. The service was conducted by Rev. Prebendary H. M. Johnson (Vicar of Ilfracombe). Mrs. W. Brownscombe was the organist, and the hymns were, 'Lead us, Heavenly Father'; 'O Perfect Love' (sung to the *Londonderry Air*); and 'Praise, my soul, the King of Heaven'. The best man was Mr. Hugh Ridley Boileau, brother of the bridegroom.

The bride, given away by her father, wore a heavy ivory satin gown with a long train from the waist and an old family veil of Honiton lace mounted on tulle held in place by Tudor bonnet of the same lace. She carried a bouquet of arum lilies.

Four little girls acted as bridesmaids. They were Miss Ann Pellew-Harvey (niece of the bride); Miss Katherine Hallowes (cousin of the bride); Miss Mavis Aitken; and Miss Juliet Aitken. There were two pages: Master David Davenport (cousin of the bridegroom); and Master Adrian Hope-Vere. The bridesmaids wore white and silver organdie ankle-length dresses, forget-me-not blue sashes and shoes, wreaths of forget-me-nots in their hair, and carried posies of mixed flowers. The pages wore forget-me-not blue satin trousers, white crêpe de chine blouses and blue leather Cromwell shoes.

The bride's mother wore a black georgette gown and coat embroidered in pink and gold, and a black hat with pink and black straw flowers. The bridegroom's mother wore a light navy blue crêpe Romaine dress with white appliqué lapels and a three-quarter coat of the same material, and a blue Bali buntal straw hat with paradise plumes.

A reception was held at Langtree Rectory. The bride and bridegroom were the recipients of three hundred presents. The bride's present to the bridegroom was a hunting crop and a gold pencil, and the bridegroom gave the bride a diamond ring. From the parishioners of Langtree the bride received a blue enamel and silver toilet set, from Langtree Gymkhana Committee an oak bowl and tray; other presents were from the officers of the 2nd Battalion of the Somerset Light Infantry, a case of cutlery; from the officers of the Camel Corps, a silver salver; officers of the Sudan Defence Force, cheque.

The honeymoon is being spent at Affeton Castle, lent by Sir Hugh Stucley. The bride's travelling costume was a navy blue dress with white satin collar and cuffs, three-quarter coat to match, and a blue Bali buntal straw hat."

From the Western Times Friday 24th May: "Under the arch of welcome, surrounded by hundreds of villagers who had come to wish them well, Mr. and Mrs. E. H. T. Boileau were welcomed by the bride's hunter, "Penny Royal," after their wedding at Langtree Church on Saturday afternoon.

The bride, who has taken an active interest in parochial affairs and follows the Stevenstone Hunt, was Miss Rachel Louisa Hallowes, daughter of the Rev. Bernard Hallowes and Mrs. Hallowes, of Langtree. The bridegroom was Mr. Etienne Henry Tudor Boileau, The Somerset Light Infantry (P.A.) and the Sudan Defence Force, eldest son of the late Col. J. Ridley F. Boileau, Royal Engineers, and Mrs Spencer-Smith, of Fordlands, Northam.

The History & Murder of Mary Richards

Paula Fuller has researched the following story and I am grateful for her permission to include it in this book:

'Mary was the eldest daughter of Elizabeth (Betty) née Leach of Newton St Petrock and the late Richard Richards of Langtree and was baptised at Langtree Church of England church on 21st April 1833. Mary had a sister called Joanna who was baptised at Shebbear Bible Christian Chapel on 4th March 1831. She may also have had another sister called Maria, born approximately 1823, who died of a fever in 1842 at the age of nineteen. Her grave lies next to Mary's at Siloam Chapel. Interestingly, buried the other side of Mary's grave lies another Richard Richards, who it is thought, may have been a brother. He was born around 1829 and died in 1913 at 84 years of age. His headstone states he was a preacher.

Mary lived in Langtree with her mother Betty and her sister Joanna. She was a glover by trade and did out-work for a factory in Torrington, as did many young girls and women at the time

Mary, her mother and sister Joanna all lived at Berry Cross by the 1841 census. Her mother was in receipt of Poor Relief, which was paid by the parish to the people who were unable to work and in receipt of little income, very much like unemployment benefit paid by the government today. Some less fortunate were reduced to go into the Union Workhouse in such circumstances.

In 1851 they all lived at Siloam Cottage. The *North Devon Journal* states she resided at Langtree Week at the time of the murder, but there are no available records to check this information. However, her mother and sister were not on the 1861 census for Langtree Week, so must have moved on, but I have been unable to trace where. Maybe her mother ended her days at the workhouse? This I have not looked into. Her sister may have married, but we do not know for certain, and it is time consuming to trace when unsure of the parish of marriage. Neither of Mary's parents are buried in the Parish.

I have been unable to classify with first source evidence the exact location of Siloam cottage. Ordnance Survey maps of this area do not state the names of individual properties and it is not on the Tithe Map, dated 1841. However, I have come to the conclusion that 'Siloam Cottage' was part of the chapel we now see today.

On the day she met her dreadful fate, she had left her home at Langtree Week, a small hamlet in the parish of Langtree, around eleven o'clock. She was to return her finished gloves to Stoneman and Willis, her employer in Torrington. She carried

Siloam & Stairy Lane near where Mary lived

with her two baskets, one of which belonged to Mrs Anne Tucker, wife of Thomas Tucker, yeoman who resided at Rivaton, also in the parish of Langtree. Mary had an order of 2lbs of currants, 1½ lbs of sugar and a dram of saffron to fetch for Mrs Tucker from Mr Mallett, the grocer in Torrington.

On reaching Torrington she proceeded to the grocers to purchase the goods. Elizabeth Balkwill, apprentice to Mr Mallett, served Mary as instructed by the letter from Mrs Tucker. She had other items to purchase for her mother and other neighbours including some blacking and blue, a 1penny loaf, ¼lb of soap and 1½ oz of tobacco. Mary then went on to her employer, and was paid 4*s* 7½*d* for the finished gloves she had returned, and collected the following weeks work, this being 11 pairs of tan leather gloves.

Mary made her way back home to Langtree Week, passing through the village of Taddiport, at around 3 or 4 o'clock in the afternoon. She fell into the company of a man who was hanging around the bridge. He fell into conversation with her and asked if he might walk with her, which Mary did not object to. On ascending Cross Hill, Mary had to make a stop at Mary Martin's house, the last house on the left, to collect a parcel containing two dresses.

The man, whose name was Harvey, asked Mary if this was her journey end. She replied, "I have several miles further to go". She then bade him farewell and went into Mrs Martin's house, leaving Harvey to continue up the hill. A man named Stacey, driving his cart, passed Harvey on the hill and noticed he was occasionally glancing back, as though he was waiting for somebody.

Mary stayed for five or six minutes and then left to continue her journey home, carrying her two baskets and a further parcel, which she had collected from Mary Martin.

Unbeknown to Mary, Harvey was lying in wait for her, where the two roads meet, near a clump of fir trees.

He struck her with a claw hammer and then dragged her into the field known as Colwill's Meadow, which belonged to Mr Martin. He robbed her of her wages and assaulted her. She begged him for mercy on her knees; he struck her again, the blow penetrating her straw bonnet. Bleeding profusely, he dragged her into the catch-pit, which was about 15 feet from the gate and there he left her. Harvey then fled towards Bideford across the fields.

John Stacey, the driver of the cart who had observed Harvey behaving oddly, passed the spot where the vicious attack took place on his return journey and, in spite of seeing signs of blood on the road and picking up Mary's comb, he went on his way unaware of the poor girl who lay suffering so close by.

Mary was not discovered until the next morning. At around 5.30am on 17th May William Milford, a shoemaker of Taddiport, discovered Mary. She was in great distress and her clothes were covered in blood and dirt from the field. Milford stopped a passing cart, driven by a man named Ward, and the two men lifted Mary from the ditch and rested her against a trough while Ward went to prepare the cart.

They then saw a woman approaching. It was Mary's mother who had waited anxiously for her daughter to return from her errands. When Mary did not arrive home by nightfall her mother became very worried, as Mary was a reliable and trustworthy girl. As soon as it was light she set off in search of her daughter, and was greatly distressed to see the two men and the poor beaten girl.

Her mother asked "Mary, how came you here?" Weakly she answered, "Mother, I don't know".

Mary was taken on the cart to the Union Workhouse in Torrington where she was examined by the surgeon, Mr John Rouse. She had thirteen wounds to different parts of the head, and her skull had been smashed. Such was the violence of the blow that part of the straw bonnet was imbedded into her head; there was little hope of any recovery.

Leaving Mary for dead, Harvey had taken what he wanted from the baskets and continued on foot to Bideford. By chance he met with his brother-in-law, James Goodenough, around 6 o'clock. In court his brother-in-law describes Harvey as "being flurried about something". Harvey left with Goodenough, and another man named Prouse. He did not reach home till 11 o'clock.

It was later discovered that Harvey had given the currants, sugar and saffron to his wife, who was quite unaware of how her husband had come by these goods. She baked cakes with them the following day while Harvey went to Torrington and then on to Barnstaple. In the afternoon of the 17th May, he visited Abraham Land, a hairdresser and barber in Maiden Street, Barnstaple where he paid a penny for a shave and to have his whiskers removed.

There are no more accounts of his movements until he was duly arrested at Myrtle Place, Barnstaple, in a house of disrepute kept by a Joseph Griffiths. At 1am on the 18th May, he was taken into custody after a violent struggle in which he attempted to escape. The police were quite sure they had the right man, as so many witnesses had come forward with a description of Harvey seen loitering around the area on the day in question.

After later searching his residence, a lone farmhouse on Thornhillhead Moor, in the parish of Buckland Brewer, they had all the evidence they required, for concealed in the bedroom upstairs was the murder weapon; one claw hammer still carrying marks of its use. Harvey denied any knowledge of it.

Mary's baskets were discovered in Cross Woods on Thursday 18th May, by Elizabeth Turner of Burrington. The contents were recognised as the belongings of Mary Richards. Harvey was actually taken to the Union Workhouse for Mary to identify. Although she was still in a critical condition, she was able to identify him as her attacker and noted that he had removed his whiskers.

Two weeks later Harvey was sent to trial. On the bench sat Sir Trevor Wheeler, Lord Clinton, Rev C D M Drake, John Solely Esq. (Mayor of Torrington) and George Braginton.

The trial lasted nine hours, whereupon Llewellyn Garrett Talamage Harvey was formally committed to the County Jail, to stand trial at the next Devon Assizes. On the afternoon of the same day, Mary Richard's fight for survival ceased. Without pain she passed away around 3 o'clock, 14 days to the hour after suffering her fatal injuries. It is thought her fight to stay alive was just to see her attacker Harvey committed for his crime.

On Friday 30th May Mary's body was taken from the workhouse to the Bible Christian Chapel Siloam, at Langtree. The bearers were Joshua Vanstone of Stowford, William Hackwill of Collacott, Joshua Copp of Suddon, Thomas Short, Thomas Banfield and Fredrick Stacey. The chapel was full. Rev Snell preached the sermon and as requested by Mary they sang her favourite hymn as the service finished.

Her grave can be seen in the churchyard to this day, the inscription telling the sad tale of her demise:

*MARY RICHARDS
of this parish
on whose person a murderous
assault was committed on
Cross Hill Little Torrington
May 16th 1854
she lingered till the 30th instant
when her spirit left this world
to return to God who gave it
Her body here rests in sure and certain hope
of the resurrection to eternal life
The Saviour Our Lord Jesus Christ
Age 21 years
Her years of probation were few
But Jesus had taught her to pray
And Jesus her Saviour she knew
Before she was summoned away*

As to Harvey, his trial lasted two days. The judge, the Hon. Judge Wightman presided over the court. The prosecution was carried out by Mr Valleck and the attorney in defence of Harvey, a Mr Fryer, a solicitor of Exeter. It took the jury ten minutes to decide and they returned with the verdict of GUILTY.

On Friday noon, the first week into August, at Exeter jail the execution of Llewellyn Garrett Talamage Harvey took place.

It was approximated that ten thousand people came to watch. It was said he spoke just before the executioner covered his head and the rope was placed around his neck, "The Lord have mercy on my soul".

Harvey's brother-in-law Goodenough, after the execution, travelled with waxworks of the culprit and his victim, dressed in authentic clothes, giving a narrative of Harvey's history.'

Footnote. There are varying conclusions as to where Siloam cottage is. I have been told there was a cottage on Stairy Lane which runs beside the chapel, part way along, near the clump of trees; also there was a cottage opposite the bottom of the lane and a little towards Shebbear Cross which some can still remember. Different people believe that either of the three cottages are a possibility. Since Paula researched this article I have received evidence that the Richard Richards, who is buried next to Mary, is her brother He lived at Langtree, in a long since disappeared cottage on the corner of Langtree Moor Lane. He was the father of 14 children; the youngest of these was Archie Richards, builder of this Parish and member of the Home Guard. Archie's granddaughter Sylvia has contributed to the memories section near the back of this book.

Gymkhana

Langtree Gymkhana was held for a few years in the early 1930s on a Wednesday in early August. In 1930 the Social Club sold a set of skittle balls to the Gymkhana committee, and the School log book tells us that in 1934 a number of children were absent from school as they were picking wild flowers for the Gymkhana the next day. Alma Carter remembers that there was a prize for the child with the best bunch of flowers. Bill Brooks remembers one year on Gymkhana Day there was a problem and the gate to the field was locked. Thankfully it was all sorted out and the day's events were able to proceed successfully. Mr and Mrs Joe Bond have a copy of a newspaper report of the time and it is reproduced here, as many will remember the people referred to in those long gone days:

"Langtree's second Annual Gymkhana and Sports were held at North Park, a beautifully situated field near the village (by kind permission of Mr George Bond snr) on Wednesday, and the premier credit for the great interest taken in the event rightfully belongs to Miss Rachel Hallowes, the Hon. Secretary of the committee and the foremost organiser. Her enthusiasm and energetic efforts on behalf of the horse sports resulted in there being over thirty competitors, an unusually large number when compared with figures reached at contemporary meetings. The attendance was very satisfactory, being about 700, and among the spectators were many visitors from Bideford, Torrington, Northam, and Westward Ho!

The esteemed chairman of committee was the rector (Rev B Hallowes), Mr W Brownscombe filling with aptitude the elastic office of hon. Treasurer, and the following comprised the committee: Messers F.J.Webber, W Box, J Ford, F Dymond, P.B.Jones, W.H.Hackwell snr, A.J.Tucker, H Harris, G Bond (a most useful member), W Brooks, W Burrows, S Cole, W and R Goss, A Soby, A Westcott, W and, A Burrows.

For the horse sports Brig Gen. Gwyn-Thomas (Monkleigh) and Col. C Didha (Bideford) were Judges, with Mr Webber as Starter and Mr Harris as Clerk of the course, and Mr R.E.L. Penhale (Torrington) Hon. Veterinary. There was keen competition for the silver cup (generously given by an anonymous donor through Mr G Bond) open to residents in the Torrington and Bideford districts, for mare or gelding not exceeding five years, and exclusive of all previous prize-winners in show rings judged on points, paces and over six low hurdles. Mr W. J. Cory (Bradworthy) was the winner with Mr Cleverdon of Bideford second and Mr Hearn of Langtree Week third. Those successful in the children's pony class for ponies 13h.h. and under, to be ridden by children under fourteen years of age were: 1. Miss Heather Jackson (Torrington), 2. Skidmore Ashby (Shebbertown), 3. G Bond (Roborough). Prizes for this event were given by an anonymous donor through Mr Slee and Mr G Copp respectively.

The results of the various mounted Gymkhana events were:
Potato race: 1st. W Oke (Bradworthy); 2nd. P Ayre (Milton Dameral); 3rd W Turner (Baxworthy Hartland).
Polo bending - 1st. F.W. Heale 2nd. Miss B Moorhead (Westward Ho), 3rd. W Oke.
Bobbing for apples: 1st. Lewis: 2nd. Pett; 3rd. Vanstone.
V.C. race: 1st. Pett; 2nd. Vanstone; 3rd. Cleverdon.
Wheelbarrow race: 1st. G Bond and partner; 2nd.Chamberlain and partner; 3rd. F Heale and partner.
Musical chairs: 1st. G Bond; 2nd. M Carmoy (Bideford) 3rd. F Heale.
Jumping: equal 1st, Covey, W Brooks and Bailey.
Trotting race: 1.5 miles - 1st. H Pett, 2nd. G Bond, 3rd. M Carmody.
Flat race under 14.2 h.h: 1st. Berry; 2nd. M Carmody; 3rd. Arnold.
Flat races 14.2 h.h. and over: 1st. Pett; 2nd. Dymond; 3rd. Carmody.

The men's sports held in the evening after the mounted events resulted: -
220 yards (local): 1st. H Underhill; 2nd. C Huxtable; 3rd. W Gent.
0.5 mile (local): 1st. H Underhill; 2nd. C Huxtable; 3rd. P Kellaway.
1 mile cycle race open: 1st. P Scott; 2nd. P Dayman:. 3rd. F. L. Rice.
100 yards slow cycle race (open): 1st. A. Wheeler; 2nd. A N Elliot;. 3rd. G H Childs.

Children's sports were in the hands of Messrs Westcott, Cole, Walters and Beer, and resulted as follows:
50 yrd girls under 8yrs: 1st. G Moore; 2nd. M Sanders; equal 3rd. B Furse and V Sanders.

50 yards, boys under 8yrs: 1st. J Beer; 2nd. P Beer; 3rd. D Cox
100 yards, girls under 10yrs: 1st.G Stevens; 2nd. A Daniel; 3rd. L Underhill.
100 yards, boys under 10yrs: 1st. R Harris; 2nd. T Badge 3rd. N Ward.
100 yards, girls under 15yrs: 1st. A Cox; 2nd. M Wheeler; 3rd. M Passmore.
100yrd boys under 15yrs: 1st. E Underhill, 2nd. J Berriman; 3rd. E Glover.

Other attractions on the ground besides the sports and confectionery stalls were skittling in the charge of:
Messrs Bond, Hackwell, Box, and Goss (Devon alley)-winners: 1st. (Live pig) F Folland; 2nd. B Bridgman; 3rd. S Pett.
and Messrs Dymond and R Goss (Diamond alley) winners: 1st. (live pig) W Gent; 2nd. F Waldon; 3rd. H Underhill; and
Judging weight of pig: won by Mr F Dymond and Mr Horn.
Guessing name of the pig, no one succeeded. The name of the pig was Moses.

Public tea (including free tea for local schoolchildren) was served in the village by the following helpers: - Mrs A .J. and Miss Tucker, Mrs and Miss Boundy, Mrs Moore and Miss Blight, Mesdames Furse (2), Mrs Brownscombe and Miss Jones, Miss Andrews, Mrs Hooper and Miss Hooper; Mesdames PB Jones, Burrows and Walters, with the help of Messers Jones and Tucker at the 'gate'. Helping at the gate of show-field were the Rev B Hallowes, A Soby, A R Burrows and R P Andrews.

In the evening a popular dance was held in the schoolroom, for which music was supplied *gratis* by Miss Barwick's orchestra from Barnstaple. Messrs Brownscombe and F Dymond helped at the door and Mr A Burrows discharged the duties of M.C.

The previous year's Gymkhana and Sports had proved successful financially, and, with the fine weather resulting in a large attendance at the current event it was hoped to have a substantial reserve balance in hand to help the event over any further, future difficult period.

Parish Hall Annual Fun Day

Langtree Fun Day began as a one-day event to raise funds for the proposed new Parish Hall. It quickly grew into a whole weekend of events and became a major attraction for miles around. It was held in the field apposite Doggaport Lane, by kind permission of David and Margaret Pearce, and involved many of the people of the parish in one way or another. Credit must go to the organising committee who had the boldness to risk the considerable outlay needed to sustain such an

Lord Clinton opens the fun day events 1986 and is presented with a buttonhole by Lynette Isaac John Folland and Rev Nigel Mead look on.

event. A Parish Newsletter report of 1993 described the Fun Day thus:

'The weekend started for some on the Thursday evening with the erection of the marquee and the fixing of the toilets. Friday saw the completion of the work just in time for the Country Dance. At this stage we were panicking as at eight o'clock we had very few dancers. By nine o'clock the marquee was full and it turned into a very successful evening.

Saturday morning was misty and you couldn't see from one end of the field to the other. Then, what's this coming? No it can't already. Please, we're not ready. The first mountain biker was there at nine. "The race doesn't start until eleven" I told him. "Yes I know" he replied, "I want to ride the course once to see what it is like". The bike ride was a huge success, thanks to all the committee members and landowners who moved fences, opened gates, collected marker posts etc to create the track. The vintage car, tractor and machinery rally was well supported with a great many entries and many people admiring the beautiful old vehicles. Ron and Rita Deacon were much involved in this part of the event. There was a craft fayre, with one stallholder desperate to leave before he sold all his stock!! He had another fayre the next day. The youngsters did their part, running stalls, games and waitressing, and the evening disco was well attended and much enjoyed."

Quite a weekend, and still there was the clearing up to be done on Monday but the end result of that particular fun-day was £3000 in the kitty for the Hall funds.

One year there was a rodeo on the Saturday. On a number of years, Sunday morning saw a lunch in the marquee, and in the evening a united service with a full marquee, young musicians and a choir to help lead. This was sometimes followed by a barbeque.

Collective Farm Sale

These are held each year at Doggaport Farm by kind permission of John and Eileen Beer and family, and are another part of the Hall fundraising effort.

The first one was held on May 2nd 1992 to raise funds for the proposed new Parish Hall. At first people were invited to donate goods to be sold outright for the funds. This quickly evolved into a much bigger event and items were contributed where some, all, or none of the realised price went to the funds, but always part of the commission did. Kivells Auctioneers' generosity in this and their hard work has been much appreciated. A vast array of items have been sold over the years – from large farm machinery and building materials, to plants, cakes and toys. In fact, anything no longer needed, as long as it was saleable, found its way to Doggaport. The Beer family have worked extremely hard over the years to make this event possible and been very generous in the continued use of their field. On a wet sale day, it has often looked a very sorry sight after the event is over. Yet still they continue and people come from miles to buy useful equipment or find a bargain. Sometimes it has been accompanied by a car boot sale on the same site, and committee members also prepare and sell hot dogs, beef burgers, soup and drinks. A great deal of money has been raised for the Hall by this event.

Two photos of the sale day. Above: Inspecting items for sale are John Beer flanked by Edward and Velva Ley and Below: Crowds begin to arrive

Miss Langtree

John Soby remembers that in 1961 he and the rest of the skittles team, including Jock Mills, had been to Bideford and won their event. On returning to Torrington Jock found that his 'Missus' (Doreen Hutchings) had also won the Torrington Carnival Queen contest. Local heats had been held in the surrounding villages with the winners there going on to represent their communities in the final. We have recorded dates of these events being held in the early 1960s, and then there was a break while a different method was tried (that of seeing who could sell the most tickets and thus raise the most money). But the old way was reverted to again in the 1970s onwards. In 1964 Miss Langtree was Diane Hearn with Pat Gerry as runner-up.

A 1977 record states that the Miss Langtree dance was held in the Church Hall on Wednesday March 23rd. Dancing was from 9.00 pm. until 1.00 am. Tickets were £1, which included refreshments, and could be obtained from Mr Corby, and Mrs Mary Nicolls. Judging was at 10.30 pm. Entrants had to be 15yrs old or over, and must live in the parish. By 1982 the dance had become a disco, with 'Terry's disco' providing the music. Judging had moved to 11.00pm and the lower age limit was now 16yrs. The judges were appointed by the Torrington Carnival Committee, and during the later session of dances the W.I. and the social club had been invited to organise the event. (The earlier ones had been put on by just the W.I). In 1977 the Langtree winner was Marion Balsdon. The Carnival Queen that year was Miss Frithelstock, Diane Baker, who later became a Langtree resident as Mrs Michael Heard and achieved newspaper fame again by giving birth to their first child Natalie on the same day as the Princess of Wales gave birth to Prince William.

Doreen Hutchings as Carnival Queen in 1961, flanked by Miss Shebbear and Miss Little Torrington

Carnival

At the beginning, the Carnival Queen competition was held in the Town Hall in Torrington but in later years moved to The Plough. Over the years Langtree has submitted a number of floats to the Torrington May Fair Carnival, as well as having provided them with a Carnival Queen. We have a number of photos of the various entries, but I do not know how many won prizes. The WI entered a few times, as also did the Primary School. The most recent of the Youth Clubs has also entered.

Above: Langtree WI entry, date unknown. Below: Primary School entry, 1986: Chris Cole, Michelle Findly, Nicky Roe. Lynette Isaac as Postman Pat. Clair Mitchell as Jess the Cat

Miss Langtree Centre, Marion Balsdon, with Left to Right Jennifer Moore, Helen Mills, Susan Mills and Amy Griffths. 1977.

Sheep dog trials at Collacott

The first sheepdog trials held in Langtree were at Collacott on 29th July 1978. This went on to become an annual event continuing for ten years. Mr and Mrs Grenville and Alma Bond were the hosts, Grenville having been a member of the Devon and Exmoor Sheepdog Society since 1975. He had taken part in a number of trials before starting the event on his own farm.

The day's events started at 10am and continued through to 6pm; I am sure much work had gone on by the society, helpers and hosts for many days previous to the event taking place. Over 65 dogs were put through their paces, with neighbours, including A Tucker & D Fishleigh, lending their sheep for the day. Handlers came from far a-field, from Mevagissey to Langport and Tiverton to Bude, also from the Moorlands around, from Bodmin, Postbridge and Simonsbath, and of course from Langtree, as Mr Bond tested his dog Meg, against the best of them. The names of the dogs included, Drift, Taff, Fleece, Trim, Hemp, Flicka and Tweed, as well as the more commonly heard, Gyp, Ben, Spot, Rover and Meg. First prize was £6, second £4, third £2, fourth £1, and also rosettes. Mr Bond himself has a vast array of rosettes of many grades and colours, quite a sight to see although he is very modest about them. There were three classes - open driving, open Maltese cross and open novice.

Grenville with his dog and the sheep safely gathered

The day also included various stalls for the attention of those who came to watch. This helped to raise money for local charities and organisations. Those who have benefited over the years are the Church, Church Hall, Playgroup, Siloam graveyard, Tower Repair Fund, Methodist Chapel, Torrington Cottage Hospital, the Society's own funds, Langtree graveyard fund, Sunday School, and the Parish Hall Fund.

In a newspaper report at the time, Mr Grenville Roberts, treasurer of the Devon and Exmoor Sheep Dog Society stated that these trials were becoming a great attraction for visitors, especially foreign holidaymakers, as they do not have anything like it on the continent. He said, "There is something fascinating about the possibilities of communications between shepherd and dog". He commented that young people were also taking an interest in the activity and enjoying it as a sport, a challenge and a hobby.

In 1991, sheepdogs were selling for up to £570 each at a sale on a farm in Kingsbridge. Today they fetch up to £1000 and nationally would be even more. Langtree's very own sheep dog trial-er, Grenville, doesn't buy in dogs, though he has bought young, untrained puppies. His prize-winning dogs are mainly home-bred.

Mr Bond has helped train people through the Agricultural Training Board, passing on some of his skills to others on how to train and care for sheepdogs. One of these is a former neighbour, Graham Simms, who is now a vicar, but was at one time a shepherd at the Big Sheep, the visitor attraction at Abbotsham. Mr Bond has also given demonstrations at Young Farmers Club events, and competed at the North Devon Show. With a number of years experience behind him, he has also become a judge at trials, with Mrs Bond presenting the prizes.

Royal Garden Party – May 31st 1965

Memories of Mrs Sylvia Curtice via her daughter Mrs Pat Dowson.

DEVON FEDERATION OF WOMEN'S INSTITUTES

Dear Members,
I have great pleasure in informing you that Her Majesty the Queen has graciously invited W.I. members to a special Garden Party to mark the occasion of our Golden Jubilee. Details are given below:
DATE: MONDAY, 31st MAY 1965.
PLACE: Buckingham Palace
TIME: 4 p.m. – 6 p.m. (the Gardens are open one hour before commencement)
DRESS: Afternoon dress with hat and gloves. Umbrellas if showery. Badges.
NUMBERS: ONE invitation per W.I., and bearing in mind that I have been asked to suggest that preference shall be given to members who have never had the opportunity to attend a Royal Garden Party.
INVITATIONS: A personal invitation will be sent direct to those nominated early in May.
IT IS EMPHASISED THAT THIS IS NOT TRANSFERABLE, AND IN THE EVENT OF THE RECIPIENT BEING UNABLE TO ATTEND, MUST BE RETURNED.

BADGES: Members attending are asked to wear the W.I. Badge, the Devon Bar and a nametag. All these are obtainable from the County Office.

A special train was laid on by British Rail, running from Penzance to Paddington – W.I. Jubilee Special – leaving Exeter at 10.30 with no further stops. Nine 40-seater coaches transported Devon members to Buckingham Palace. The cost per member was £2.00. Members were requested to wear their W.I. Badge, with its Devon bar and a special disc with their name on issued from the W.I. office. This was essential for checking at the Palace gates.

The Lord Chamberlain is commanded by Her Majesty to invite Mrs Sylvia Curtice to an Afternoon Party in the Garden of Buckingham Palace to mark the Golden Jubilee of the National Federation of Women's Institutes on Monday, the 31st May, 1965, from 4 to 6 o'clock p.m. Afternoon Dress with Hat (Weather Permitting)

"It is hoped that all members will travel on this train, as I am arranging for Westward Television Units to be present at Exeter St. David's, also V.I.P. treatment from the Station Master. Restaurant cars will be placed between the Cornish and Devonshire coaches, so that light refreshments will be obtainable during both journeys. One last plea, will Devonshire members PLEASE NOT MIX WITH THE CORNISH MEMBERS otherwise my task of issuing tickets and ensuring that you all arrive at Buckingham Palace will be made more difficult than necessary."

Sylvia Curtice

The train left Paddington for home at 7.30pm, arriving at Exeter St. David's at 10.30pm and Plymouth at 12 o'clock midnight: 1½ hours to travel from Exeter to Plymouth – it must have been well into the early hours by the time Penzance members alighted from the train.

Sylvia has left us her own impression of the day written on the back of one of the W.I. letters:

St. Giles, Torrington, Beaford and Langtree left 9.30am. Coach waiting at Paddington – train had been late arriving at Exeter. Food arrangements very bad (on the train). Biggest thrill was actually going through the palace to reach the garden. Peat Moss lawn. Flowers not at their best. Most members must have spent their pennies and no queue at the toilets.
Large lake with pink and white flamingos.
2 large carvings of storks.
Lovely refreshments. Very dainty china with gold edges. Silver plates, tea and coffee urns.
Everything very informal, young policemen came from S.Devon. Even made the sentries laugh. (About 200 coaches.)
Prince Andrew's car blue.
Queen in cerise with white and pink hat (Breton style).
Princess Marina in Tangerine suit and Tangerine velvet turban.
Princess Alexandra in Peach coat with peach off-the-face hat.
Duchess of Gloucester in pink suit and Breton style hat. Duke rather thin but very brown.
The Queen and the other members amongst the crowd from 4.15 until 5.45pm."

Open Gardens Weekend

Yet another of the fundraising ideas to raise money for the Parish Hall funds was "Open Garden Weekends". This involved a number of varied gardens being open on Saturday and Sunday from 2pm-6pm, with Cream Teas being served in either the Green Dragon or the Rectory. Some years there was a best hanging basket and container competition. The descriptions which follow cover the many gardens to be visited, showing a wide variety of ideas and plants.

Bibbear– a professionally designed garden

Alfie's Garden: The old village tip transformed into a garden and play area
The Coach House: A garden in the making, often hampered by 2 small boys intent on trial biking and playing football.
Wedlands: Improving cottage garden
Langtree Primary School: Children's garden, herb garden and containers.
The Willows: Modern bungalow garden, in the process of being made over. Will it be a new TV series?
2 North Park, Fore Street: Tiny garden with an array of bedding plants.
The Green Dragon Inn: Large garden containing mainly trees and shrubs. Rockery and ornamental raised pool.
The Old Rectory: Half-acre, 150 year-old garden being reclaimed from overgrown rhododendrons over the last 3 years. Help welcome!
Barns Farm: Slowly evolving, new informal garden: mainly shrubs, young trees, perennials and conservation area.
Kerry Park: Modern bungalow garden with over 1000 bedding plants and vegetables. Main feature: fishpond.
Buckerell, Church Lane: Modern bungalow with borders, baskets and container gardening.
The Post Office: South-facing house, forecourt and raised flowerbed; wall baskets, window boxes, and containers of seasonal and perennial plantings.
Cartref, Fore Street: Cottage garden: fruit, vegetables and flowers.
The Forge: Large cottage garden, mainly perennials; some trees, interesting individual features.
West Frost Cottage: Cottage garden: vegetables, flowers – and a puzzle you cannot solve!
Penlan, Stibb Cross: 10 year-old family garden. Large lawn, borders and shrubs. Fishpond and rockery.
Hillandale: Garden and model village in the process of restoration after years of neglect.
Stapleton Farm: Large Garden with semi-wild fair-sized pond. Unusual trees and shrubs, recently planted. Parterre garden.

OPEN GARDENS DAY AT LANGTREE

13 Varied Gardens to Visit on Sunday 10th July 1994 2 pm – 6 pm

Admission £1.50 to cover all gardens (under 14 free)

Cream Teas available at Green Dragon Inn £1.00

START AT ANY OF THE GARDENS

All proceeds to Parish Hall Building Fund

Foot and Mouth

The nightmare became reality for the West Country when foot and mouth was confirmed at a farm in Highampton on February 26th 2001. There had been other outbreaks of the disease in the country before but none had ever been on this scale and none had come as close to Langtree as this outbreak did.

Two years on, those of us who lived through the situation still clearly remember the silence and the smell of burning, along with the frustration, helplessness and pain. Life has moved on, businesses rebuilt and restored, but life on the farm has changed forever because of the disease. Restrictions and record keeping have vastly increased and the weekly visit to the local market is very different from what it was.

No Admittance

We had no confirmed cases in our parish, which is a miracle. We were surrounded by parishes which had almost all their farming livestock wiped out. Shebbear, Milton Dameral, Monkleigh, Beaford, Alverdiscott, Bradford, Sheepwash - all very badly affected. Frithlestock and Torrington also had their share. Much of Langtree did however come under D category restrictions, which meant no movement of livestock, and there were almost daily veterinary inspections. There were five instances of livestock being slaughtered. Geoff and Julie Bond of East Browns, and Helen McCowen of Ashbury lost their stock in contiguous cull (i.e., their farms were joined with those with confirmed cases). Richard and Sonia Ovenall lost their vast herd of pigs because of high risk. Richard and Samantha Mills lost theirs through contact; Richard worked on a farm in another parish which went down with the disease – and Mark Priest lost his sheep on compassionate grounds, which were on Barns Farm for winter keep and the food ran out but the animals couldn't be moved nor food brought in from his home farm which left no other option but slaughter.

Langtree had its taste of a pyre at East Stibb Farm and Geoff Bond has allowed us to use photos of the devastating scenes. His own animals and other disease-free ones were burnt there. The slaughter of healthy stock, that had been carefully bred for generations with selected bloodlines, was hard to take. The stock was irreplaceable though other animals could, and were, later bought in. No one but those who experienced it can really know what it was like to see and smell their stock lying dead for days and in some cases weeks, awaiting collection for burial or burning.

Carcases

We were also caught midway between Ashmoor – the government's massive burial pits which in the end remained unused – and Arscott, Holsworthy, where thousands of cattle were burned, also Deep Moor tip where many sheep carcases were buried. All this added to the deep concern and pressure. Farm children were kept away from school to avoid the risk of contact with other families whose animals could fall victim to the disease. The *Western Morning News* launched

Pyre

the Green Wellie appeal and Noel Edmonds and Prince Charles backed it. (This appeal was to raise funds for families and businesses caught up in the difficulties) The hero of the hour for the West Country was Anthony Gibson of the National Farmers Union – described as "the one voice of sanity" amongst so much chaos and pain.

Shops, tourism, in fact everyone was affected in some way. With so many restrictions and no visitors to the area – or even amongst family and neighbours, normal social life was put on hold. Never has the telephone been so appreciated, as for many it was the one safe means of contact left available. With the crisis having begun in February, it was July/August before many of the severest restrictions in this area were lifted – but livestock could still only be moved by licence, and these were not always easy to come by. Often long waits were endured and always much paperwork. The Tarka Trail was closed and all public footpaths – even walking the dog was no longer simple or straightforward.

Nevertheless, country people are strong in spirit, and with initiative and fortitude have adjusted to the new situation and are building again a much-reduced farming industry.

Richard Mills tells us something of what it was like to be directly involved with Foot and Mouth and to have the experience of losing your stock

"On 14th April 2003, our flock of sheep were culled as part of the Foot and Mouth crisis. We had 155 ewes and 310 lambs killed. They had to be culled as I had been working on a farm which, unfortunately, contracted Foot and Mouth and I was then classed as a "dangerous" contact. We can only have praise for the men who came to kill the sheep. Neither the ewes nor the lambs suffered, and the slaughter men showed compassion. At the time we were devastated. We did feel some relief that our sheep hadn't actually got the disease, this would have meant taking out of all the neighbouring farms' animals as well. At the time this was our biggest concern. After the sheep were culled, there was lots of paper work, many visits from ministry officials and lots and lots of cleaning! On a positive note, we were young enough and had the motivation to re-stock and we are now looking towards the future."

Sam, Richard's wife, says, "I felt very sorry for Richard losing all of his sheep. He worked hard for many years building up his flock to a certain standard and they were wiped out in an afternoon.

They were culled at the end of lambing. As I was pregnant at the time, I couldn't help with the lambing, and we couldn't have anyone in to help, so after lambing them all on his own, they were killed. About an hour before they were culled, a ewe actually lambed, which was heart-breaking.

My lasting memory of the afternoon they were killed, was handing Alice, our 2½ year old daughter over the garden fence to my mum (she was going to stay with them whilst the sheep were culled). We were all crying. I shall never forget them driving away in the car with Alice, knowing that when she returned her beloved 'baas' would be dead."

Restocking

National Events

Programme for the **King's Silver Jubilee** Celebrations at Langtree, 1935 (taken from Parish Council minutes of the time).

2.00 p m United Service for one hour.
3 00 p m Children's Sports
4.00 p m Children's Tea.
5.00 p m Adult Tea for four hundred.
Sports held In North Park.
6.50 p m Adult Sports and lighting of Bonfire.
Tea to be held in the Old School Hall.

£1. Allowed for oil for the Bonfire.
£2 Allowed for the Children's Sports.
£3-1-0-Allowed for the Adult Sports.
£1. Allowed for Fireworks.
£2-10-0. Allowed for Jubilee Mugs.

Report of Langtree's celebration of the **Coronation of Queen Elizabeth II** as recorded in the *Western Times:*

The coronation celebrations at Langtree began with peals on the bells. A United Service was held in the Parish church, the Rev B Hollows (rector) officiating, assisted by Mr W R Huxtable (Free Methodist).

Parishioners then paraded to the field, led by ex-Service men, Coronation Committee and School Children. An excellent programme was arranged by Mr Westcott (Headmaster of the day school).

Skittles was included in the events, the prize being won by 1. Mr A Ayre, 2. F J Dymond jnr., 3. F J Waldron, R Stoneman, H J Furse. Ladies prize: Miss Olive Underhill. An excellent tea was provided by the ladies committee, viz, Mesdames F Mills, A Terry and J Ford, assisted by Mesdames S Gerry, J B Adams, F Dymond snr, F Ford. Mugs were presented to the schoolchildren by Mrs B Hallowes. The bonfire was lit by Mr W H Burrows. The sports field was lent by Mr S Squire. The programme concluded with a free dance in the Old Day School, Mr A Ayre being the M.C.

Maureen Richards tells us that she remembers her dad buying a television at the Union Inn in time for the coronation of Queen Elizabeth II. People came to the Inn to watch the ceremony and celebrations. Barbara Babb (née Huxtable) also remembers going to watch the coronation at Ned Vanstone's home.

Very few people had televisions then and some bought sets especially for the occasion. Others, like the school at Langtree, hired them for the day. It was a very big and historical event. I myself remember being taken the following week to an Okehampton cinema with the rest of my Primary School-mates, to see the film of the Coronation. We had also been taken in the same way to see the film of the late King George's funeral.

The **Queen's Silver Jubilee** was marked in Langtree by celebrations similar to the previous events, i.e., United Service led jointly by Rev R Wallington and Rev Brian Earley in the church, Fancy Dress Competition and Children's Sports, Presentation of Mugs by Mrs Daisy Ley (wife of Parish Council Chairman), and the lighting of a Beacon Bonfire. The occasion was also marked in a number of more permanent ways. As has been mentioned in an earlier section, a play area was purchased for the community and named 'The Jubilee Play Area', a new moveable

Daisy Ley as Queen Elizabeth I

The Fancy Dress Competition, 1977

out-door wooden Skittle alley was made by Jock Mills and Les Knapman, and an 'Embroidered Jubilee Banner' was made by Ethel Huxtable, with the names of everyone in the Parish at that time on it. It has found a permanent home in the Parish Church.

Crowds on the church green, 1977

The Parish Millennium Group was formed, on behalf of the Parish Council, in October 1999 to organise a **Parish Celebration of the Millennium** and a gift for the children of the parish to mark the occasion. The committee consisted of Tricia Shaw, Pat Dowson, Jill Mitchell, Sue Folland, Caroline Catling, Cathy Ley, Julie Bond and Gareth Reid. A lot of hard work resulted in over £1,100 being raised in just seven months. Fundraising events included a photographic exhibition, darts and skittles tournaments, a fun day and a jumble sale. There was also a lot of detective work carried out in finding out how many children under the age of 16 lived in the parish.

Unfortunately our funds would not run to the expense of Millennium mugs for all of the children, so we decided on something a little different. We used the tree from the Langtree School badge and designed a small enamelled pin badge, which we had specially made by Torrington Jewellers. We then set about organising the Parish Millennium Party. Morris Men, Circus Jugglers and a Bouncy Castle were booked and paid for, two marquees were erected in the playing field by several muscular men of the parish, straw bales were kindly loaned by David Ley, and tables and benches from the school. Bunting was put up all around the playing field and the stage was set for the celebrations. The committee had hand-delivered invitations to every household in the Parish to make sure that everyone knew about the party. The party was free to Parishioners, and everyone brought along a plate of food for a bring-and-share tea. The weather was glorious, and the entertainment excellent. Jill Mitchell and Matthew Barnes organised games for the children, including tug-of-war. Helen Mellody presented the Parish Badges in gift pouches to the children.

The committee had decided to mark the Millennium in a more permanent way, and in April 2000 applied to Millennium Awards for All, for a grant to equip the playing field. We were delighted to hear in June 2000 that we had been awarded a grant of £4,459. A few new faces joined the re-named Millennium Playing Field committee, and we said good-bye and thank you to some previous members. David Shaw, Mark Highet, Fritz Takken, Jane Beaumont and Brett Kingston joined us.

We set about tidying up and renovating the playing field, cutting hedges in the pouring rain, removing conifer trees in preparation for the new equipment, removing rubbish that had been dumped in the playing field and removing old equipment, which had been condemned by RoSPA. At the end of March 2001 Victoria Sawmills began installing the new equipment, which consisted of a climbing frame unit, two flat swings and one cradle swing, all with new chains, and two picnic benches. The total cost was £4,513, and the newly prepared playing field was ready in time for the Easter holidays.

During the autumn of 2001 it became difficult for some of the committee to continue, and regrettably the responsibility for the playing field was handed back to the Parish Council, along with the small amount of funds that were remaining.

More families with young children have since moved into the Parish and hopefully are enjoying the facilities that are available to the community. It would be nice if a fresh group could be formed to continue the good work already done and to ensure this valuable Parish facility is available for future generations.

The Queen's Golden Jubilee was marked by a United Service in the Parish church on Sunday morning, then various sporting and entertainment

Ben Copp, Langtree's oldest life-time resident, arrives for the village photograph to celebrate the Queen's Golden Jubilee on Monday 3rd June 2002 (see page 62). Ladies are, left to right, Sandra Juniper, Pam Watson, & Helen Cole

events the following day. These were held in the Jubilee Play area and included a talent show in which a considerable number of children and teenagers took part with some very good 'acts'. A bring-and-share tea followed in the primary school and it was all much enjoyed by those who came, though on a much lower key than previous celebrations had been.

School Camp

School camp was something that Mr Alan Edgcombe introduced into the school calendar and became a highlight of the junior class each year. I know our own children loved it and saw it as a great adventure. There weren't so many opportunities for children to do such things as this in the 1970s as there are now. Camp was held at various places, Wembworthy Centre being the first place that was tried, then Loxhore in North Devon and Slapton Ley in South Devon. Each child was allocated jobs to do and this rotated through the week so every child had a taste of the different tasks.

One or two parents went to help share the responsibility with the teaching staff and to do the cooking, and each child kept a diary of the week's events. I have a copy of the diary kept by Neil Folland for the week June 16th–23rd 1978 at Loxhore. It is interspersed with drawings and sketches of the various 'nature studies' they did (plants, rock formations, and a cat) also postcards that he'd been able to buy, and a written record of what he had to do each day. The children had to help put up the tents and prepare for camp to begin then generally 'muck in' with whatever needed doing.

"Sat 17th June: First full day at camp," the diary reads, "we woke up very early. We had a game of football at 5.00 then, at 6.30 Mr Edgcombe came and played cricket with us. He did not get anyone out, but I did! Thursday 22nd June, I woke up at 6.40. We had an early breakfast. It was raining hard that morning. After breakfast we put our beds tidy, then in a break between the rain we did our jobs. Friday 23rd: When the bus came we started packing. We were 3/4 hr late leaving. When I got home I had fry for dinner. The End."

Summer Daze

For a few years Langtree had its own Pop Festival. It was held at Stapleton Farm and was the brainchild of Alex Duncan who had a music group of his own. It all happened in the early 1990s. Named Summer Daze, it was sponsored by DARF Records. A number of pop groups were taking part, large crowds of young people came, and the event was from 10.30am until midnight. Held at the end of July, there was also a Craft Market, Bouncy Castle, Kids Corner, Jugglers and a bar. Something to keep the people enjoying themselves all through the day.

Cook of the Realm

Langtree was brought well and truly into the National spotlight in 1972 when farmer's wife Gwen Troake of Thatton in this Parish won the final of the BBC Nationwide 'Cook of the Realm' Competition. There had been twelve regional finals, culminating in the championship contest at the BBC studios in Shepherds Bush, London. Not only did Gwen win this but also she became the Nation's favourite cook and appeared in most women's magazines of the day as well as on various TV programmes. She had won two other National contests in 1969, namely 'Cooka Duck' at the Brighton Pavilion, and later in the year, an 'Open Sandwich' competition.

The TV programme 'The Big Time' became popular in 1978, when an amateur was given an opportunity to test their skill in a professional capacity. Gwen was chosen to cook a meal at the Dorchester Hotel in London to celebrate Edward Heath winning a literary prize with his book. Many celebrities were among the six hundred and

Camp Fire. Sing a long with Allan Edgcombe

Gwen Holds the Cup and is accompanied by daughter Theresa and husband Dudley

fifty guests including Lord Mountbatten. The meal was deemed to have been an outstanding success. "Gwen had never had a cookery lesson in her life," said husband Dudley. She learnt from her mother to begin with, and the rest was self-taught as she experimented in her own kitchen for the family and with friends.

In another contest held in London called 'Golden Menu Competition,' Gwen found herself competing against her own daughter, Theresa, who was representing the London area. Gwen came first, with Theresa taking second place, a real family effort. In one of the contests there was a confrontation with Fanny Craddock who was critical of Gwen's chosen dish. When she returned home there were over 1000 letters of support and encouragement for her and the telephone never seemed to stop ringing.

Langtree also has two other media stars. Bernard Hill has been on TV on a number of occasions concerning his work of Fox Calling. Bernard has written about this in his own book so I will not repeat the story. Tim Ley is also working in the media, having been with Lantern Radio as a Disc Jockey for some years. Before that he worked with Tarka Radio at the North Devon District Hospital. He has now moved on to Somerset, still with radio, but we in Langtree can no longer hear his cheery voice each day.

Airship R101

Bryan Ley has an unusual memory that must surely have been rare for this part of the country. He tells us, "Many years ago, about 1930/31 I was at Bibbear when one of my uncles (can't remember which one) came running in excited and said 'come out yer.' I went out with the others and there in the sky was the airship R101 travelling West to East. It had come in from America and was heading for London. Two or three days later it travelled from London to Paris and caught fire on landing. The Airship was destroyed. Only some of the people on board escaped alive."

Transformer

Also from Bryan and Daisy Ley we have a picture of a giant Transformer, which passed through Stibb Cross in 1982. It is believed to have started this part of its journey from Plymouth, though where it had originated from is not known. It was on its way to Alverdiscott. A great deal of planning had to be done before the journey could commence, special road works were carried out at Woodford Bridge and sections of the road were closed to other traffic until it had passed through. Travelling from Anvil Corner through to Holsworthy Beacon, it made its way to Stibb Cross, then took the Bideford road to Frithelstock, and thus on to Torrington and its final destination.

Transformer

Among those watching it pass are Bryan Ley with his young grandson Timothy, and daughter-in-law Cathy. On Bryan's left is Bridget Horn, and is it her then boy-friend (now husband) Colin Larkworthy by her side?

Residents Association

I have found one reference to a residents association at Stibb Cross, time has not permitted me to uncover more facts but I'm sure there are people out there who remember it. I believe it's important to record the fact that it existed.

Maureen Richards has seen records at the Northam records office of Hussars, stationed in Torrington, coming to Langtree and training in the old church hall. The article was in an old Bideford Gazette but she did not record the date. Something for us to look into later perhaps!

Skittles at the Church Fête in the early 1970s

Church Fête

This happens every year on the first Saturday in August. It was always held on the Rectory lawn, and continued for some years after the Rectory was sold, at Terry and Sue's invitation. It then moved to the social club for a few years until that also was sold, and is now held either at Lake Farm by invitation of Colin and Ruth Wood, or in the village play area. We have a number of photos, which perhaps depict the fête better than words can.

Above: Anna Folland in charge of Pony Rides in the 1980s
Below: Busy With The Stalls

Sam & Ella

New Year's Eve.

Some years there is a United Watch-night Service at St Michaels church Shebbear, to which Langtree people are invited.

Celebrated each year at the Green Dragon with fancy dress, then as the clock strikes the midnight hour and a New Year dawns the patrons all go outside and dance around the old beech tree singing 'Auld Lang Syne' One year Sylvia Smith and Rose Issac utilised some costumes from a Langtree Player's event and went to the celebrations as two chickens, Sam, and Ella at the height of the Edwina Curry 'Salmonella in eggs scare', (I'm told on good authority that their husbands refused to own them for the evening - see above). The New Year's Eve Celebration is depicted in the Map on the front of this book

Young people celebrating New Year's Eve at the Green Dragon
Left To Right, Back Row Keith Taylor, Nicola Langmead
Middle Row Jeremy Jollow, Averill Kinsman, Sue Smith,
Martin Soby Front Row, Bob Soby, Sarah Dowson,
Julie Langmead.

Wedding of Laurence Metherall and Madeline Tucker in 1935. Standing, L-R: ? , Bill Metherall, ?, ?, ?, Grace Metherall, Arther Metherall, Bride and Groom, Rev B Hallowes, Noel Knapman, Miss Smith, ? , Miss Smith (2), Jim Adams, ? , ? , ? , Janie Knapman. Seated: Mr & Mrs. Metherall (bridegroom's parents), Mrs. Brown, Mrs. A Tucker & Mrs. J Adams (Bride's mother & sister), ? , Dolly Copp & Leslie Knapman (age 4 years) whose elder brother, Aubrey, was at school

Above: Church Lane Langtree, often called 'Teapot Street'. Note the Clock Face is painted white. The Clock is the Village War Memorial

Below: Zion Methodist Chapel Langtree Previous to 1950, with carbide gas lamps still in place

*Above:
Dick Harris in the late 1960s. At the time he was living at the Union Inn Stibb Cross*

Left: A Women's Institute event in the Church Hall in the early 1950s. L-R: Nancy Hearn (who had just cut her finger) Florrie Adams, Ethel Huxtable, Mrs Scott, Mrs Frank Mills, Janie Langmead and Florrie Moore.

Below: A Rememberance Sunday Parade of the Royal British Legion at Newton St Petrock in the mid 1960s. Rev Wallington of Langtree is in the white gown, and among those in the parade are Charlie Walters, Dick Harris, John Barker, Reg Glover and Stan Mitchell.

Above: Golden Wedding celebration of Mr. & Mrs. Hutchings of Southcott, Langtree, probably in the 1930s or 1940s. Back row, L R ? , Dr O'Flority of Torrington, Mr Noot, ? , ? , Mr E Moore, Miss Hunt, ? . Middle row: Mrs Noot, ? Mr & Mrs Hutchings, ? , ? , Front row: Mary Glover, the rest are unknown except the last one who is Miss M Boundy. Joyce Vanstone's mother, before her marriage, 'lived in' with Mr & Mrs Hutchings for a number of years.

Below: Leslie Knapman receives his long service medal at Barnstaple Civic Centre in 1986 from Chief Constable D Elliot.

Charlie Walters Langtree's longest serving 'Special'. For many years he was a sergeant, and is pictured here in the 1950s

Chapter Twelve

SOCIAL CHANGES

Population of Langtree

1801	Total	583
1850	"	941
1851	"	878
1861	"	839
1878	"	820
1881	"	735
1891	"	672
1901	"	621
1911	"	589
1921	"	543
1931	"	504
1961	"	463
1971	"	451
1981	"	525
1991	"	647
2000	"	654
2001	"	677

Population ages in	1991	& 2001
0-5yrs	38	31
5-9yrs	58	26
10-14yrs	58	45
15-19yrs	41	48
20-24yrs	33	33
25-29yrs	39	24
30-34yrs	49	43
35-39yrs	52	39
40-44yrs	58	53
45-49yrs	55	50
50-54yrs	37	55
55-59yrs	21	59
60-64yrs	29	49
65-69yrs	32	26
70-74yrs	19	22
75-79yrs	20	21
80-84yrs	8	15
85-89yrs	3	6
90-94yrs	2	2
95+ (no individual no. for '91)		0

Number of Households in 1991 was 218
Number of Households in 1998 was 247
Number of Council owned dwellings in the Parish in December 1999 was 6

Old Stibb Cross

Number of house completions was:
1991/2	4	1992/94	0
1994/5	3	1995/6 3	3
1996/8	0	1998/9	2
1999/0	2	2000/01	7

I have no later official figures than these except to say that 46 dwellings are in the process of being erected at Stibb Cross during 2002/2003.

Tenure – Households. Survey dated 1999 but working on earlier years figures
Owner occupied   184
Private Rent   29
Local authority   8
Holiday accommodation   9

Number of chargeable dwellings by Council Tax Band
A   20,   B   41,   C   83,
D   54,   E   35,   F   17,
G   3,   H   0.

Car ownership at September 1997 (most recent figures available)
Households with no car   12
"   "   One car   100
"   "   Two cars   84
"   "   Three cars   25
Total number of cars   343

144

Community buildings closed or sold off

Lord Clinton agreed to 'give, grant, convey. . . the old School. . . to the church' in 1949. It then became known as the Church Hall. Names that were on the official document include Rev Gibby, S G Cole, Ethel E Soby and J H C Bond. It was sold with planning permission to convert to a dwelling in 1998.

Stibb Cross Market closed in the mid sixties.

Siloam Chapel was sold in 1973 and used for storage.

Old Methodist Chapel Langtree sold for housing 1979.

The Rectory was sold for development in 1987.

Stibb Cross Chapel sold for housing 1994.

School Nativity Play in the Church Hall - early 1990s

Housing Development

Local Authority Houses in Langtree Village. First four built in 1948, by Ned Vanstone, other two built in 1953 by Beers of Bideford.

These were followed by two bungalows in Langtree in early 1960s and then later in the 1970s further bungalows at Stibb Cross. I have not been able to ascertain precise dates. More recently in the mid 80s, development of Heathland View Stibb Cross, and now in 2002/2003 the latest development of part of the old Horns site at Stibb Cross has brought many new homes into the Parish. There have been various individual developments over the years, but one of the most important means of housing development in the past twenty years has been barn conversions. Perhaps one of the first conversions would have been Langtree Mill many years ago, but in recent years there have been twenty-nine barns or similar turned into homes, plus some holiday lodges.

Traffic and Roads

It's hard to imagine roads without many of the signs and instructions that we take for granted today, but clearly they have not always been there. Halt signs were introduced in the early 1960s to the Browns Lane junction with the Torrington to Holsworthy road, Sandy Lane Cross coming from Lake Farms, and also where the Stibb Cross Junction met the Holsworthy to Bideford road. The priority of that junction was different then, it was changed to its present state in December 1985. 30mph signs were first requested for the village in March 1963 and fixed some while afterwards. Various road-widening schemes have taken place in the Parish over the years. In July 1962 the top and bottom of the road from Watertown Cross to Stapleton Cross was widened. In February 1964 dangerous corners at Berry Cross were dealt with, and Birchill corner improved in August 1982.

The first request for something to be done about Withacott Corners was made in 1965, the work was eventually completed on that stretch of the Langtree to Stibb Cross road in March 1990, but the worst of the danger was dealt with in the 1970s. There had been a hard-fought battle to get the work done, eventually Hills Bus Drivers threatened to go on strike, giving the authorities two weeks to begin action to remedy the situation or they would not be venturing into Langtree with their buses. Reg Curtis and George Dymond were the spokesmen for the drivers saying that they were 'dead scared' to take their buses along the road. £100,000 had been spent on the very bad corners but still there was a problem with a narrow piece on the hill, lorries and caravans were jack-knifing, causing massive hold-ups. It was not helped by the fact that this road was part of the specially designated 'Holiday Route'. The narrow stretch of road was dealt with shortly after this.

Reasons for absence from school

Apart from sickness and weather conditions there were a number of other reasons why children missed school that seemed to be considered normal for the times.

July 27-28, 1932 Chapel Sunday school outing followed next day by Church Sunday School outing.

Children would leave school early – or maybe miss a day altogether for the Sunday school anniversary at any of the three chapels, (Stibb Cross, Langtree, Siloam), or for church or chapel harvest festivals.

Christmas Markets at Bideford and Torrington in 1939.

In the first year of the school being open, the children were asked on April 20th how many would be going to Torrington Mayfair. 50 out of 66 said they would, so it was set in motion to officially close the school for Mayfair. I believe this has continued for many years but has not been observed for a long time now, though some other schools do still keep to the tradition. Sometimes play breaks were re-arranged so children could leave early for some event and if the hunt was meeting at the Green Dragon, morning break would be changed to coincide with the time of the meet, then the children would be allowed to come out of school and watch.

On June 15th 1938, a batch of artillery vehicles was passing through Stibb Cross at 9.30am. Only 13 children arrived at school – the rest having gone to view the unusual event, no doubt many parents went also.

Summer holidays were much shorter – sometimes only 2 weeks. In 1941 it was from August 15th to September 1st and in 1943 from 29th July to 16th August. V.E Day, Princess Elizabeth's wedding, Prince Charles' Birth and the King and Queen's Silver Jubilee were all occasions for a day off school.

July 1945 brings the first reference to 6 weeks summer holiday beginning on 26th July – September 9th The previous year, 1944 had been 4weeks August 3rd – September 4th.

School daily opening times were not always as they are now. In August 1943, school ran from 9.50-12.50, then 1.50pm-4.20pm.

School Health

Throughout the 1930s and 40s, there was a great deal of sickness. The word epidemic was often being used. Illnesses included Scarlet fever, Impetigo, Mumps, Whooping Cough, Ringworm, Measles (60% absent in one bout in 1949) Diphtheria and Influenza. In 1941 immunisation for Diphtheria began, there having been a number of cases, including adults (my future mother-in-law was one of them, having 2 sons at school where possible contacts were made.).

Some children were off school for months at a time through illness, with a Doctor's certificate, because it was considered they were better off at home, or simply not well enough to be in school.

There were regular visits from the school nurse who checked the children's hair for head lice, and the school doctor also came, and school dentists were there all day. In the 1930s children with suspected sight problems were sent to Torrington Bluecoat School to be examined at the eye clinic. Head teachers sent notice to parents that this was happening (it seemed to be the schools decision, backed up by the parents permission.) Later on, eye tests were carried out at Langtree.

By 1986 the situation was very different. With the coming of the Health Service many years before, the school now had less responsibility for this aspect of the children's welfare and their role

New school entrance to safeguard the children when arriving and leaving school

was a preventative one. They had someone to come and talk about drug misuse and educate about its dangers. There was a video for girls on "growing up" and a talk about "stranger danger".

Free milk was supplied to the school for those who wanted it over the years, and in 1955 an experiment with milk tablets was put in place but didn't last long. (I distinctly remember banana flavoured milk tablets.)

September 1990, an educational psychologist visits the school and extra help has become available for children with special needs – physical or educational

In the late 1800s there was a very serious outbreak of Diphtheria in Langtree and a number of people died. They are buried in the village churchyard. Immediately by the steps you will find the graves of four of the Furse family who died within days of each other over the Christmas and New Year period. A few yards along are the graves of the Holman family, including the only son of Elias Holman of Langtree Week, bringing to an end the family name in the agricultural implement industry.

Wells in the Parish

Before mains water came to Langtree and other rural areas, people were dependent on wells. Farms and cottages away from villages had their own. Sometimes in the village, a number of cottages shared a well. There were known to be wells in various places in Langtree Village. There was one at the school in the "veg garden" area. It was 26ft deep and used regularly until 3rd June 1956 when it was realised there was only 3ft of water left in it. On 7th June that year, Torrington Fire Brigade carried 2000 gallons of water from Watertown to the school. A tank was filled and the rest put in the well. By July 9th the well was again considerably decreased and it was suggested a

Village Well preserved for the future

tank (maybe a larger one) was placed outside the fence in Mrs Squires' field, North Park. This must have seen them through the week or so to the summer holidays with the hope that autumn rains may improve the situation. In November 1956, mains water was connected to the school and the well was later filled in with stones.

Ethel Huxtable remembers there were wells in various places in the village, and sometimes tensions developed over them. There was one at the far end of the Crescent area and another near the top of Church Lane – opposite Twosome Cottage. There were two along the row of houses at the Stibb end of the village and one in the driveway to the recently built bungalows off Church Lane. This area was known as Willypath, it has also been called Lennies Lane. Stories are told of the day when the circus came to Langtree, and pitched tent at North Park field, then the elephants walked down the village streets to this well where water would have been drawn up with buckets and rope to enable the elephants to drink. I'm sure many gallons were needed and maybe the elephants squirted some of it over the hard-working water gatherers as they playfully refreshed themselves. The place of this well has been marked for future generations by Terry Fallon who has built an ornamental well structure above it.

There was also a village pump in Fore Street. Alma Carter (née Daniel) remembers the day when problems arose over the pump and no one could get water from it. (See her memories in the final section) There may well be other wells; these are just the ones I've been told about. Stibb Cross would also have had its fair share of wells. Bernard Hill remembers there was one at Hills Garage. He remembers they found an old container with stuff in, no one knew what it was, but thought it might be carbide - so they chucked it down the well for safety. It exploded with a loud bang, which he heard whilst working at Southcott. This often used to happen, rubbish thrown down old disused wells, no one was aware of environmental dangers then.

Standpipes

Having all become used to mains water and very dependent on it, in 1976, we began to get a taste of what it might have been like before that service came to our villages. Of course when people were dependent on the wells it was a way of life and they were well prepared for coping with it. When the drought came, and the standpipes with it, we were not prepared for such a way of life. Two people who lived in the Crescent, Langtree tell us what it was like for them. Ethel Huxtable tells us that at first the standpipe for the Crescent was outside Mr Medland's house, across from the old Chapel, then after a while an extra one was placed between the two end houses in their close, just outside, and between the homes of Mr and Mrs Northam, and Mrs Box and family. This was because of the age of three of these people; it was not thought reasonable for them to have to fetch water from further away. Of course every-one in the Crescent benefited from this new arrangement. Pat Dawson also fetched water from the same standpipe. She says "At first it was a novelty, but after carrying many, many buckets and bowls of water the novelty soon wore off. I don't think any of us realised how much water we used or how much we had taken it for granted".

Stibb Cross from 1930 to the 1950s, as remembered by David Hill, lifetime resident in Langtree Parish.

David has built a scale model of Stibb Cross as it was in his younger days. With the model he has written a record of all the people who once lived in the houses that he has re-created, and that record is printed here. David worked in the family firm of Hills Buses all his life and was a driver for them from the time he was able to hold a licence to do so, until his retirement. David knew all these people and has very fond memories of them, in fact quite a number are his relatives.

"**No 1.** Occupants 1930, Mr & Mrs Arthur Horn, their son Peter and Mr Horn's brother Wilfred. 1950, Mr Arthur Horn, his second wife Ethel, son Peter and Mr Wilfred Horn. The first Mrs Horn, Emma, died in 1933. Mr Horn later married Nurse Quick, the district Midwife. She delivered many babies in the parish during the late 1920s and early 1930s (including myself). We were told she always delivered her babies in a large leather bag,

Hill's Garage in earlier years

which she strapped to the carrier of her bicycle. The Horn family moved to Stibb Cross in the late 19th Century.

No 2. Occupants 1930, Mr Albert Hill (grandfather) Mr & Mrs Frank Hill, their son David and Mr Kenneth Hill. 1950, Mr Albert Hill, David Hill, Reg Curtice his wife Sylvia and their daughter Pat. The Hill – Sanders family moved to Stibb Cross in 1868.

No 3. 1950, Mr Kenneth Hill and his wife Laura.
No 4. 1930, Mr & Mrs Charles Hill, their son Norman, and daughters Mary, Margaritte and Ethel. 1950, Mr & Mrs C Hill and lodger Walter Harris.
No 5. 1930, Mr Mitchell and his housekeeper. 1950, not sure, probably the Baron family.
No 6. 1930, Mr & Mrs Jim Fowler and son Clifford. 1950, Clifford Fowler. The Fowlers were a Newton St Petrock family.
No 7. 1930, Mr Bill Fishleigh and his wife Lucy. 1950, Mrs Trusdale, a widow, she drove a 1934 Wolsley Hornet car.
No 8. 1930, Mr & Mrs John Stoneman. Mr Stoneman was a farmer and his wife Nellie kept the shop. 1950, Mr & Mrs Scott. The Scotts with their daughter Eileen were Bakers; they moved from Langtree to Stibb Cross in 1939 and built a modern bakery. Their vans covered a large area delivering bread and confectioneries.
No 9. 1930 Mr & Mrs Sam Beal. 1950, Mr & Mrs Jollow and their son Walter.
No 10. 1930, I think it was Mr & Mrs Bill Johns. 1950, Mr & Mrs Sam Beal and son Ken.
No11. 1930, Mr & Mrs Frank Blight, son Arthur and daughter Ida. 1950, no change. The Blight family had been Blacksmiths in the village for many years
No 12. 1930, Mr & Mrs Jenkins, son George and daughter Mabel. 1950, Mr Richard Harris wife Vera and daughter Maureen.

During the 1930s, 40s, 50s and 60s Monday was Market Day at Stibb Cross. Farm animals were bought and sold in the market area, which was roughly between the chapel and the pub. Cows, steers and sheep were driven along the roads to the village, one person at the back and two or three in the front, to prevent the animals from straying in the wrong direction.

Cars were parked at the rear of Hills Garage; a charge of 6d was made for the privilege. One of the Torrington banks hired a room from Mrs C Hill for the day and another bank a room from Mrs F Blight. Farmers were able to pay into, or draw money from them.

Stibb Cross has for many years provided employment for a number of people, in 1950 Horn's, Hill's, and Scott's Bakery employed in the region of 20 persons. Most of them lived in the village or close by, they either walked or cycled to work. The market provided some part-time work, auctioneers, drovers, cleaners etc."

Hill's Buses today, with present owner Mr Hearn, and David Hill nephew of the founder, a driver with Hills until retirement

David Hill with his scale model of old Stibb Cross. When displayed the model takes up a space 16 feet by 4 feet

Langtree from 1935–1946, as remembered by Bernard Hill

"I lived in the village for over fifty years and there were many good people living there, but very little was available for the children's recreation – not even the playing field, so we had to play in many different fields and sometimes on the roads, when we got into trouble.

I was born in 1931 at Stibb Cross but moved to Langtree the following year and I was lucky to be born with a wonderful memory, so now I am going to tell of many of the old people and some of the old characters of Stibb Cross and Langtree.

The first of them was a little dapper man by the name of Charlie Blight who lived in a little old wooden hut with his wife just two hundred yards from Stibb Cross on the Holsworthy road. His gift as a stone hedger was widely known and he did lots of jobs for the council and local people as well. When working for the council he was paid monthly and his pay day was a time for a booze up at the local. When arriving home drunk one night the wife refused to let him in, so his reply was 'I'm on the right side of the ruddy door with all the money and the pub to go to.'

The next dwelling was a farm owned by Will Fishleigh and his sisters, and there are two things I remember here: Riding on their donkey, and the noise made by the Glennies. (A kind of poultry)

The Bible Christian Chapel was very near to the market place and one of its greatest supporters was an Uncle of mine, the late Nath Gilbert of Binworthy Farm, who was also a local preacher. He once told me that he made up his sermon for the next Sunday when working on the tractor. He also had one of the first motorbikes in the area and I have heard my dear old mother talk about her bumpy ride on the back. I think this one would have had solid rubber tyres.

Stibb Cross Market was supported by farmers from a wide area and during the war years it was one of the busiest in North Devon. It also brought great trade to the Union Inn nearby which in those days was owned by the Jenkins family. Just opposite the inn was the blacksmith's shop, where Mr. Blight shod local horses and made iron implements for farmers. He lived with his wife, daughter Ida and son Arthur, who was a rabbit trapper during the winter months. One of his proudest possessions was his H.R.D. Motorcycle. There were two farm cottages next before we came to the shop owned by Mr. and Mrs. Jack Stoneman, who were a lovely couple and whilst his wife ran the shop, Jack had his little bit of farming whilst my father trapped his rabbits. There were two cottages that backed on to the market. One was

Hills charabanc sets off on a trip

owned by Grandfather Bill Adams who worked on local farms. He was a good craftsman and when retired he worked at the market doing the cleaning up. In the next cottage lived the Sanders family who made clothes pegs and other things to sell locally. Mr & Mrs Stoneman sold the shop to Mr & Mrs Scott who had begun a bakery shop in the parish; this was now moved to Stibb Cross.

Continuing up through Stibb Cross my aunt Lucy Fishleigh, who was a schoolteacher at Thornhillhead and later at Langtree as well, lived in the house with the monkey-puzzle tree at the back. In the next house lived Jim Fowler and his son Clifford who worked for Hills Services most of his life.

My Uncle, Mr. Charles Hill, lived in the house next to the garage where they brought up their family of four and Norman the son, worked at the adjoining Hills Garage for a while, after leaving the forces. Hills Services and Garage served the area well for many years with taxis, buses and garage repairs, where my brother worked all his life until retirement.

Just across the road was the Corn Mill Merchants, Horn Bros. who had a milking herd and a large number of poultry and pigs, so Stibb Cross had four important things, a cattle market, Hills Services, Hills Carpenters Shop and Horn Bros.

Leaving Stibb Cross we now come to Withacott where the two farms, Higher and Lower were farmed by the Leys and the Beers. The Beers also farmed some of Muffworthy where I spent many hours picking up potatoes as a boy. Father Tom Beer suffered arthritis for as long as I can remember and the sons, Philip and John, were hard workers and good farmers, whilst their sister Elizabeth did the milk round.

The Ley family home was Bibbear Farm where Grandfather Ley lived and farmed with his son

Part of the Ley Family. Grandfather Charles holds baby Edward, with dad Henry on the left And Uncle Percy to the right

Percy. Another son, Henry lived at Cholash, and a third son, Stanley lived at Withacott. The Leys were great Chapel supporters and also helped with the Parish Council.

At Withacott crossroads a large garage was built by the Adams family. Fred, the youngest son, had a lorry and did some haulage, and also delivered coal. When the war came Fred had to join up and the 'War Agg' took over the garage as a repair shop. It was also a machine store where machines were hired out to farmers to help with the harvesting etc.

On towards Langtree we come to a house that was once a Baptist Chapel and still goes by that name. It had once belonged to my uncle Kenneth Hill. Now on to the Frost Cottages where our shoe maker, Mr. Denford lived, and we used to call him "Bid Bid Denford" because this was the sound his motorbike and sidecar made because he drove it so slowly.

In the adjoining cottage lived a grand old couple, Mr. and Mrs. Fred Mitchell, friends of my mother, who farmed just a few acres and he was an excellent maker of wooden mouns (a kind of basket) for potato picking and for carrying meal and roots when feeding bullocks. I always remember the little Dartmoor Pony and Trap that he used.

Next we come to Doggaport Farm, where old Mr. Netherway lived with his daughter who married Bill May. He now did the farming. Mr & Mrs May had two daughters, Joyce and Doreen, and all the family came to the village chapel. Father and I caught his rabbits and also helped with their harvesting and corn threshing. Doggaport was then two farms, Father Latham and his son farmed Lower Doggaport, that was not a very big farm.

Now into the village. In the first row of cottages lived the Badge family, Mr. and Mrs. Folland, then Mr. and Mrs. Fred Ford, who worked on the council and was also a good bell ringer. Next came Mr. and Mrs. Bert Ayre, who was a smallholder with just a few cows. He was another rabbit trapper. He followed a local football team at Shebbear. In the next cottage lived another real old character, Bill Sutton, where he and his wife reared a family of seven children. Bill was a hard working-man, another rabbit trapper, he also worked at the Clay Mine at Petersmarland. He was an expert gardener and won many prizes at local horticultural shows. One of his sons, Jack, owned a threshing machine and did most of the threshing on farms for miles around. Unfortunately Jack passed away about eighteen months ago (April 2002).

Just across the road, in a big house, lived Butcher Nichols, who served the village for many years. He also was a farmer whose rabbits father and I caught. Further along the road, lived the Sanders, then the Walters family who had a small farm with a milking herd and the father, Charlie, was our local postman for many years, he also was a bell ringer.

Thomas & Nora Nichols with daughters Edith, Ethel, Alice and Emily, and sons Hedley on Mum's lap, who died at two years old, Arthur, Tom, and Oliver standing by his Dad

Coming now into the village where the Cox family lived. Dudley, the son played in our football team. Fred Cox was a good and tidy farm worker and Dudley worked at Stapleton Farm, for the Bond family, for many years.

In the next cottages lived the Daniel family of five, and the Scott family, who had the bakery there right through the war days. Across the road was the home and blacksmiths shop belonging to the Gerry family who had about eight children, one of which, John, along with this brother-in-law, Sam Hinks, played football at Shebbear. They were both good players. Another brother, Reg, kept the shop in the village during the war days when almost everything was rationed.

We (the Hill family) lived up at Latch Lane for many years, until father retired to a cottage down in the village. Father was a rabbit trapper, something that I also loved doing, and for years we worked hard for the local farmers and for our living.

In the village there were more Vanstones than any other family and the old people lived at Judd's Farm at the bottom of Latch Lane. One of the sons, Ned, followed his father's profession to be a builder, carpenter and undertaker and I worked for him for a few years where I learned much about the trade. I also dug graves for many years.

Ned Vanstone was one of the most respected men in the village, and was always on call when trouble or tragedy came. He was also a keen supporter of our football team and one of his relations, the late Arthur Stevens, also played with us when we won the Holman Cup at Lynton in 1952. He was also a good bell ringer.

The sale of Ned Vanstone's Estate

In the next cottage lived another old character 'Cockney' George Daniel, and his wife, who was a huge lady. Mr. Daniel was in the First World War and I do not think he had a constant job afterwards, but he did a lot of cycle repairs which were very helpful to the villagers. He also helped a few with their harvesting and threshing. Mrs. Daniel brought up her grandson, who was called Roy. During the war days we boys used to play at soldiers with our camps built down in 'Bonds Break' that adjoined our fields. We used to pass away hours down there with our camp fire having tins of soup and boiled potatoes, but unfortunately they used to taste a little smokey.

In the centre of the village, at the crossroads, was the meeting place for all we children, right outside Mr. and Mrs. Hutchings' house. We would often stay talking and making noise until after dark and sometime disturbing their sleep. Then we would get a jug of water thrown down on to us out of the bedroom window.

Wedding Of Audrey Daniel & Les Prouse.
This scene shows how different this corner used to be

The Methodist Sunday School was across the road, where we had our Sunday school, also socials, parties etc. Right on the corner was a shop owned by Mr. and Mrs. Alf Burrows and after they died, Mr. and Mrs. Reg Baker lived there with a son Derek who was one of 'us boys'. As years went on this house was demolished to give space for lorries and buses to get round the corner. (See photos above and overleaf for how the corner used to look.) The Mills family lived next door, I think that there was a family of five, and two sons, the late 'Tinky' and Gerald, were great friends of ours both in childhood and adult lives, working together and sharing many sporting and recreation things in the village. Across the road lived Mr. and Mrs. Douglas Brock. He worked for Hills Services after being demobbed from the services. Their son, Roger, worked for John Coles, Contractors, for many years. He was a good and tidy workman doing a lot of tractor work.

Next to this was the Methodist Chapel, which we attended. The village shop and post office were the next buildings that were run by Reg Gerry and Reg Jones. At one time the post office was a separate business, run by Reg and Mrs. Jones, but later he had the shop as well. Mrs. Jones was a Miss Down before she was married and was one of my first teachers along with Miss Major and Miss Bow. I had the pleasure of meeting Miss Bow recently after over sixty years. Mr. Westcott was the headmaster and was a good but very strict teacher and there was not many who left his class without feeling his cane across their backside.

On the other side of the road Ned Vanstone built his bungalow about the beginning of the war, where he ran his business for many years doing lots of building in Langtree and in other villages as well.

The Green Dragon Inn was run by Mr. and Mrs. Dick Vanstone and she was a bit of a 'dragon' to we children. If we played or made a noise around

View of the corner and Teapot Street, Mr George Heath has managed to find out the names of some of the people. In the first doorway Mrs Davey and Charlie Davey who were shoemakers, then Jack Davey with James Matin. Further on are Annie Sussex and Annie Vanstone.

her house or the tree beside it, she would soon appear with her whip. Adjoining the pub was a house where Sid Gerry and family lived. His son, Sid was one of our footballers, he died recently, about two years ago.

Before the war Mr. Hallowes, was the parson at the Church and when he died, a Welshman, Mr. Gibby, took over. The men's club was near the church and a good thing for the village to have.

Down the bottom of the village lived Joe Ellis and his son-in-law Horace Furse, who worked at his brother's farm at Burstone; he also was a good skittler and member of the men's club. Old John Vanstone and his son-in-law, Edric Moore, farmed Wedlands. Edric was a grand chap, a likeable character of the village [see page 184].

We come now to Church Lane or Teapot Street as it was called and I believe it got its name because if strangers were walking by, one or two residents would come outside and empty their teapot in the drain just to see who the visitors were – just being nosy. The two cottages by the Church were occupied by Reg Madge who was also a good ringer and he worked for the Clinton Estate, before he unfortunately got killed at Buda Double Corners by a milk lorry. Two old sisters lived next, Pol Sanders and Dobby Oaman, who we used to tease quite a bit. Ned Vanstone's carpenters shop was at the top of the lane where he also stored lime for white washing houses and cowsheds as well. Then came the Box family, father Barney was the local chimney sweep and he also dug graves. How he used to manage it with a wooden leg was a marvel – and he rode his bicycle as well! They had eight children and some still live in the village.

Old Mr. and Mrs. Heal and their daughter Florrie lived next. Mr. Heal was always called Neighbour Heal, and he, like many people, had a field, where he kept a cow and just a few sheep. Bill Waldren lived next door with his wife and son Fred, and I always remember when we were shooting rooks at the rookery, Mrs Waldren would have some to make 'rookie' pie. One of the Vanstone family, Tom and his family, lived next with Michael, who grew up with us. Tom worked on the roads. Across the road lived Ned Johns and family, they had two children, Bill and Edna. They had nicknames of 'Dippy and Dobby' names that they carried all their lives. Ned was a grand chap and he worked for his relation, as a mason, labouring with Vanstone Builders. The last house in the village was owned by Ronald Stoneman, and his wife with their children Vera and Tim. Ronald was in the war and was a prisoner of war until the end of the war. I can remember taking him down a lovely glass of cream as a welcome home present from our family. Tim was a great pal of mine and we were a pair of mischievous devils together.

There were many farming families living around the village that I must mention, starting with the Moores of Southcott, and then there was Studley Squires, also of Southcott, who was known widely for growing flatpole cabbage plants that were tilled and fed to cattle. Thousands of these were sold at local markets. The Bond family lived at West Wooda where old Joe Bond had a stallion for many years; also he broke in colts and was a good horseman. His sons Joe and Eric farmed locally until retirement.

Birchill was farmed by Jim Huxtable and sons until they gave up and sold to Mr. Ley. Higher Collacott was farmed by Bill Wilton who was also a keen skittler at the men's club.

Lower Collacott was the home of the Knapman family. Unfortunately father had a bad leg and walked with a stick. The two boys, Aubrey and Leslie were good workers and managed the farm. The farm was later sold to the Folland family who

Picture taken from Wedland's yard, believed to be Rachel Hallowes and Dick Adams

Stanley & Gladys Mitchell, who lived in Church Cottage, Teapot Street

still farm it today. Farmer John and his wife were great helpers with the Church, School, men's club, and the WI, also father loved his hunting.

One of the Adams family farmed at Lake and one of his loves was his steam engine that he used at his quarry for stone crackin'.

Watertown Farm was owned by old farmer Jones who was one of the leaders at the Church and also the men's club owned Watertown Farm. Mr. Fred Dymond lived at Beara Cottage and worked at Watertown. His son George was one of the areas best footballers. He worked for Hill's Services most of his life. Another of the Dymond family, Jim lived at Buda where he farmed for several years. Burstone farm was the home of the Furse family who were good followers of the local chapel and father caught their rabbits for years.

Chapples was the home of the Mills family where father Fred once worked for the Council. There were eight children, five boys and three daughters, who all came to Langtree Chapel.

Bill 'Dippy' Johns (Taken from a Video Still)

There are still some of the family alive today and one of the grandsons farms Chapples at this present time.

We now come to what the villagers used to call 'the higher end of the Parish' where the farmers were the Sobys at Badslake and Berry, the Coles at Week, the next were the Copps, the Faceys at Thorne, the Balkwills at Lambert, the Troaks at Thaddon and the Brooks at Suddon, followed by the Fishleighs and the adjoining farm Rivaton farmed by Grenville Bond and his father. Most of the Berry Cross and Langtree Week people were supporters of the Parish Church. Near Berry Cross is Siloam Chapel that was closed down many years ago.

Jimmy Adams with wife and daughter Ruth, with his steam engine

Now we come to East Browns Farm that was farmed by the Brooks family for many years. During the war days we spent hours at their lake fishing and boating. Many lovely memories. The last little farm to talk about is Putshole where George Hearn and his father farmed. They had an engine, for grinding corn and for electric light, and when we in the village could hear the sound of it playing it was a sure sign of rain. (There are more of Bernard's memories in the end section and the war/evacuees section).

Changes at Berry Cross over the past 150 years

The following is a small part of a history project on Berry Cross researched by Paula Fuller in the early 1990s.

"Berry Cross is situated on high ground, many of the fields are sloping away. A stone post between the crossroads and the chapel still remains as the highest point. From the earliest map available all the fields were enclosed, some smaller than they are today. Smaller fields were more common in the 1800s. Today the dividing hedgerows have largely been removed to allow the large farm machinery. The fields have changed ownership through the years, with large farms in a position to buy land off smaller dispersing farms.

Stowford Moor was taken over by the war office in the Second World War, and tilled with potatoes. This was done by the German prisoners-of-war, and then re-grassed after the war as it is today. Berry Cross is a small hamlet today. It consists of nine houses, two of which (the bungalows), have been built recently, within the past seven years.

The 1841 census shows that there were twenty-two families living in Berry Cross and on the surrounding farms. There were 57 children under sixteen, today there is just a fraction of this number, 13. Family sizes have been decreasing gradually over the years. Today the average family size two or three children, but in the nineteenth century it was not uncommon to have five or more children. Many offspring stayed with their parents to an older age as the 1841 census shows 42 single males in this area and 26 females. It is interesting that the male figure is somewhat higher to that of the females. Often young men were doing an apprenticeship and were not in a position to marry, or in this area the females were not of an age to wed. People married locally from the surrounding farms and neighbouring villages. Peters Marland, Shebbear, Langtree, Merton, Frithelstock are listed as parishes, which women came from.

By 1881 the number of unmarried people had changed, with more single women than men. Men were going further afield to work after apprenticeships had finished and young men sought work in a prospering town. It was not uncommon to have generations of families living under one roof. Grandfathers, Mothers, Sons and Daughters, and their children all shared the small accommodation. This was common on farms when a father retired and his son and family were now running the farm. The father was still living within the family unit with the son now becoming the head of the house. This has continued through the generations. Family life was important, a way of surviving and they didn't go out much or travel far.

Often children lived with their Grandparents. An unmarried daughter with an illegitimate child would stay within the family getting support from them. A male child born in the 1800s may well have been called John, William, Thomas, James or Frederick, as these were all popular boys name, as they still are today. For a girl, Elizabeth, Eliza or Anne was all equally popular.

Often there was not much between the children's ages and the woman quite often had a child when she was into her forties. The mortality rate

The three photographs in this column, although not taken at Berry Cross, represent the kind of farming that would have gone on in the latter part of the period Paula writes about.
Above: Howard Balsdon's father and helpers gather in the hay
Below: Colin Nicholls and family harvest the corn
Bottom: The Ley's of Withacott with horse and cart

in infants was quite high in the 1800s. This may explain the need to have so many children so close together. With cholera and similar diseases caused by drinking polluted water, many children especially, died from this in the nineteenth century.

Society could be thought of as having three classes; farm workers and general labourers; craftsmen and tradesmen; farmers and squires. In the 1800s the rural hamlet of Berry Cross was made up of all three classes of people. The main industry for this area was, of course, farming. The farms in this area varied in size from 60 acres to 160 acres, employing two or more farm labourers. The chief crops grown were barley, oats, and wheat with the soil being loamy, and the sub soil full of clay.

These farms gave work and homes for the local people. An agricultural labourer often lived-in on the farm, especially if single. A married labourer was often supplied accommodation in a separate dwelling nearer to the farm, for their family's use. These labourers moved around to wherever work was available. I noted many changes in the tenancy of the tied cottages in Berry Cross. There were both male and female farm servants some as young as twelve years old. Agriculture undoubtedly suffered through some of these changes. With modern machinery and improvements in farming methods, the agriculture labourer's work was becoming less. Today none of the cottages are tenanted by labourers.

The rest of the male population who lived in Berry Cross shared various occupations: a tailor, 1870–1910; a shoemaker, 1857–1910 (two generations); a shopkeeper, 1914–1939 (this was situated in one of the cottage's front rooms); a carpenter, 1893; and a thatcher, 1914–1939. These people were very much a part of the community. Carpenters were always kept in work doing their normal jobs such as table making, gate construction plus of course, the coffin making!

The trades were passed on through the generations with their children or local children by apprenticeships learning the trade. Unfortunately these trades are dying out and we certainly don't have many of these alive today in Berry Cross. The local Blacksmith was always busy as horses were the only power available then. A farm of any great size would have had three or more horses and one best horse, which were used for riding to market or hunting.

The women of this community were employed as servants as stated earlier; this would be as dairymaids or domestics. The majority of the females in Berry Cross the ages varying from ten to fifteen to fifty-eight and sixty, were employed as glovers in the gloving trade run by Stoneman &

Berry Cross in the early 1990s

Wills, the glove manufacturers in Torrington. This gloving would be in the form of out-work. Cutouts were to be sewn by hand as very few machines were then available, then returned weekly by the ladies where upon they were able to collect their earnings, which were around 5s for a weeks work.

A young woman by the name of Mary Richards (referred to elsewhere) was a Glover living in the area in 1800s. her week's earnings of just 4s.7 1/2d. There are no Glovers in the area today, the factory is closed.

There are no shops in Berry Cross today either.

In 1851, there were 15 houses at Berry Cross including 4 on Stowford Moor, of which one remains. The tithe map shows these cottages, and others which have also disappeared. Obviously the cottages today have been much improved and modernised, but from outside look much the same. It is strange to think that such large families lived in these same cottages well over 150 years ago. How overcrowded they must have been by today's standards.

Land Sale

Ground formerly owned by Clinton Estate and sold off in 1958

Acres	Farm	Tenant
50	Gortlage	Mr P Gordon
145	Birchill	Mr A.W. Ley
7	Emmys (Hammas)	Mr J E. Sutton
176	Lower Doggaport	DCC
	Buda and Chapels	DCC
40	Smallridge Down	Mr C. J. Huxtable
53	West Wooda	Mr J & J.C.Bond
16	Accommodation Fields	Mr A.J.May
2	Arable Field	Mr G Daniel
10	Doggaport Brake	Mr M Harris
176	Watertown	Mr W J Balsdon
102	Burstone	Mr W L Furse
11	Bitterstone Fields	Mr H J Dale
11	Newbuildings	Mr S G Furse

228	Suddon	Mr C Fishliegh
105	Thatton	Mr D S Troake
186	Lambert	Mr A Balkwill
40	Thorns Farm	Mr W L Facy
149	Stowford	Mr T W Goss
217	Langtree Week	Mr N Cole
14	Earlswood smallholding	Vacant

D Cott	Langtree Week	Mr W Gent
D Cott	Sandy Lane Cross	Mr W H Walsh
Parnacott Cotts		known as Parracott Cotts
Plot Berry Cross		Mr W J Lucas
S D Cottage Berry Cross		Mr C Bale
Green Dragon Inn		Wickham & Co
Green Dragon Cottage S.D		Mr R Vanstone
22 Fore St.	D Cott	Mr S Vanstone
23 Fore St.	D Cott	Mr F Sanders
24 Fore St	Terrace	Miss R Luxton
25 Fore St	Terrace	Mrs Kellaway
26 Fore St	Terrace	Mr W Sutton
29 Fore St	Terrace	Mr F Ford
30 Fore St	Terrace	Mr K Brock
32 Fore St	Terrace	Mr M J Badge
Church Cottage		Miss L Bond
Pound, Workshops, Sites 8.5a		Mr E C Vanstone
Rose Villa S.D. Thatched		Vacant
Hockridge Cottage S.D Thatch		
Watertown cottage		Mrs J Luxton
Forches Cottage		Vacant
Cottage at Buda		Vacant

Allotment Fields as follows,
2 Fields at Berry Cross	4.5 Acre
1 Field Moor Lane	3.75 Acres
1 Field below Doggaport Farm	2 Acres
3 Fields North of Rose Farm	7.5 Acres
1 Field, brow Wooda Hill, Southcott Lane	1.6 Acres
1 Field at Southcott cross	4.8 Acres

Tenant for these fields Langtree Parish Council
At Gortlage Farmbuildings-Priestacott Corn Mill
Mill Leat running from near Gortlage house to Mill.

Grenville Bond on the right at Collacott Farm with his father (centre) and father-in-law

Farming

The hours were long, the commitment total and the work hard, but the satisfaction of working close to nature and being your own boss were great, and a wonderful environment for family life. Farming has long been described as a 'way of life 'where the whole family were involved together in caring for the stock and planting, tending and harvesting the produce of the soil. It was sometimes a battle against the elements, yet always also a working with the elements, through the changing seasons, and on a day-to-day basis. For centuries things remained much as they had always been, though there would have been minor changes taking place. At the end of the 19th century changes began to increase, then in the 20th century speeded up considerably with increased mechanisation. With the coming of Supermarkets, the Common Market, and the Common Agricultural Policy the farming way of life the people had known for generations began to disappear.

Langtree in the early 1900s

Grass silaging at Bryan and David Ley's Farm

Chris Ley, as one of the decreasing number of younger generation farmers, tells us something of how it is now.

"Throughout the generations agriculture has played an important role in the life of the parish and has faced many challenges and changes over the years. This process accelerated dramatically towards the end of the twentieth century with agriculture, like many other industries and professions having to take a responsible approach to the environment as well as becoming increasingly burdened with new rules and regulations".

David Fishleigh combining corn

1st April 1984 saw one of the first big changes with the introduction of Milk Quotas. Initially dairy farmers faced no other option but to cut milk production or face large fines. After some time quota became easier to trade, so as some farmers gave up milk production others could increase. In the mid 1980s South West Water began a campaign to clean up the River Torridge with most livestock farmers in the parish having to install dirty water systems of some form or another. In 1993 the Integrated Administration and Control System or IACS was introduced which meant nearly every farmer had to obtain detailed maps and grid reference numbers for every field they farmed in order to get any subsidies. These changes also saw the introduction of arable set-aside and limits on stock numbers per hectare in order to claim livestock subsidies. Dairy farmers faced turmoil again in 1994 when the Milk Marketing Board was abolished, the milk selling system deregulated and

Harvesting maize for Geoff Folland

farmers beginning a roller coaster ride of profitability. The spring and summer of 1996 was one of the hardest hitting times for cattle farmers when it became largely accepted that BSE could be passed to humans. All meat from cattle over 30 months old was banned from the food chain and every newborn calf had to be registered and given its own individual passport. This system changed again in 1998 when double ear tags and new 'improved' passports were introduced. Traceability and farm assurance soon became a familiar, although somewhat despised, part of agriculture. The start of the twenty first century was not any less challenging with the foot and mouth outbreak of 2001 and in 2003 the governments of the European Union have agreed to implement a complete overhaul of the Common Agriculture Policy. The change and uncertainty goes on.

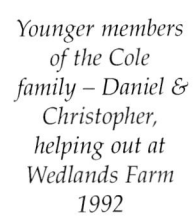

Younger members of the Cole family – Daniel & Christopher, helping out at Wedlands Farm 1992

Chapter Thirteen

BUSINESS AND EMPLOYMENT

From being a mainly agricultural Community in the long distant past Langtree now has many different kinds of business. Many of these were listed in the first part of the book in appendix 5.

I am not going to try to cover all the things that now exist in the Parish, I don't have the means to do it, but what I have tried to do is bring you the stories of some of the long established, or unusual businesses that have flourished here, or been more recently established.

Scott's Bakery

Tony Glover tells us of its how his grandparents started Langtree's very own bakery. "Granfer Scott came from County Down in Ireland; we don't know why they decided to move. Gran was a Miss Issac from Black Torrington, and they met at Newton St. Petrock. Granfer cherished an ambition to start his own Bakery.

At first he worked for Giffords at Hartland, a famous Bakery in that day. Then he worked for Hockin and Greenslade at Shebbear, where Frank Buse learned his trade. In approx 1934 he left them and started up his own business at Langtree. Mr and Mrs Scott rented/leased rooms at the end part of Thorne house. There wasn't a lot of space but they had a bakery at the back part with a shop in front, and from there they proceeded to supply the people of Langtree with bread, cakes, pasties etc. Not only did they sell from the shop, but daughter Eileen, their only child, delivered around the village in a specially made Cart. She used this cart for six years. As work increased they took on a baker at Thorne house.

During the war (exact date not known) they moved the business to Stibb Cross. The shop and premises there were much bigger. From there they eventually operated 4 delivery vans. As soon as daughter Eileen was old enough to drive she used the first van. The other drivers were Bill Brock (who stayed with Scott's much of his working life) Arthur Hutchings of Clements Hill, Charlie Harris, and sometimes Gran took a turn. Their 'rounds' included Berry Cross and Langtree Week,

Eileen Scott and her cart

Langtree Village, Thornbury, Buckland Brewer, Bulkworthy, Petersmarland.

Eileen married Reg Glover in 1946 and he helped part-time in the bakehouse. He also serviced and maintained the vans (bakehouse mornings, vans afternoons.) Granfer Scott built a bungalow for the family and named it Galway after his native Ireland. He was so proud of having achieved this ambition of starting his own bakery that he determined from the beginning that it should be a model example of how a bakery should be. He even incorporated it into the name and to this day it is still 'Scott's Model Bakery'."

Granfer Scott died in 1950 aged 60.

Eileen and Reg now had a young son, Tony to care for. Reg's first love was mechanics. It was recognised they could no longer carry on as they were, so in September 1952 the bakery, shop, dwelling house and a van was rented out to a Mr Fred Beck who ran the business from then onwards. Eileen continued to work for them – 30 years in all – at the Stibb Cross Shop and then later in Bideford (I think for many of us locals she epitomised Scott's Bakery). Gran Scott died in May 1981 and Eileen in July 2001. Reg pursued his own work from 1950 as the local Ferguson tractor representative, and he died in 1979.

Mr Scott Bakes Bread at Stibb Cross

Mr Beck rented the Bakery from Mrs Scott – 1st September 1952 – from this point on he ran the business. He had an extension built at the back (now removed) and this work was done by PHC. At about the same time, he bought the house on the corner of Fore Street and Church Lane in Langtree for £460 from Mr Ned Vanstone.

The bread was cooked in two steam ovens. This involved a furnace with a number of tubes running through the bottom of the ovens. They were full of water. The furnace was kept burning all the time, clinker and ash would have to be cleaned out each morning and the fire stoked up for the day's baking. These ovens were eventually replaced with electric ones. Mr Beck got up at 3 am each morning.

Each morning two mixes of dough were made – with 315 lbs flour in each mix. Flour came in sacks of 280 lbs each – 1 sack of flour made 216 loaves of bread. Cooking fat was rationed and there was a subsidy on bread. "We had to keep meticulous records as there were regular checks to make sure the number of loaves made and sold tallied with the amount of flour used. This happened until about the early 1960s, as far as I can remember".

Bill Brock, Derrick Gould, Wreford Leverton, Eleanor Broad and Doreen Hutchings worked for us. Wreford and Doreen lived in until our growing family meant we no longer had room for them. We bought the house next-door with barn and ground in the early 60s.

We sold bread in our shop on the premises and also had three bread rounds, travelling by van to the remoter farms and homes to deliver bread, groceries, butter, Typhoo tea and cream crackers, which we also sold in the shop. On market day at Stibb Cross, we sold pasties and cups of tea to the farmers.

We moved to Bideford in 1964. The baking was still done at Stibb Cross. We leased/took over No 21 The Quay and traded from there. Bill Brock took charge of the shop. The shop at Stibb Cross was closed and we sold off the delivery rounds. I had been starting the days baking very early and getting back to Bideford much too late, it was becoming too much!

In 1977, we bought the former Boots store at 85 High Street, Bideford. There was warehousing behind the shop, which we turned into a bakery and closed down the Stibb Cross one. It took three months to make the transformation before we had Bideford set up and fully working. There were still a few finishing touches required, but it was soon completed. We kept the Quay shop until three years ago. At the peak, we employed 22 people in the High Street. This has now reduced to 12. People used to do a large shop on Saturdays, which kept us busy. But we lost our weekend baking when supermarkets began opening on Sundays. We still use the last mixer we bought new at Stibb Cross and I still do four hours each morning (to help my family) in the bakery.

When we sold the Stibb Cross premises, it became a Carpenter and Joinery business. We never had any complaints about noise all the years we were there, not even with all the very early hours activity, yet I believe there were complaints for the woodworking business. How times have changed! 90% of our trade now is cakes/confectionery. The supermarkets can sell bread for less than it costs us to make it."

Scotts were the first bakery in North Devon in 1959 to implement deep-freezing with baking in raw state.

Horn's Flour to PHC

Jeremy Horn tells us the story of Horn's. "They originated from Rowden, Moortown, down the lane. There was a Methodist Meeting House there. The family parted up and a married couple left in the night and went to London. They changed their name by adding a 'T' into Thorn (Horn was deemed not to be a good name to have at that time, during the First World War, as it could be presumed to have German links).

Joan Sanders, Geoffrey Beck, & Pam Ford, making pasties

Peter Horn With One Of The Early Lorries

Samuel Horn was a tailor. He bought some land at Stibb Cross from the Stevens-Guile family. He and his wife had three children – Arthur, Wilfred and (I think) Emily. Emily died of Diphtheria or similar when she was approx. 14–15. I think that was around 1912. They were farming at this time (I don't know how they changed from tailors to farmers!) and had a shop in one of the rooms of the house where they lived. It's the one just before you turn into Hills, (the shop was against the road). It was a general grocers shop, previous to the 1950s

Out of the farming developed the sale of chicken feed and meal. In the early 1960s, they bought a grain drier and local farmers would bring their grain there at harvest-time for drying, then take it home again to use or store for later sale.

Three men, Wilson Harding, 'Bungy' Broad and Ron Neal were working for Alan Lock of Shebbear. When that business folded, my father Peter Horn took them on. They continued to do the same kind of work, amongst other jobs. They erected cow kennels for us, but made by other firms. Ron Neal was inspired to come up with what he felt was a better design so Horns made their first cow kennel and installed it at Thornhillhead (Mr Barron's Farm). In approx. 1964, they decided to go to the Devon County Show at Exeter and as 'late entrants' couldn't get a stand with other similar trade stands so were fitted into a spare space near the dairy cows. This turned out to be the perfect place and they received a huge number of orders, although were not quite sure how they would be able to fulfil them. They went to see the Bank Manager and launched into this new line of business, and proved to be very successful at it! By the 1970s the firm had begun to supply and construct steel sheds as well and the two areas of business ran along together well. The kennels work faded out in the early 1980s and the last steel shed was erected in about 1990 at Penzance.

Ready to deliver another load of Ly Dry Kennels

The construction work had taken Horn's to many parts of the county. The business had incorporated selling building supplies in about 1987 and this now became their main focus. The name Ly Dry Cow Kennels took over from Horn's and then later it became Peter Horn Construction, but soon became known simply as PHC Building Supplies. At its peak, the firm employed over 100 including drivers and was a good source of supply for many miles around.

The new sheds were built, and Bideford Toy Factory used one for storage for some time. Trevor Gents Steel also functioned from there prior to the 1990s.

Stibb Woodcraft, having outgrown the former Scotts Bakery shop, also operated out of one of the sheds for a time, and Harpers Animal Feed started up their business there and stayed for about five years. Both the old buildings (Mill and farm) and some of the newer sheds have now gone and a residential building development is nearing completion on the site. This summer the business has passed from local hands into a national company."

Horn's had operated out of Stibb Cross for four generations – Samuel; brothers Arthur and Wilfred, Peter, and lastly Jeremy. Between them they have contributed to 100 years plus of Stibb Cross history. That has now come to an end as Horn's has been sold to Travis Perkin this summer (2003).

Harris's Hauliers

Colin Harris started up this business thirty-one years ago. He was the first driver and was soon joined by his father-in-law Marwood Wheeler. Later Colin's wife Hazel also became one of the drivers, taking on the smaller 7 1/2 ton lorry. When Marwood had his accident, son Martin took over as soon as he was of age. At the peak of the business there were three lorries, starting with two singles then a trailer. Colin, Hazel and Martin all travelled locally and further afield going as far as Scotland. Hazel frequently drove to Brecon Market in Wales. Ten years ago Colin had a heart attack and was not allowed to drive for twelve months, so they cut back to two lorries. Not only did the family transport animals to and from markets, but they also kept cattle themselves. This developed into an interest in showing at Christmas Fatstock Shows. By being regularly at some of the best markets around, they could 'take their pick of the best available when purchasing, but they also bred some of their own cattle, keeping a Limousin bull. The family began winning prizes, and in 1989 won three championships and one reserve champion. These were at the following Markets - Champion at West of England Tavistock, Chipenham, and Bideford; Reserve Champion was at Barnstaple Autumn Sale. Not bad for one season's work. Colin also won outright the championship trophy at Bideford in 1997, having taken the title four years non-consecutive-

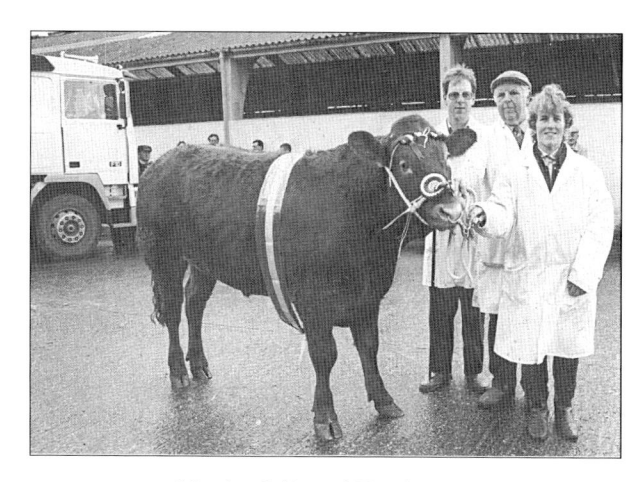

Martin, Colin and Hazel Harris with one of their Champions at Bideford

ly. Since then he has won at High Bridge in Somerset. Reserve Champion in 1998, and Champion in 2002.

Unfortunately the business came to a sad halt eighteen months ago when Martin suffered a fatal accident while working on his lorry doing routine repairs. This happened in March 2002, and then six months later Hazel died.

Colin is still carrying on with his show cattle in spite of these devastating blows, and is planning to be competing again this season, Christmas 2003

The recent history of Stapleton
by Peter Duncan

We moved to Stapleton in September 1966 from a small farm in the Midlands. My parents, Keith and Margaret, paid about £100 an acre. We moved lock, stock and barrel, bringing our herd of Jerseys, with their followers, and all machinery with us. The buildings were then in some disrepair, so a barn was converted into a herringbone parlour, and cow kennels were erected by Buckland Filleigh Sawmills. In those days milk was still in churns, and in the early morning you could very often hear clearly the loud rattle of empty churns as milk lorry after milk lorry from Torridge Vale rounded the corner over a mile away in Langtree, on their way out to start their rounds. I've often wondered how it sounded if you lived right next to the road. Of course it was not very long before churns gave way to bulk milk collection, and a refrigerated tank was installed at Stapleton as at all other dairy farms in the area. It was better for the producer and the processor, but not such good exercise for the driver!

During the 1970s and 80s my parents continued to build the herd, peaking at around 120 milkers. They always followed a strip grazing system, with winter fodder provided by vacuum silage. The intention was to minimise purchase of feed, so we always grew about 40 acres of either oats or barley for feeding in the parlour.

I suppose it was in my early twenties that I realised that I was far more interested in making milk into other products than I was in producing it, a calling for which I had no aptitude. This was to bring great changes to Stapleton. We began yoghurt making in 1975, in two converted loose-boxes generously provided by my parents. Later they must have wondered what they had started, as the manufacturing business gradually grew and grew. When they reached retirement, the herd was sold, and the remaining buildings gradually converted for use in manufacturing both yoghurt and ice cream. The land was rented to neighbours, and then sold to them, so that milk is still produced from the same fields. The former farm buildings at Stapleton now house a modern manufacturing plant, albeit on a modest scale, supplying yoghurt, ice cream and desserts to customers all over Britain, including the big supermarkets, and abroad. We take Jersey milk (staying true to our roots,) from local producers, and we provide employment for about 45 people. In fact, after a much longer than predicted useful life of 30 years, the cow kennels from Buckland Filleigh were removed to provide extra car parking for staff. At an original cost of £10 per cow, they had certainly given good value for money!

Tarka Springs – water from the rocks

It's not every day that broken bones lead to an entirely new enterprise and way of life, but that's what happened at Little Comfort. Neil Folland – recovering from surgery to repair an injury sustained through rugby – decided the time had come to do something different. Along with his wife Sarah and sister Anna a whole new business was established, Tarka Springs. Knowing that there were two natural springs on the farm, he decided to have them tested and was delighted when they came back with the result 'exceptional quality'.

With the help of grants from the former MAFF and the E.U., they were able to convert a farm shed into a bottling plant and storage. It was a huge

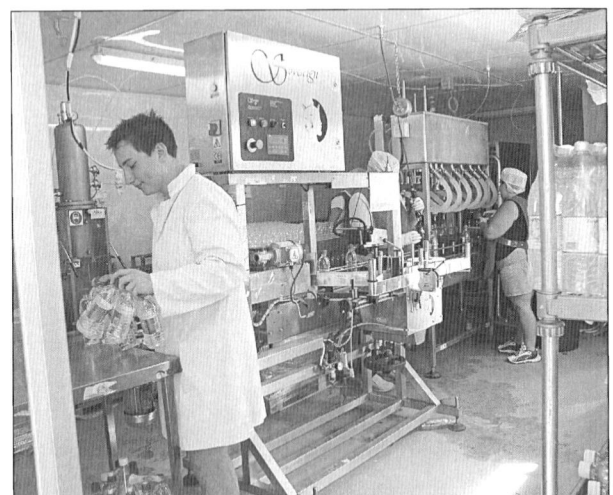

Tarka Spring bottling plant

step to take but the family were soon seeing the results of their bold decision to make a break from farming. There is a 10,000 litre tank on the springs and it pipes the water into a holding tank, where it then goes underground to be filtered. The spring water is exceptionally clean and is being sold locally as well as further afield. Bottling began in August 2001 after 18 months of planning and organisation as well as the upheaval of all the structural changes and rebuilding. The water comes out of the ground naturally without the aid of a pump – all helping to maintain the 'natural' purity. The next stage was to move into flavoured water with a choice of three – peach, forest fruits and lemon and lime.

Leisure centres and holiday attractions are among the outlets for the water – and of course it's been available at our local village lunches twice a year and is sold in the village shop and two local inns. Even the builders who worked hard to

Above & Below: Stapleton Yoghurts in the making

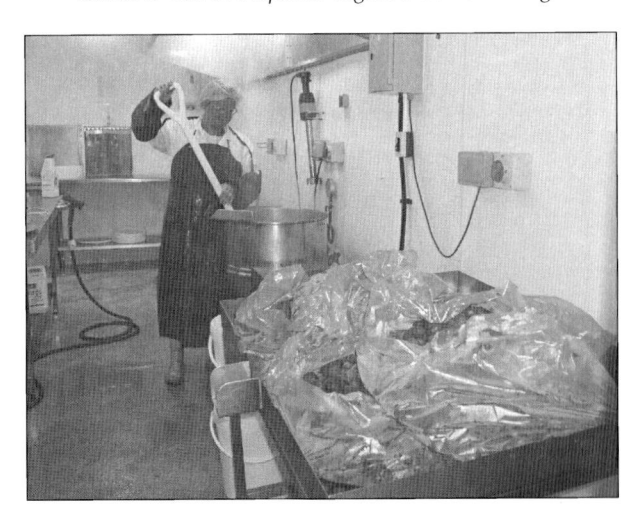

Neil's sister Anna and wife Sarah at a 'Taste of the West' event

convert the buildings were local – in fact from our own village – the Langmead brothers. Tarka Springs water is now sold in 4 sizes and with the distinctive 'Tarka the Otter' symbol on each bottle, is clearly recognisable as from this area. Other than family, three people from the community are employed there.

Withacott Dried Flowers

Glorious colour everywhere – arranged on shelves, stacked in baskets on the floor and hanging from the ceiling, dried flower in a riot of colours – pinks, oranges, greens and scarlet. Withacott Dried Flowers started out as a hobby and grew into a business when former farmer Andrew Payne–Cook was recovering from a cataract operation. With his wife Jane they started growing a few everlasting flowers amongst the vegetables in 1984. At first they grew all their own – 10,000 seeds each of statice and helechrysum plus 25 different grasses, and achillea. From 1986 they bought in things that they could not grow here.

The family in the shop

Up until 1986 it was just Andrew and Jane Payne–Cook. The business grew and from 1986-88 they were employing 25 people.

Seed was bought from Thomson and Morgan. At the beginning they experimented with posies and sold them from their dining room. In 1985 a grant was obtained from CoSIRA (Council of Small Industries in Rural Areas) to convert one of their barns into a shop. Next the granary was made into an office, and then in 1986 another barn was converted – next to the shop – into a workshop for making the posies. "In the beginning we grew everything from seed and pricked out thousands of plants, then planted them out into their growing positions at the end of May – then they had to be harvested. We picked 10,000 helechrysum heads which we had to wire up within 24hrs of picking, as sap from the stalk causes a reaction that firmly glues the flower to the wire stem. No artificial glue is ever used". Perfumed oils were used to give the arrangements their lovely smell.

"My husband did all the growing and I handled the P.R, delivering leaflets in a wide area all over North Devon and at various tourist attractions." Roses and several other species that our climate was not suited to growing were brought in from Holland – a firm called the 'Flowering Dutchman'. Our hobby had become a successful business.

Flowers were slowly and naturally dried

Sadly Andrew died in 1988 after being ill for 15 months, and our Dutch suppliers went into liquidation owing us a lot of money. Nevertheless I carried on till 1989.

One feature of the business was visitor tours – these happened from 1985 – 1989 but holidaymakers and locals enjoyed being shown around and buying gifts and souvenirs. Items were sold locally and all over England. We made posies for Boots, Growers, Retail and Wholesale."

Nicholls Pounltry Appliances
Another Stibb Cross business of some years ago was that of Cedric Nicholls and the Poultry Appliances he made. Our picture shows his prize-winning exhibition at the North Devon Show in 1950.

Above Left: Cedric Nicholls sharpens a scythe in a recent photograph

Above Right: A relative of Marion Hearn (nèe Balsdon) feeds the fowls

Left: Competition. Which is the loudest, turkey gobbling or cockerel crowing?

Chapter Fourteen MEMORIES

In this section you will find a whole mixture of people's memories on many subjects, giving us a real insight into how life used to be, and also of some long-disappeared parts of Langtree's social history, as well as some fairly recent memories. Some people's memories are scattered throughout the second section of the book, others are contained in one place here, and some are part of each. There is no specific order, I have simply tried to keep variety of interest for the reader.

John and Eleanor Folland

John & Eleanor have very many happy memories of being involved in many aspects of Langtree life. John was Church Warden along with George Heath, & school governor for many years, Eleanor was in the WI where she was a founder member and continued until she moved from the village not so long ago. They still enjoy coming back to the village meal and visiting the new hall. They were the first people I interviewed for this project and happily turned out old photos for us to enjoy.

Eleanor Folland, Margaret Knapman, John Folland. Eleanor and John were the first couple to share their memories and photographs for the book

Joe and Joyce Bond

Joe & Joyce were also early interviewees. They had many photos to show me, both of old Langtree and of many of more recent village activities. Joyce remembers there was a produce show at Langtree, possibly in the 1960s. It was held at the School and Joyce's sister was one of the judges. They both remember many activities held in the Church room across the years, including Harvest Suppers when the tables would be well laid with food, and a large turnout of people to partake of it.

Joe remembers living at Wooda Farm as a boy. "The ceiling in one of the rooms at West Wooda Farm was rather ornate. There was a dome with a special edging. There were also two angels which were taken outside while redecorating/refurbishing, and they got wet and fell apart. It was the same architect involved with creating this ceiling as had worked on ceilings in Lanhydrock House Cornwall – I believe he came from Frithelstock."

Young Joe Bond cycled to and fro to Bideford Grammar School each day. He reckons he must have cycled more miles than any other schoolboy in his day.

John Folland, Rev R Wallington, & George Heath

Copy of a page of Joe Bond's father's account book for wages paid out in 1895

Richard Bray DSM

Contributed by Eileen Arundle-Timms (née Ley) who is a close friend of Dick Bray's daughter.

"Dick Bray, a former parishioner of Langtree, can be remembered with pride as an engineer of outstanding ability and a wartime hero.

Dick Bray came to Langtree in the 1920s from Instow and lived, first at Berry Cross, and then at Rose Cottage. He worked at the agricultural engineers, Popes of Torrington, but it soon became clear that there was a need for work to be carried out nearer to the farms in the Langtree/Shebbear area. Dick was offered a small piece of land on the edge of Bibbear Farm. He built a wooden shed for his workshop, an asbestos bungalow for a dwelling, and Wayside Garage became established.

In the words of his daughter Pat "My father was always 'called by the sea'. He often left his business in the care of his sons, Donald and Douglas, and employee Russell Furze, while he worked part-time for the Merchant Navy; as an engineer on the Lundy boat the Jerina, and on coasters in the Bristol Channel.

When World War II broke out, Dick was transferred to the Royal Navy, where he served as chief engineer on minesweepers. In 1942, the vessel on which he was serving was damaged in enemy action and his wife received the dreaded telegram 'missing at sea, presumed drowned'. However, due to Dick's engineering skill, the minesweeper with its crew arrived crippled into Lowestoft two or three weeks later. He was subsequently decorated with the Distinguished Service Medal by King George VI for his skill and determination."

Jock Mills

"I remember the dances that were held in the Church Hall. We used to call them Six Penny hops because it was 6d to get in. Somebody would play the accordion, the old type that we called a squeezebox. Sylvia Harding (our present Newsletter Editor's mother) could play it lovely.

I remember us boys used to build 2 camps and two groups would play at fighting against each other. My group built their camp in the Rookery (the strip of land against Dragon Hill above the Rectory entrance and now belonging to Nick Nack Cottage). There was another group and they had their camp in Bonds break. We made our own fun and games in those days and were never bored.

Children would not be allowed to join the social club but sometime when P.B Jones of Watertown was there and we were hanging around, he would count how many there were of us, then give one of us some money and say 'go to the shop and get x number of oranges (1 each) and some fags.' When the boy came back if the change had been 1/2d he would say, 'you keep that'. That was a lot of money for the lad – he could buy quite a few things at the shop for 1/2d.

I remember working for Ned Vanstone, I learnt my trade with him. He had up to forty people working for him at one period, there were two gangs of Builders. He 'worked' a quarry near Beaford, at Post Bridge. I recall Ned had a Saw-Bench, which was run by a motor, you had to wind the bench back and forth. During the war both Ned Vanstone and Arthur Horn had a 'nearly new' lorry 'taken over' by the government for official war duties. They never saw their lorries again. It is rumoured that whilst they were being transported across to France for Army use the ship they were on was sunk.

Miss Hellings, Mrs G Mills (Jock's Mother), Horace Furse, and in the front, Frances Mills, and Marg Gent (nèe Cox) who all worked at the Rectory when this photo was taken.

There was a lime kiln near Ned's workshop, it was perhaps about twelve feet by nine feet, and about four or five feet high as far as I can remember. He used the lime mainly for whitening ceilings and the outside of houses."

Jock Mills and H & E Daniels

"There used to be a 'lock up' in Langtree in the 1920s at what is now 24 Fore Street. There were three cottages there at that time, occupied by Bill Sutton, James Vanstone and Kit Luxton. There was a piece built out in the front of one cottage and this was the lock-up. The windows had bars on them I believe. That piece and the cottage it joined to is now gone and the other two cottage have long been made into one."

Edna and Harold Daniels

"We became interested in vintage tractors in the mid 1970s. Our son, David, started it off by doing up an old 'Fergie'. It was much easier and cheaper to get parts then – you could pick them up cheap at sales as scrap or at scrap yards. It has become harder and much more expensive. Many more people are doing these restorations now and those with parts to sell realise the value of what they've got. Sometimes we have to get parts from America. A company in Derbyshire imports them for us. We have 23 vintage tractors now, including Edna's brother, Dippy John's, Field Marshall."

"We (Harold and Edna) went to the 'new' school at Langtree. It was our only school and children stayed there till you finished 'schooling'. Tinky Mills and George Dymond were two of the first to go to the new Secondary Modern School in Torrington at 11yrs old. We, who were an older age group, left school at 14 years old."

Harold says, "I was in the air force in 1941 – then they transferred me to the army just before D Day. I was in the Tank Corp. and travelled through France, Holland, Belgium and Germany.

Archie Richards was a builder and he came to Langtree and built the houses known as Flat Tops at Wonders Corner. I believe he also helped build the Social Club - voluntary labour contributed to this building. The skittle alley was added later. (Jock remembers it was a draughty place). Samuel Furse and Algie who lived at Burstone helped dray stones from the commons to do the foundations. Tinky Mills and Reg Glover built up and re-roofed the skittle alley building in the 1950s.

I remember Langtree Choir practising in the old school and the band used to play at the fête.

At the Gymkhana there were children's races, which we enjoyed in the field next to North Park and across the lane.

I remember when Scott's Bakery started. They had the end part of our house, Thorne House, (they lived across the road where Mr Ellis lives now). My father, George Daniel, parted the room off for them. They had a shop as well as the bakery. The first wedding cake they did was for Reg Gerry. Then the shop got too small so the partition was taken down. They then bought the shop at Stibb Cross. Mr Scott started it up from nothing."

"We (Harold and Jock) remember firework nights. People used to come from all over the place to join in. We had some fun, but not everyone saw it that way. We got up to some mischief really with the fireworks but we meant no harm. Some years, Policeman Scott from Monkleigh came over – our firework nights had made a name for themselves. He came over to keep order and everything was reasonably quiet while he was there – when he went home on his motorbike; then things began to happen. Sometimes it would be midnight when we let off our fireworks."

Edna Daniel

"I remember Colin Wood dancing the broomstick at their Ruby Wedding Party last year. He is really good at it."

Bryan Ley

"Withacott Farmhouse burnt down on 9th May 1943. It was a Sunday morning and we had all gone off to chapel. Someone came into the chapel and told us the house was on fire. The service was stopped and the people came to help us. We managed to get all our furniture out. Once the Fire Brigade came it only took 1/2 hour to stop the flames. There were 6 engines & pumps from Bideford/Torrington (more than they have now). They got the water from East Browns lake – piped it all the way with pumps at various intervals.

While our new farmhouse was being built, I

used to sleep at my Uncle and Auntie's house at Bibbear each night. One night walking back I had almost arrived at the house when I heard a plane roaring overhead – a bit later I heard a big explosion and flames shooting up in the air. I realised the plane had crashed but couldn't tell where – it had gone over the hill from where I was. We found out it had crashed at Buda Farm.

Two cottages were burnt down at Stibb Cross on Shebbear road – no one died. There was also a fire in the shop at Stibb Cross. Thee were quite a few fires in those days. Bibbear farmhouse also burnt down.

The District Council was responsible for local roads and the County Council was responsible for main roads.

Fred Johns and Jim Luxton worked for District Council, while Tom Vanstone and Fred Mills worked for County Council."

Jack Beer

"There was a shed at Withacott, it was built before 1935 and used by Jimmy Adams to keep his lorries (his father lived in the cottage where Bryan and Daisy are now, Withacott Cottage).

The War Commissions Committee took it over and as far as I can remember it was used for excavators. These were used for ditching and draining the land in order to help with the production of more food, such as growing potatoes on Thornhillhead Moor. In the 1940s my father had bought the shed, and we used it to store potatoes.

Jimmy Adams dug a well 47ft deep and drifted back under at the bottom. This was all done with hand tools. There was a pump there for many years to get the water up but my father sold this – it was no longer used once the mains supply came.

I remember father's first car was a Chevrolet.

Father used to deliver milk to Torrington by horse and trap. The day before, milk would have been scalded (very slowly heated in a large, wide top pan on the stove to bring the cream to a head), and then he would sell the cream, the scalded milk and new milk. It was carried in churns. People came out with their jug, and father had various measures to give it to them with. At that time, brothers Wilfred and Alfred Horn at Stibb Cross had seven or eight cows and they made butter. Father took their butter and sold it in Torrington along with his milk and cream. The Horns also had some pigs – they later went on to start the corn mills.

I remember once Father and Mother were coming home from Bideford one Tuesday – it was a rough afternoon, wet and windy. They travelled by horse and trap. The horse was a fairly recent purchase and very lively. Father had bought a new hat in town and was wearing it. Coming through Saltrens, a sudden gust blew it away. He said, "Here Mother, take the reins while I find my hat – I can't afford to lose it". She answered, "No way, he's too frisky for me." Father turned the horse and cart around and went back to look for his hat in the growing darkness of a winter day. He found his hat, very wet, with water in it. He tipped it out and put it back firmly on his head. Money was hard to come by in those days and nothing was wasted – a new hat was to be valued and looked after – it had to last a long time.

I remember Archie Richards building the houses at Flat Tops when I was about 12 years old. He had bought the ground from Cholash.

Life was hard in those days. I remember a number of families getting into trouble financially. They just couldn't pay their bills. I remember one family being 'put on the road' (evicted), when the bailiffs came.

I remember Dick Bray setting up business at Wayside. It was a repairs garage – people bought their machines to him and also he would go around to farms etc doing repairs.

Father had six horses and carts. In Father's account book for 1924, he bought a cow for £26.15 and another for £27.10. These would have been very good cows at that money.

I remember walking to school from Withacott, starting when I was 4 years old, with my brother Philip who was 5. We had no adult to accompany us. We went to the old school at first, then later on the new one.

I remember Billy Ackwell driving his car too fast down the road past the school and not being able to take the corner, he crashed into the wall. He was quite a bit the worse for the drink. This would have been before 1929 – while I was still at the old school.

I used to cycle to school at Shebbear College in all winds and weather. It wasn't very nice sometimes; we got very wet. I remember Hill's who ran a charabanc service from Stibb Cross, would take seats out when it was not being used to transport people and use it to spread manure. The manure came in cloth sacks then.

I remember there was a Young Farmers Club in Langtree thought I never went to it – I think it was during the war)."

Mrs J Beer

"Thrashing days were very hard, I don't like remembering them. We had no fridges or anything then. We would cook a large joint and cater for up to a dozen men. Sometimes it would come into rain and the job couldn't be finished. We would have all this food left on our hands.

"The kitchen floor at Withacott was very rough when we first went there – it would wear out my floor cloths very quickly as I scrubbed it. (I remember the day it was cemented over, (3 Bills came to do it – Bill Daniels, Bill Box and Bill Ellis) They worked for Ned Vanstone. I thought it was wonderful – so much easier to wash. Then I remember when we had tiles put on it. This really was something, I felt like the Queen. I remember us planning to buy some carpet for a front room, then a new shed was needed outdoors so the carpet had to wait. I was disappointed at first but that's how it was in those days. You didn't have

Emily Nichols, Rachel Hallowes, Thomas Nichols with workman Dick Adams. As Jack Beer reveals in his memories on the previous page, horses were the only real means of transport for most people

anything unless you could pay for it and, as it was the farm that brought in the money, that always came first."

Ben Copp

Ben's father had Langtree Mill built in 1900, where he ground wheat into flour and barley for animals. He farmed at Clements Week and collected rent for the Rolle Estate of Stevenstone. Most properties in Langtree belonged to Mark Rolle. Mr Copp Snr died in 1917 of a stroke, aged 57 years.

Ben went to the old school near the church. Mr & Mrs Kelly and Mrs Cooper were the teachers. The pupils aged 5 to 14, were put into six groups, with a curtain separating each group. There was very strict discipline.

Ben can remember the Green Dragon burning down. Mr Westcott allowed the pupils up the road to look. The fire engine came from Bideford. They ran hosepipes down to Watertown stream for the water supply. There were so many holes in the pipes most of the water was lost before reaching the fire.

When Ben was 14 he was sent to Wallingbrook School, Chumleigh. It was like a prison, he hated it. After a football injury Ben had osteomyalitis (inflammation of the bone). This affected his life, i.e. in hospital for many months, and ulcers on his legs even today. He had wanted to be a motor mechanic but he was not strong enough so he helped on the farm. He had an operation in Exeter in 1936, pre NHS. This cost was £35 plus £5 for consultation.

On July 17th 1927 he had his first driving licence, it cost 5 shillings (25p), no test and no insurance. Petrol cost 18d (8p) a gallon. His first car was a Lagonda, 4 seater, and 4-door tourer. His second was an Austin 7. He drove the preachers to and from Siloam chapel. Sister Dolly played the harmonium organ for 40 years.

At Stibb Cross market he bought ewes for £2, and sold fat Easter lambs for 25 shillings (£1.25) each. Cow and calf sold for £14, Devons or Shorthorn. Men walked fat cattle to Torrington Station, and then they were sent to Exeter. Sometimes by lorry at Venn Green for Butcher Tucker at Holsworthy. The auctioneers were Wards at Torrington.

There were two shops in Langtree. The Post Office, run by Mr & Mrs Trigger, and a shop run by Mrs Curtis. There was a blacksmith Mr Gus Gerry at The Forge, builder Bill Vanstone and son Jim. They had a saw pit and shed at the bottom of Church Lane.

When there was a bumper catch of herrings at Clovelly, a horse and trap with big wicker baskets would bring herrings, 12 for a shilling (5p).

The Hearn Brothers of Frithelstock had four threshing machines, which travelled from farm to farm. Charlie, George and Walter Hearn were helped by Jack Sutton, Jack Buse, Ned Johns, Bruce Lock, Reuben Maine, Charlie Marshall and Cecil Call. Bruce Lock was still combining in 2003 at the age of 83 years!

Early tractors in the Parish were a Fordson, costing £150 from Whitlock's, Holsworthy. One owned by Mr Sam Cole at Week, and one by Mr

Jack Sutton's old tractor

Nath Gilbert at Binworthy. Mr Brooks at Browns had two Allis Chalmers at £200 each.

In the winter Frank Hill, Bert Ayre, Bill Sutton and Joe Bond Snr went trapping rabbits. They were gutted and then taken to Torrington Station to be sold in the cities. They sold for 1 shilling (5p) per rabbit.

Early cars from Heamen's Garage, Torrington included a Chevrolet bought by Sam Cole for £500.

In 1928 Mr Hackwell offered Ben North Park (the village hall field) for £500. He thought it was too much and declined. Land with a house sold for £25 an acre, without a house it was £20 per acre. Eggs were 6d (2 1/2p) a dozen and pig meal was 7 shillings a cwt (30p for 50k). People kept their own pigs and Dick Adams of Buda and Alf Soby of Berry would come and kill the pig. Mrs Osbourne of Mount Pleasant would hold a bowl under to catch the blood to make black puddings. Intestines were washed out in the stream and used for skins of hogs puddings and sausages. The bladder was blown up and use as a football."

Ben Copp's 90th birthday
Back row, seated Mrs Dorothy Cole, standing Raymond Kellaway, Micheal Knapp, Ruth Wood, Colin Wood, front row, Audrey Kellaway, Keeley Mills, Ben Copp, Jock Mills

Ethel Huxtable

Ethel came to Langtree in 1948, newly married. She moved into a newly built council house in the Crescent.

She started work in the school canteen in 1955 as a helper, working under Mrs Mitchell as supervisor. The school dinners were bought from Holsworthy at the time.

"In 1975 Mrs Mitchell retired and I took over as cook. By this time we were making our own meals (started in April 1956). In 1966, I applied for, and got, the job of cleaner and did the two jobs together till I finished at the school in 1990 (with Tinky's help in later years). He was taken on as caretaker when I gave it up. I think I am the school's longest serving employee – 36yrs.

We could feed the children for between 9p and 14p per meal in 1975."

Below are some of the prices of food taken from records Ethel kept at the time:
Chuck Steak cost 35p per lb
Leg of lamb at 46p per lb
Hock (ham) boned and rolled 27p per lb
Chicken at 24.5p per lb
Cod Fillets at 28p per lb
Pig's liver at 34p per lb
Sausage meat at 19p per lb
Streaky bacon at 36p per lb
Cheese 31.5p per lb
Eggs 3.5p each or 37p for a dozen
Pork Sausages 23p per lb
Topside at 49p per lb
Leg of Pork 44p per lb
Steak and Kidney – skirt 47p
Kidney 30p per lb
4lb tin luncheon meat £1.05 per tin
Smoked Halibut 30p per lb
Pilchards in tomato sauce 20.5p per tin
Tongue 30p per lb
Turkey 49p per lb
Between 400-450 meals were provided per week.

Desserts included:
Chocolate sponge and vanilla sauce
Lemon meringue flan
Prunes and custard
Pineapple upside down and custard
Semolina
Stewed apple and custard
Fruit crumble and custard
Fudge flan
Trifle and cream
Rice pudding
Jam puffs and cream
Cream buns

Ethel continues, "I remember going on WI outings. We used to take a milk churn with water in and primus stove to boil the water and make ourselves a cup of tea. I remember a trip to Coombe Valley – then to Duckpool for our picnic. Later in the day we went in to Bude for our fish and chips. Another trip was to Tarr Steps. There were no toilets. Our bus driver said 'not to worry, take up some floorboards from the bus while others were out sightseeing.'

I remember going to Quick's chick hatchery on the edge of Okehampton and back into town later for fish and chips. One little girl (who is now an active part of Langtree and a Grandma) kept asking for some likly lowlords (liquorice allsorts).

We also had a trip to Barnstaple visiting Brannams Pottery and then a show in one of the picture houses. There was a man there, entertaining with some balloons and making them into animal shapes. We'd never seen it done before and were fascinated. (I can't remember what show we went to see).

When I was four years old I remember my Dad being in Torrington Hospital because his blood was out of sorts and leeches were used to draw the bad blood. I remember hearing about the nurses being told off because they had thrown the leeches away afterwards. They should not have done this. They should have placed the leeches in salt water where they would have vomited the blood up and then could have been used again. My Dad had to wait some time to continue his treatment.

Dad left for work early in the mornings – when he was up my sister, brother and I would all get into bed with mum, and dad would bring a cup of tea and two pieces of bread and butter (for mum) before he went to work. Mum used to tell us stories and use her hands and fingers to make shadow shapes on the wall. She would make shapes of birds and animal heads. We loved to listen to these stories and believed it all. There was a magical innocence about our very long childhood in those days. Things were tough but we enjoyed very simple pleasures together as a family.

One day, Dad bought me a little tin aeroplane. You had to wind it up then it would just lift off the ground and drop back down again. We used to play hopscotch and a game called dodge the ball.

During the war, in Meeth, the village where I grew up, there was an evacuee teacher. In the holiday she gathered us together and taught us different crafts. This is where my love of knitting and other needlework stems from. She taught us how to weave a piece of cloth, then put a lining to it and make it into a tea cosy. We went into a local farmer's field, where there were lots of thistles. We gathered the thistle down, brought it back and used it as padding between the two layers of our tea cosy. It really helped to keep the tea warm.

On Easter Sunday we would have boiled eggs for breakfast, which had been made bright colours for us. Then Dad and Mum would take us down

Ethel at School in 1979, with the children and staff of that time: -Top row L-R. Linda Mitchell, Mark Fishleigh, Sharon Buddle, Janet Beer, Mark Sutton, Debbie Willey, Hilary Prouse, Sammy Mills, Katrina Pengelly, Scott Glover, Judith Ley, Mark Squire. 2nd row: Shaun Stowell, Adrian Folland, Matthew Rowe, Andrew Fowler, Julie Balkwill, Sue ..?... Robert Bewes, Jason Ford, David Johns, Rachel Clayton, Catherine Earley, Louise Angrave, Darren Richards. 3rd row: Caroline Woolridge, Ben Rowe, Sharon Fishleigh, Theresa Wonnacott, Bridget Horn, Amanda Squires, Marie Fisher, Sharon Harding, Nicola Langmead, Marcus Moore, Zena Penticost, Richard Horn, Stephen Horn, Mark Leonard, Christopher Ley, Richard Harding, Stuart Mills. 4th row: Brenda Horn, Elizabeth Prouse, Glen Johns, Mark Dowson, Justin Bent, Joanna Shepherd, David Mitchell, Lorraine Brown, Ian Goaman, Louisa Cooper, Joanne Richards, Haley Barber, Anthony Westall, Philip Earley, Mark Willey, Catherine Goaman, Linda Palmer. Front row: Sylvia Smith, Mr Allan Edgcombe, Mrs Thomas, Anthony Palmer, Denise Wonnacott, Stephen Mumford, Martin Palmer, Geoffrey Williams, Kim Penticost, Mark Glover, Paul Cooper, Alistair Hughes, Sarah Dowson, Steven Woolridge, Mr Harry Cornish, Ethel Huxtable

to the chicken house and we would find chocolate eggs, all wrapped in shiny paper in the nesting boxes, it was so exciting. It seems strange now, looking back that we didn't realise our parents put them there. We were young and it was part of what made childhood special."

Daisy Watkins

Daisy has records of Stibb Cross Sunday School showing that in 1925 there were 44 children (20 boys and 24 girls) on the register – 10 years later it had dropped back to 24. Still a large number when you remember there would have almost certainly been Sunday Schools at Rowden, Langtree, Thornhill-head, and maybe Siloam chapels as well as Langtree Church. The Sunday School teachers at Stibb Cross in 1923 were John Blight, Nathan L. Gilbert, Ethel Annie Andrews, (Nathan Gilbert's future wife) and Mary Ellis. By 1928 the two women had been replaced by Winnie Andrews and Ida Blight.

"I remember the circus coming to Langtree. I went, Mrs Horn took me, we were good friends with them and I was often over at her place. There was someone called Buffalo Bill in the circus but I can't remember anything else about it – not what I saw or anything.

I remember the dentist coming to Stibb Cross, in Mrs Beatrice Glover's cottage. I sat in an ordinary chair to have my teeth seen to. They had to wind up by hand to get power for the drill etc. I think we had some form of anaesthetic to numb the pain.

I remember the bombs falling at Binworthy – there were 8 of them – the peacock was killed and a chicken house damaged with the chickens killed.

There was a fire in the shop that later became Scott's Bakery. Stonemans, then Blights, then more Stonemans lived in it. I think they were all related to each other. The fire happened in the time of the first Stonemans – the house/shop was gutted. There were also some cottages on the Shebbear road, on right side as you leave Stibb, that were burnt down – no one was killed but the houses were finished – the ruins were there until the site was cleared to build two bungalows.

There was a family in Stibb Cross whose child became very ill. It was before telephones. My Uncle Nath Gilbert went to Shebbear to fetch the doctor but he wouldn't come. He said, 'they owe me money already.' I think the child died.

I remember reading in an old book that at one time there was no road from Bideford to Holsworthy – I'm not sure when the road was made.

Mr Mitchell was a rabbit catcher – he called his house Three Gates because it had three gates on the premises. One day he offered to sell the house to my uncle for £100-00 on condition he could stay living in it for the rest of his life. Uncle thought he was just joking. Then he offered it to Mr Ley who realised he was serious and bought it. I remember a prisoner-of-war being with the Beers at Withacott. I think he is still in the area and in touch with them.

I remember the Shebbear group of Methodist Chapels were with Torrington for a time. I remember some ministers from a long while ago, Rev James, Rev Neale, and Rev Pattee. My Grandad Fishleigh gave the ground for Stibb Cross Chapel. He was asked later if he would give more land for a graveyard, but said no. Later on in life he regretted it and felt that maybe he should have made the second gift also. My Uncle William Fishleigh married Lucy Andrew – she became a schoolteacher at Langtree's new school."

Gran and Grandad Fishleigh, (Leonard and Maria), 3 Daughters – Mary youngest (next to dad), Annie and Bessie (not sure which is which) Son William married Lucy Andrew. Photo taken at West Stibb before 1891 They were Gran and Grandad – Uncle and Auntie to Daisy's mother Emily.

Nath Gilbert's wife Annie surveys the bomb damage at Binworthy

Barbara Babb (née Huxtable) remembers her mother Dorothy telling her that Mr Westcott, who was the Headmaster at school when she was a child, used to begin the school year in September with a new suit each year. By the end of the year it had become ink-splashed and worn so would

Wedding of Jim and Gertie Huxtable (parents of Cyril) approximately 1900. Top left are Bill Huxtable, Emily (nèe Huxtable) and Archie Richards. Apart from the bridgeroom's parents on his left, the rest of the group are members of the bride's family, the Reddaways from Torrington

need replacing again. Barbara was a little girl when Smallridge Farmhouse where she lived had its thatched roof replaced with slates. The work was done in summer, in dry weather. One night when they had all gone to bed it started raining. "We were awakened by a strange noise and could not think what it was, then realised it was the sound of rain falling on the roof, a new experience for us."

"I remember my dad speaking of Butcher Oliver Nichols (father of Hedley) at West End Villa. Dad used to take sheep there to be slaughtered. Mr Nichols had a dog, it was ginger in colour and very fightable. Dad's dog got to know, he would happily take the sheep as far as the Forge in Langtree Village but wouldn't go any further. He wanted to avoid the butcher's dog, and getting into a fight. The men knew they had to manage the last bit of the journey by themselves. Butcher Nichols had a brother who lived in the cottage near West Ford Farm. He used to come home from Torrington on the train. As getting off at the official stops of either Watergate or Yard would have meant he had to walk some distance to his home, he persuaded the train driver to let him off at the viaduct, then he just had to scramble down the bank and he was home." (There is now a set of step in that place so people can access the Tarka Trail from there.

Ron and Sandra Juniper

Ron: "I remember seeing a horse drawn bus soon after I arrived in Devon in 1940, it belonged to Marshall Haulage. It was just moving into petrol-driven vehicles at the time. Jack Hoyles had them – they travelled from the station and took people up into the square, dropping them off by the Post Office.

We farmed at Taddiport for a short while and owned the long strip fields of the leper colony – we nicknamed them 'the Junipers'.

I was a plumber for some time – we did a lot of work for Clinton Estates. I worked in a number of houses in Langtree – I remember what is now Twosome Cottages, and Doggaport when Mr Eric Bond was there – putting in bathrooms etc.

I remember 'Onion Johnnies' as they were called, travelling around in the area by bike with strings of onions around their neck. They had come across from Roscoff to Plymouth. I don't know where they kept their onions for each day's supply.

I remember buying a decent sized bun for 1/4d and taking it to school for lunch.

As a young man I travelled to Bristol twice a week by motorcycle and studied for (and got) a degree in Ballroom dancing. I taught in various places around the area including Little Torrington Village Hall. Some Langtree youngsters came to those. Many people met their marriage partners through these dances. My brother's wife used to help as my partner till I met Sandra, and then we shared it together.

My Dad drove a delivery van for Popham's bakers from Torrington – the round included the Berry Cross Area.

Sandra's Grandfather, Mr Bowden, travelled this area as a representative for Co-operative Insurance."

Bernard Hill

"I remember Jim Scott and Reg Glover, who were very popular people, and when the football team at Shebbear was formed in 1946 they were two of our keenest supporters and several of us Langtree lads played in the team.

Those were happy days, with the war now over and people were glad to get out and support all sporting activities. In the first Shebbear United team there were three of us Langtree boys, Dudley Cox, George Dymond and myself, who was the boy at sixteen. Later on, others who were being demobbed from the forces joined us. They were John Berry, his brother-in-law Sam Hinks, Arthur Stevens, Sid Gerry and also Walter Harris and Leonard Harris played for a while. We had a good team with some happy memories.

I must tell you about this very funny, once in a lifetime, happening. We were down at the camp one day. With us was young Roy Daniel, he was the youngest lad, and his grandmother came looking for him. When coming down our very steep field that adjoined the woods, she must have fallen down, and being such a big round lady, she rolled to the bottom. Nobody saw this happen, or knew she was there, all caught up in the brambles, until the late Peter Horn who came down looking for us, just could not think what he was seeing – was it a sheep, or a bullock? Then when getting a closer look, saw it was a woman. He was frightened and ran home to tell my mother and Mr Horn, his father, who was at our small farm delivering corn and meal, what he had seen. Mother said, 'That must be Mrs. Daniel'. She had seen her pass by looking for Roy. They hurried down, to find the dear old lady so entangled in thorns and brambles that Mother had to run home to get the scissors to cut her free as her long hair was really caught up in the brambles. What a job they had to get her up and help her up over the steep field and down to her home. I have told about this very funny and unusual happening to many people.

Playing at soldiers was one of our favourite pastimes and we had tin helmets, imitation guns, camouflage clothes and we used Mother's old box type pram, that was used previously for all us five children, as a 'bren gun carrier' with my brother sitting in with his gun poking out the front and me pushing it at great pace down the lane and through the village making a fair noise as it had no tyres. Some lads down the lower end of the village had their camp down by the Rectory and at times we would attack each other. Well, we made our own fun.

The Methodist Chapel was well supported in the old days. Many of the large families attending regularly and Mr. Francis Moore of Southcott was the organist for years and the Chapel caretaker Mr. 'Bommy' Hellings was required to blow the organ until he became so old and shaky we were getting breaks in the playing! He was a man with a temper and we children used to play tricks on him sometimes, and I have seen his whiskers well bristling with temper. We used to have our anniversary and harvest home services which were well attended with good singing and very often a good Cornish male voice choir gave a concert. These were the good old days for both churches and chapels but now with most of the old generation gone it is quite a different story.

The Men's Club was a very good thing for the village for recreation and during the war it was the headquarters of the Home Guard. My father was a member and I can remember him going off at evening time with his shotgun tied to the crossbar of his bicycle off to Thornhillhead Moor where parachutists might choose to land. They also had a small guard shed in the village, they would take it in turn to keep look out over the area.

The War Days. The first we heard about being at War was when our neighbour stuck his head over our garden gate and said to mother, 'well, Missus – us be at it again then'. It was not long before the evacuees flooded down from the cities seeking safety from the bombs. It was rather a sorrowful sight with hundreds of children carrying little more than their gas masks, and with a few schoolteachers to look after them. Many of them come from the Bromley schools, as did the Clark family, whom we got to know very well. Charlie Clark lived at the adjoining Judds Farm with the Vanstone family where he learned to milk cows, feed the pigs and poultry and pick up the eggs, catch the rabbits and moles and became a good help on the farm and he loved his work. We became friends and remain so today – over sixty years on, and still meet occasionally. We both loved catching rabbits with the ferrets, also chasing them when the corn was being cut – it was great sport. Charlie had two sisters, Iris and June, and the last lodgings for all three was at Mrs. Hearn's at Putshole before returning home to London at the end of the war.

At Judd's farm Mr. Vanstone had an old spaniel called Victor that became attached to Charlie and followed him everywhere – even to Sunday School one day – so we took him up into the gallery before the preacher came. We started the service with a hymn, then things went silent for a prayer and just after Mr. Ley the preacher said 'let us pray' a loud howl came from the dog who thought we had gone and left him. Mr. Ley looked up to see the dog's paws and nose looking over the balcony, then knowing that I was always the ringleader he came and gave me a hiding. I was rather disappointed getting a hiding for someone else's dog, but it caused much laughter later and something funny to remember. There were many evacuees in the area and we all got together to play football against each other. To meet in the Church Hall, for what we used to call our 'two penny hop' for dancing. Two dances I recall were 'Anytime you're Lambeth Way' and 'Underneath the Spreading Chestnut Tree'.

Just to mention some of the evacuees in the village. The Clarkes at the Vanstones, the Haineys at Mrs. Tom Vanstone, John Savery at Mrs. Burrows, The Taylors at Mrs. Walters, Trevor Westbroom at Mrs. Gerrys, the Everitts at Wedlands; Winnie, Hazel and Marjorie Warner at the Bonds and many others. We all joined together at the Chapel and Sunday School, went bird nesting in the woods, picnicking at Brooks Pond and down by the stream, although the war was on life continued much the same in the country and we all enjoyed ourselves. Harvest time was always great fun in particular cutting corn and chasing the rabbits, also riding on the horse and carts. Well, in those old days it was a hard living with very little money to spend but we had the peace and quiet of the lovely countryside, we knew how to make our own fun and to enjoy the simple things of life. That is worth more than money.

Looking back over the years – like most people of my generation – we thank God that we were born when we were for we had many of the best and most enjoyable years."

Norman Hill

"I remember Langtree was the birth place of myself and my wife and we were both taught at Langtree school by Miss Down in early classes and Mr Westcott in later years. He was a wonderful man and teacher and admired by those he taught in later years. When war broke out, the Home Guard unit was formed and our headquarters was the Church Hall where the time between shifts on watch was spent. When we were on watch we were, at first, using an old stone shed opposite the Green Dragon pub. Later a small wooden shelter was placed near the Post Office on the pathway in front of the school and only 2 went on duty and changed every 4 hours. My shift included William Daniel, myself, Ned Johns, and Harold Ford. I well remember the day the evacuees came to Langtree Parish as I drove a coach to Torrington station where I saw all the small children varying in age from about 4 to 16 just carrying a small bag or case, gasmask and a label tied to their clothing for identity. We took them directly to Langtree old school room where the waiting committee was ready to sort them out for fitting into all the different homes previously arranged to take them. My mum took 2 boys Alan & Norman Barum. When the war was over Norman returned to London, but Alan stayed and took a job on a farm and eventually met and married my sister and now lives in Dawlish.

I remember one amusing episode when Henry Gerry persuaded Nick Beer to go and see a film by telling him it was all about harvesting, as he had never been in a cinema before. The film was called Random Harvest. He gave Henry a good telling off, but admitted he enjoyed the film.

I think our main interest centred around the Sunday school, church and the Men's Club held in the Church Hall where we all met and played snooker, billiards, skittles and table tennis.

In the 1920s Langtree had 2 football teams, Langtree United and Langtree Locals. United played in a field next to Mr Nicholl's house in the village, the Locals at Stibb Cross in a field behind Hill's Garage." (The Social Club was also referred to as Church Hall whilst the old School existed.)

Olive Hill (Norman's wife) comments:

"Langtree as I remember it, was a good village to grow up in. Most of our entertainment centred on the chapel and the church also there was a Men's Club, which was popular.

I remember my teenage years. We had social evenings in the Sunday school, Guild meetings when we had debates on different issues.

Mr Westcott our Headmaster arranged concerts, in which most of the youngsters joined in. We also had a choir, which was trained by Mr Noot, later taken over by Mr Reg Baker.

For a village there was quite a lot going on.

After the war broke out we had First Aid classes in the old schoolroom, also lots of the ladies knitted socks and balaclavas for the troops. The night the German plane crashed at Buda, Dad was on duty with the Special Constables, it was frightening. It sounded as though the plane was going to crash on us. Mum and I hid under the stairs. Dad came back to see if we were O.K. and then went to Buda on guard for the rest of the night.

We had Air Force men staying (I don't know where). They stayed about 2 weeks and dances were arranged, also some of them came to our homes. When Plymouth was bombed we could see the sky lit by the flames and Plymouth is about 50 miles away.

We were lucky in Langtree we had our local shop, we had a Post Office and later we had a Bakery.

I can remember my Grandfather helped Mr Scott to get started in the business and also rented him a house to live in.

I can remember having a wonderful childhood growing up in Langtree."

Peter Johnson

"I am glad of the chance to record my thoughts about Langtree. I have nothing but fond and grateful memories of the village that was such a safe haven for myself and many others during World War .II As probably the longest evacuee resident in Langtree, I am privileged to say 'THANK YOU' from us all.

I started at the village school being taught by Mr Westcott the headmaster and Mrs Mills. I made many friends including Roy Moore of Southcott, Maurice Hellier, Terence Slade and Billy Brock. Mr Westcott was very keen on collecting salvage and Langtree won the area prize for collecting waste paper. Billy Brock and I were busy collectors pulling a borrowed trolley all over the place.

My school work was going well and my farming education was coming on in leaps and bounds. Auntie taught me how to cook tubs full of potatoes for the pigs, Joyce & Doreen taught me how to milk (by hand), and Uncle involved me in as much of the farm work as I could help with. Before long, I thought myself as a 'local', and spoke like one as well!

Many happy memories return as I am writing this. Arguments with Mr Walters the postman as to who's cow was the champion milker, running to school with Billy Brock pretending we were either cowboys on horseback or policemen on motor-bikes, bringing in the cows on my way home from school, and bringing home some shopping items from Mr Nicholls the butcher, Mr Gerry in the village shop and Mr Scott at the Bakery.

We used to hear regularly from my parents and indeed they both came to Dogaport to see us but it was an expensive trip in those days. I was extremely lucky in forming such a close relationship with my 'other family' especially Auntie! We got on very well and she would take me to Bideford pannier market where she sold some of the farm produce. In those days the Hill's bus ran twice a week (Tuesdays and Saturdays) to Bideford. Very often, I used to take her home wild flowers from the hedges – honeysuckle was her favourite – to please her. A lot of the lessons I learnt at that time have stayed with me since and have stood me in good stead.

Village life in Langtree and family life with the Mays was based on hard work, honesty and high standards of behaviour! These were all reinforced at Chapel and Sunday school.

I have only one memory of injustice relating to Chapel. On my way home one Sunday lunchtime, a fire engine came along and the driver asked me directions to a farm at Withecott. It was easier to show them so they took me in the cab. When we got to Withecott the farmhouse was on fire. Needless to say, I was late for lunch! Auntie was not amused and ticked me off because she had the Preacher round for lunch that day and I had held up proceedings. Auntie was no pussy-cat!

It was about this time that I learnt some new skills. Trapper Hill, who used to trap on Dogaport (with Uncle's permission!) had a son called Bernard and he taught me how to trap moles, skin them and then he would then sell the skins, if memory serves me right, for a shilling.

We used to have some great family parties at Dogaport with the May family members from Hollamoor and Frithelstock. Harvest-time parties in the summer when everyone helped, then stayed for the evening, and rabbiting parties in the winter.

One not so happy event in the village was when an RAF aircraft crashed at Buda and the crew were killed. It was a reminder that whilst life in Langtree was good, there was a war on. We were also reminded of this when we had prisoners-of-war helping with the potato harvest.

Mentioning the harvest reminds me that my favourite event at Chapel was the harvest festival, which was wonderfully supported. Remember, this was wartime, with rationing and restrictions on killing your own livestock, and when all the work on most of the farms was done with horses or by hand. Only very few farmers had a tractor and even fewer still had mains electricity or water.

At the time I was too young to realise just how fortunate we were. Incidentally, at that time, Uncle was a Special Constable and Ron Harris was in the Home Guard. Langtree too was at war. Uncle cracked his biggest case when he apprehended a boy stealing peas from his garden! It was me ... I loved fresh raw green peas.

By 1943 I was going on 11 and my father wanted me to go back to school in London. I had to take the London Scholarship exam in Langtree school on my own with Mr Westcott invigilating. One boy; one teacher! I passed – much credit to Mr Westcott who taught me a great deal. I then had to leave Langtree to take my place at St Marylebone Grammar School in London in September 1943.

By this time my brother Dennis had joined the R.A.F. and my sister Joan and her friend Joyce had gone back to London.

The end of Peter in Langtree?... No. I was back at Dogaport in the summer of 1944 as a result of Hitler's 'weapons of mass destruction' – the V1 flying bomb and the V2 rocket. Auntie & Uncle took me back - I think with open arms – and I started school in Torrington, going in each day on Hill's buses.

I like to think at this time I was very useful about the farm. Uncle had taught me well. The only cloud on the horizon was a flashy young footballer from Pyworthy who was tempting Joyce May with his luxurious Austin 7. Auntie took me to a village dance one evening so that we could check him (Reg Hambly) out. Auntie thought he was OK but I thought he should stay in Pyworthy! Auntie and I then walked back to Dogaport on a beautiful night singing 'The stars at night are big and bright deep in the heart of Texas'... Wonderful.

When Joyce & Reg were married in 1945, Dogaport was sold, breaking the Nethaway/May connection with the farm. Doreen went to work in Holsworthy and my sister Anne and I moved to Pyworthy.

PS. 58 years on and I am still in regular contact with my Langtree 'sisters', Joyce & Doreen. Last year I went to have a look at Dogaport and the school; much changed, but both still clearly recognizable."

Karen Pollard tells us, "It was not a difficult decision to leave a busy area of West London and head for a new life in Devon. September 1980 saw us arriving in Langtree with 2 young children and an ambition to improve our lifestyle and enjoy a more peaceful existence. The main features we had looked for when viewing properties were – 4 bedrooms, a large garden, a nearby primary school and a business we could enjoy running together and possibly improve in the future. Our daughter Claire (5) soon settled in at Langtree School and Martin (3) went to the Play Group 2 days a week, run by Linda Westall in the Chapel room.

John and I got down to the job of learning the Post Office transactions and expanding the retail business. We had ordered a new refrigerated counter to be delivered the week after our arrival and local residents who probably thought we were a bit modern viewed this with great interest! Gradually we got to know all our customers and find out their likes and dislikes.

A village shop is a great meeting place for all the locals and conversations of great variety took place – the latest cake recipe, the new teacher at school, how to make green bean chutney (very important), last night's television programme etc.

Claire and Martin did well at Langtree Primary School under Alan Edgcombe's headship and enjoyed Ethel Huxtable's wonderful school lunches. Martin, when he was 9, was fortunate to be chosen to learn the flute at the Music Centre in Torrington School and Claire subsequently took it up at her secondary school.

Christmas 1989 was a sad and worrying time for us all as a family when Claire was critically ill and an inpatient in N. D. D. Hospital until March 1990. The comfort and strength we gained from the community was a great help at this very difficult time and practical assistance came from many people. Churches and Chapels locally and all over North Devon prayed for her recovery and we felt enveloped in kindness and good wishes.

The years went on and many wonderful Langtree characters, who had been our customers, passed on – Reg Morrish; Harold, Tot and Johnny Ford; Marwood Adams; Alice Box; Reg Wheeler; Bill Daniels; Jack Walters; Bill and Brian Andrews and many more all remembered with great affection.

Our stay in Langtree saw many local events – additional street lighting in the early 1980s, the retirement of a resident rector at the Church, the water shortage that nearly gave us a standpipe outside the telephone box before rain saved the day, the great storm of 25 January 1990 that blew away our greenhouse and caused much damage to many village properties, and the greatest benefit to young and old alike – a proper daily bus service to Bideford and Holsworthy.

During our residence in Langtree John served as a Parish Councillor for 8 years and I was a school governor for 4 years. We managed to increase the Post Office business and tried to sell 'everything' in the shop, including plants raised in our own greenhouses. Unfortunately we had to retire early in 1998 due to John's ill-health at the time, but we are pleased to see that the Post Office is still surviving in these difficult times."

Sylvia Martin – (Nèe Richards)

"I was born at Redlands, which was built by my father, Reginald Richards and my grandfather Archie Richards, about 1933-34. They were builders by trade, and started their own business building many houses in the district, including 'Marsland' for my Uncle Bill Huxtable who was my grandmother's brother. It originally had a flat roof as did Flat Tops. The council houses were built by A Richards & Son at Annery, about twelve or fifteen local men found employment with Richards' Builders: as carpenters, plumbers, bricklayers and general labouring.

My Father, Reg, used to work alongside the men, driving them to the building sites in an old army lorry. 1947 was a very severe winter with deep snow and making the roads almost impassable, but Reg got around with his army lorry taking groceries and essentials to some outlying places, as so many people then did not have cars. It was that year that the council houses at Annery were under construction; work was put on hold for several weeks whilst the cold weather lasted.

Archie Richards was the youngest child of a family of 14. He was born in a cottage somewhere

Redlands, or 'Flat Tops' as it is often known, in the process of being built

down Langtree Moor Lane (I have tried to find the remains of a cottage there, all I can find is what could have once been a garden). He married Emily Huxtable of Birchill. Her parents were Richard Huxtable and Emily (also). Emily was a Short by maiden name, sister to Ginger Short. Red hair runs through the family to this day. Reg and Ethel Richards had two children, Sylvia, (that's me) and David, who is now a blacksmith in the Cotswolds."

Mary Geary (née Harris)

The Harris Family of Rivaton. "My grandfather, Herbert Harris and his wife Ettie moved from Berry House, Shebbear to Rivaton in 1923. They had four sons and one daughter, Herbert, Walter, Christine, Robert and Arthur, they attended Langtree School, and later the boys went to Shebbear College.

Ettie, my grandmother died in her 40s when her oldest son was 18, and Arthur was a small child. Arthur earned the nickname of 'Tacker'. Nancy Hearn called him this to his dying day! They had a maid working in the house whose name was Mary Underhill, and another whose name I do not recall.

Herbert (junior) was very keen on sport and billiards, darts and skittles, he won quite a few trophies which were kept in a cabinet in the Men's Club, where he spent many an evening. In Langtree, my Dad was known as 'Bert'. Many of the lads from the Men's Club would ride their bikes to Rivaton where one of the rooms had a Bagatelle table in it, and a dart board. I remember my dad talking about the good times they had rabbiting and fishing. Herbert was Captain of the Bellringers, so I have been told. He also helped with keeping the Churchyard tidy and he made the Arch of Welcome at the church when the Vicar's daughter, Rachel Hallowes got married. It was in May and they had a flurry of snow.

Herbert Harris jnr at Rivaton with a Monkey Puzzle tree near the top of the lane

When the family left Rivaton in 1939 to reside at Southcott Marsh in Westleigh, near Bideford, Walter, the second son was not with them. He had gone to lodge with Mrs. Hill at Stibb Cross and had found a job with Hill's Garage. He was at Hill's until 1969. Walter loved to have a chat, as the Glover, Dymond and Hill family well know, many an evening they had to stay up late listening to Uncle Walter's escapades on the buses! For many years he went to Exeter and Bideford regularly. It was a treat for me to go to Exeter on 'Uncle Walter's bus'. People would give him a shopping list and some money to do errands for them in Exeter, one lady even used to ask this 'ole bachelor' to get her underwear – must have been embarrassing for him at the time, but he never complained. On Saturday evenings he drove the late night 'Picture Bus', which took passengers to the Cinema in Bideford and back.

During the Second World War, he drove buses with blacked out lights, there were no signposts around during this time. I remember him telling me about the time he had to drive some soldiers all through the night to an unknown destination, with a sergeant telling him where to turn. It must have been during this time that Walter developed his lifelong habit of blinking rapidly and screwing up his eyes.

Walter played football for Shebbear, where he earned the nickname Snaily from his father. Tony Glover was the little mascot then. Walter used to go fishing at weekends with Bernard Hill. Everyone who knew Walter can remember some anecdote, he was quite some character."

Walter Harris at Stibb Cross

The Holmans (by Mary Geary)

The Holman Family of Langtree Week. "Elias Holman ran a machinery business at Langtree Week, Langtree for 44 years, from 1878 to 1922. During that time he must have produced many reapers, corn-drills and other agricultural machinery for the local farming community. Some remember that he made threshers and I know that he was an agent for Massey Harris binders. Name plaques, wheels, seats and machinery that were made by him are still in existence. His workshop was situated on the left side of the dwelling house.

Elias was born in Peters Marland on 26th October 1851. He was the youngest son of John and Grace Holman. He had six brothers and two sisters. His brother, the oldest son was named John like his father and grandfather before. By the time Elias was old enough to remember, most of his siblings had flown the nest; some to their own farms, and two had emigrated.

Towards the end of the 1860s, Elias's parents moved from Peters Marland to Langtree Week. By this time only Elias and Thomas lived at home. The oldest brother had married a Sarah Folland from Brushford in 1858 and was already living in Langtree. Both father and son John, Thomas and Elias were machinists and carpenters. The first mention of the machinery business run by John in Kelly's Directory is in 1870.

1866 was a tragic year for the Holman family. In January, Grace, wife of John Senior died, aged 56. Then in June, three of young John and Sarah's family of five died of diphtheria. Little John, aged 4 died on the same day as baby Joseph aged 17 months, the next day Elizabeth, aged 7 died. The two children who survived were Deborah and (Polly) Mary. Deborah lived in the cottage beside the church in her adult life. Then on September 17th 1866, Elizabeth the grandmother of Elias and his brothers and sisters died, aged 87. There they all lie in a sad row in Langtree Churchyard a short distance from the main entrance.

After their father died in 1871, Thomas and Elias planned to emigrate to America, I still have the wooden trunk my great-grandfather Elias made to take with him. However, only Thomas eventually went away. Elias stayed at home to help his brother John, make machinery in the workshop at Langtree Week.

Young John died in 1877, aged 45. The business now belonged to Elias.

Elias married Bessie Blight on June 22nd 1882; she was one of the three daughters of farmer William Blight and his wife of Down Farm, Newton-St-Petrock. She was 11 years younger than him.

Bessie and Elias had two children, Margaret and William John. One day Margaret 7 years old, had a very sore throat, little William also became ill and died of diphtheria a few days before Christmas in 1893 aged 3 years 3 months. He has a little grave near the Church path at Langtree Churchyard.

Elias Holman was a well-respected man. He was a machinist and carpenter who also made furniture, he employed some apprentices in the workshop, and I think one was called Isaacs. He employed a man to plant the large garden. Elias and his apprentices made a large cupboard with a glass front for his daughter Margaret on her marriage to farmer Frederick Folland at Langtree Church in 1906. She was elegantly attired in a cream silk gown with a wide brimmed hat trimmed with cream flowers. Her bridesmaid was Emily Folland who wore a navy silk gown.

Both Bessie and Margaret wore beautiful dresses for 'best'. Bessie had a lovely singing voice and Margaret played the piano and violin. As a child Margaret went to School in Langtree, in her 'teens' she went to a School in Torrington and lodged at

Mary Geary, Elias's great grand-daughter with Philp Jenkinson and one of Elias Holman's reapers, 1987

Elias & Bessie Holman, with daughter Margaret. Picture taken in the early 1900s

Mrs. Bell's house in South Street. Mrs. Bell was a photographer.

I was seven when my great-grandmother Bessie died. She told me that she used to find brass candlesticks and brass saucepans among the scrap metal that had been sold to Elias, she would clean them up and polish them until they shone, then use them as ornaments for the mantelpiece in the house!

Thomas Holman often came back to Langtree Week from the States to visit his brother at Langtree Week. Grace, his daughter remembered that she and her parents stayed with Elias and Bessie for 4 months in 1920! Grace said that she used to sit among the pea rows and eat the peas from the pods, if she was missing that is where she was to be found. She said Bessie and Elias were very kind people, and that Bessie was a wonderful cook. Bessie had Kimmy Ayre to help her in the house, 'a little treasure' was how Bessie described her.

On Torrington Market days, Bessie would be seen sitting in the Pannier Market, with other wives from the countryside, selling garden produce, fruit, 'dressed' poultry, and eggs. She would go to a nearby field to catch her pony early in the morning, to fix him to the Jingle; this is a two-wheeled cart that was loaded with baskets. The townspeople were delighted with the fresh food. There was a large shed at Langtree Week; part of it was used as a stable. Grannie Holman's pony preferred to trot on the earth and stone lanes, the 'new' tarmac was too slippery.

Towards the end of his life Elias had heart trouble and was ill. He had to rest. There was no son to carry on the business, so it ended in 1922. Elias had to spend much of his time now resting in bed, and on warm days he would be seen sitting outside his beloved workshop. He died in 1927.

Bessie sold Langtree Week and went to live with her daughter and son-in-law at Broomhill Farm, Peters Marland. She died in 1950, when she was in her late 80s. Both are buried at the top end of Langtree Churchyard near the line of yew trees."

Alma Carter (née Daniel)

William Henry Short, my grandfather was born on 27th March 1858 in Langtree, his knowledge of life and Langtree, and his wonderful way of talking about it, educated us to our heritage and ways of the village. He lived to be 88 years old.

He always distributed the Maundy money (Phipps Charity) to the less fortunate members of the village community on the Thursday before Easter.

He was an average size man, and as I remember him, he had a lovely white beard, and hair. He

W H Short is in the centre, with his father Thomas Short on his right, and Jim Vanstone on his left with grand-daughter Iris Moore, now Iris Andrews, on his knee.

went by the name of Ginger Short, being ginger in his early days.

Another name he went by was Lawyer Short, if anyone was in trouble with the law they would always come to him for advice, and he would help them, and speak for them at the courts. I remember his solicitor, Mr Wright saying to him in the court once, "you know more than I do, you take over."

There was the case of the village pump, the man that owned the cottage opposite him, said the pump between the cottage and Mr Gerry's forge belonged to him, having owned the cottage at one time and having old deeds in his possession. My grandfather said the pump was the village pump, consequently the man in the cottage locked the pump so that no one could help themselves, Imagine how we felt, when my grandfather took a digger and cut the lock off and helped himself to a bucket of water. Nothing was done, because he was the sort of man that everyone believed and respected.

The village school was another of his projects, being, along with my mother, a school manager.

He did not agree that the old school was suitable for children, as the view from the window looked out onto the Church path and, with funerals passing by, this was not a happy environment for children in the classroom. Being a member of the higher education committee, held each month at Exeter, he applied for a grant to build a new school for the village in a different location. All was agreed, the new school was built in 1927, and is still running today. I do not know if anyone else was involved with him, but I know he was thanked for his part in making the school possible.

He did not work in his later life, but had a small pile of rent books to pay his way. His father Thomas Short who was married to Lydia Thorne, a relative of James Thorne built the Methodist Chapel; Catherine Thorne held a school in the dining room where he lived (before my time), that's why the house was called Thorne house.

In those days cottages, rents were 6 shillings per week, and he owned quite a number of the cottages in the village, hence the pile of rent books.

He was a member of the parish council and voted on each time there was an election, gaining the full majority of the votes, occasionally a few less, but still back for another 4 years.

He was a staunch Liberal, and at election times he chaired a lot of the Right Honourable George Lambert's meetings.

He lived all his life in Langtree, his integrity was known and the respect of people he maintained all his life."

Torridge Vale Milk Factory with churn lorries 1962

Rose and Ray Isaac remember how busy it was preparing for the annual Fun Day. Rose recalls, "I was secretary when we first started to do them, there was a lot of sorting out to do and no pattern from the previous year to follow. Our children enjoyed the sports and the cycle race. I was also involved in lots of other things in the village." Ray remembers his years working at Torridge Vale and was happy to supply the picture of the lorries (opposite). The last day that milk was delivered to Torridge Vale Creamery from local farms was 30th march 1993.

Alice Beckley (née Gerry) remembers that her mother used to do 'gloving', and as a young girl Alice used to stay up and help when the younger ones had gone to bed. "The light wasn't good in those days and it was hard on the eyes but we had never known anything different. I remember parties at Doggaport with the May family, and Chapel Picnics at Trathens field. After our food had been enjoyed we paddled in the stream and played games like Rounders. Those were happy days, we all learned to be content with what we had."

Shirley Clegg (née Knapman) remembers going on 'Nature walks' with the School. It was when she was in the infant's class and the teacher was Mrs Metherell. "From the school we walked towards Torrington a short way then went down the back lane towards Wooda. It was a good road then and cars could travel on it, we studied the plants and flowers, and any other natural things of interest then took them back to school and did a project about them. We learnt what the different plants and flowers were called, and also noted the birds and insects. I used to really enjoy those times. Sometimes we went down Beara hill for our walks and my parents could hear us laughing and chattering from our home at Burstone.

I also remember going to evening classes at Langtree School when I was in my late teens. I went to art classes with Margaret Peters as the tutor and did some charcoal and pencil drawings. I believe there were other sorts of classes but these were the only ones I went to. I only went for one series, though they continued for a number of years."

Sam Braunton from Cheddar in Somerset visited me while I was compiling information for this book, to trace where his mother had lived. She was Lillian Annie Horrel. Sam has contributed a school photo taken in 1922 to our growing collection, and he has vague memories of coming to Langtree as a very little boy to visit where his mother grew up. He doesn't know which house that was, and as his mum has long since died has no way of finding out, unless anyone reading this remembers her and can let me know so I can pass it on.

Edgar Pett remembers being at Langtree School when Mr Jenn was Headmaster and used to keep a hive of bees. "There was a privet hedge which separated the garden from the playground, the bee-hive was behind the hedge. Mr Jenn used to allow three or four of the older boys to help with the bees and I was one of the ones who volunteered. I used to enjoy it. We all had special white protective clothing, including the hat and veil, but one day some bees got inside my clothing and I was stung a few times. Mr Jenn took me back into school, removed the beekeeper's clothes and treated my stings. Then he gave me a very serious look and said, 'Do you realise how many of my bees you have killed?' I didn't do any more bee-keeping after that."

Bill Brooks remembers that "Jim Luxton who lived in the thatched cottage in Browns Lane would cut his hair for 3*d*. There used to be a copse all the way up to the crossway at Stibb Cross on the right side of the Shebbear road. I remember when me and my mates came home from school at Shebbear College we used to tie small branches to the back of our bikes and ride all the way down Burstone hill with them behind us stirring up a real cloud of dust."

The Hancock Family

Mr & Mrs Jim Hancock came to Rose Cottage many years ago. Above are Alan, Leslie, Raymond, Trevor, Dick & Marion. Jim was at one time a mechanic with Dick Bray at Wayside then later with Russell Furze at Rose Hill. Three of the family still live in the Parish: Raymond with wife Rosalyn were much involved with the Social Club. Dick & Trevor still live at Rose Cottage, busy with farming & gardening.

Eric Bond

Eric Bond remembers Bill Sutton who was the father of Gordon, Jack and the rest of the children (it was a large family) He loved to do his garden. In those days someone could earn enough from their garden to pay two men's wages. "We used to call in at that home and catch up with the latest news of what was going on in the neighbourhood.

Ned Vanstone as undertaker had a very unpleasant job. Once, I remember, there were two sisters and a brother who farmed at Hollamoor. One was called Joyce May, she married a Squires (there were Mays at Higher and Lower Hollamoor and at Doggaport – three separate families, no relation to each other). One day the brother had been out in the field working with his tractor and whatever machine he had behind it. At the gate, on the way back to the farmyard, he got off the tractor to knock the machine out of gear, and slipped. He fell under the wheels of the tractor, and was fatally injured. Ned had to go and get him out and attend to things, It upset him badly…A few weeks later I was out in the field after dark working, when he came out and asked me if I would stop. He couldn't rest or sleep with the sound of the tractor still in his ears at that time of the night. The memory of the other lad was still too fresh on his mind.

Barney Box was another character of the village – He was a good chap, a good worker. He pulled mangles for us, and pitched corn, as well as doing his regular job of sweeping chimneys. One evening Ned Vanstone was in his carpenter's shop making a wooden leg for Barney Box (he had lost one leg at some point). I was there with Ned when someone (I can't remember who) came in and said 'Barnabus has broken his leg'. Oh dear what a predicament, what would Barney do now? The one who brought us the news let us puzzle over the problem for a while, and then he said with a grin 'It's ok – it's his wooden leg he's broken'. Phew! What a relief that was to Ned and me, we had pictured Barney with his one good leg broken and were wondering how ever he was going to manage.

Breeding was and is an important part of keeping farm animals. When father needed to take a cow to the bull I would be expected to see to it. I would take the relevant cow and one other to keep it company, to Monkleigh and then back again the same night. I rode my bicycle, and took the dog with me. One man, a bike, a dog, and two cows from Wooda Farm to Monkleigh and back.

On other occasions we would drive cattle to Stibb Cross Market, just one man and a dog. Of course there wasn't any traffic on the road, and the North Devon cattle were quieter, more docile. They ambled along and we managed all right.

The best fat cattle (which would be the Devons) at Stibb Cross Market went to Wales for the miners. There was a man from Torrington called Barney Hutchings – he was a big man and used to drink heavily, everyone called him 'Fat Barney'. He used to drive the cattle to Torrington Station, up to forty or fifty at a time, to be taken to their destination for slaughter by the butchers.

Eric Bond's stallion

Father 'broke in' horses for people, it could be up to eight in a month. It was all horses used for the farm work then. Father trained these Shire horses; he also kept a stallion, which he took around to farms to service their mares. One trip he used to do was to set out from Wooda and go to Merton, getting there about 1.00pm – 1.30pm, then on to Beaford Mill, then to Coombe Farm where he stayed the night (the Wickett family lived there). The next day he went to Port Bridge, then Higher House, St Giles in the Wood, then on to Torrington, and after that back home by about 5.00pm. He would have called at various farms along the way.

Above is a photo of Father with one of his stallions. It was taken in the field at Town Park, Torrington before the Dartington Glass Factory and housing were built there. Father took the stallion there to attract more customers. This stallion was called 'Colehill Perfection', the photo must have been taken somewhere around 1927. The car that can be seen the other side of the horse belonged to the Mayor of Torrington at that time. He was called Captain Starkey. By about 1940 tractors were coming onto farms and horses were no longer required. I told Father I didn't want to carry on with horses but wanted to get a tractor. He said, 'If you get the tractor you must get work so it will pay for itself', so I did some contracting work around on other farms, helping with the hay harvest etc.

Along with Father we also caught rabbits for the meat market, we were paid twenty-five shillings for one hundred rabbits. They had to be 'gutted', and then a dealer who came from Taddiport collected them. His name was Ned Short, he came once a week. He also collected eggs from the farmer's wives around about. After the war the market for rabbits went, and Cobbledicks took over the egg collection when Ned Short finished."

The following verses were in a comic, many years ago – maybe 70 years or so ago, yet Eric recited them to me from memory. M.K.

I went to the pictures tomorrow
I took a front seat at the back
I fell from the pit to the gallery
And hurt the front part of my back.
I walked home in a taxi
And I bought a plain currant bun
I ate it and gave it back to the lady
And that was the end of my fun.
It was a fine October's morning
Last September in July
The moon lay thick upon the ground
And the mud shone in the sky.
The flowers were singing sweetly
The birds were in full bloom
As I went down the cellar steps
To sweep the upstair room.

One fine day in the middle of the night
Two dead men began to fight
One blind man to see fair play
Two dumb men to shout hurray
A paralysed donkey came walking by
Kicked the blind man in the eye
Into a dry ditch and drowned 'em all.

Bill Balsdon whose generous gift made it possible for the Church Bells to be restored. Photo taken c1995

Edric Moore at the Church Fête held in the Rectory grounds. c late 1970s

Below: Brian Andrew bringing in the Cows for milking c1990